The Consort and Keyboard Music
of William Byrd

THE MUSIC OF WILLIAM BYRD

Volume I (*in preparation*)
The Masses and Motets of William Byrd
JOSEPH KERMAN

Volume II (*in preparation*)
The Songs, Services and Anthems of William Byrd
PHILIP BRETT

Volume III
The Consort and Keyboard Music of William Byrd
OLIVER NEIGHBOUR

The Consort and Keyboard Music of William Byrd

OLIVER NEIGHBOUR

UNIVERSITY OF CALIFORNIA PRESS

Berkeley and Los Angeles

University of California Press
Berkeley and Los Angeles
Printed in Great Britain by
Western Printing Services Ltd
© 1978 Oliver Neighbour

ISBN 0–520–03486–4
Library of Congress Catalogue Card Number : 77–76184

Contents

Contents

Foreword

The present volume is one of three covering all the music of William Byrd. This comprehensive study originated in an unusual way. It was not the outcome of a grand project conceived in advance by a single scholar or editor who then recruited the present authors. Nor would it be true to describe it as the fortuitous convergence of three entirely independent projects. The authors have long been friends. Over the years they have been engaged with Byrd's music at various levels of intensity, sometimes alone and at other times in conjunction or in correspondence with one or both of the others. There came a time when each began to see that his sense of commitment might lead to an individual monograph, and the larger design then took shape quite naturally. The initial plan to produce one composite volume was emended a little later to encompass three smaller, associated ones.

What it has entailed, then, is not so much a formal collaboration as mutual encouragement, consultation and criticism – for the authors a uniquely valuable and sustaining experience. Whatever the differences between their interests, casts of mind or modes of expression, they share certain assumptions, and these are worth outlining here since they are not spelled out in the books themselves. Most important, we all believe strongly that great music of the relatively distant past deserves the same degree of critical attention regularly accorded to that of the recent past or present. That Dufay, Josquin, Byrd and Monteverdi are on a plane with the greatest masters of later years is a commonplace of the history books, but one that can have little meaning unless the music is more widely heard and understood. The performance of Byrd's music has taken great steps forward in the post-war period. But the growth in popularity of early music that has benefited Byrd has tended to promote general enthusiasm rather than more searching appraisal.

Of course special difficulties arise when one attempts to reach a reasoned critical account of early music, as they do in trying to perform it convincingly. The further back one goes in history, the greater the leap of historical imagination required; and one of the tasks of musicology – perhaps the main task – is to prepare the way for this enterprise. These studies contain much discussion of sources, chronology, authenticity, influences, modal theory and so on. Without such a basis the contemporary sensibility can go very wrong in respect to the past. But without a vital link forward to the present, musicology risks losing touch with the essential nature of the art which is the object of its study. We address the music as music, mediating as best we can between historical vision on the one hand and contemporary aesthetic expectations and attitudes on the other. There is today and has been for many years much generous if somewhat unfocused admiration for Byrd's genius. We have tried to lay the foundation for its fuller understanding and appreciation.

Philip Brett
Joseph Kerman
Oliver Neighbour

Acknowledgements

My greatest debt by far is to Philip Brett and Joseph Kerman. The present volume owes its existence to them, for it was they who first planned a new study of Byrd and subsequently invited me to contribute to it. Moreover both of them patiently read my entire draft, and their criticisms and suggestions have enabled me to make numerous improvements. I am also extremely grateful to Alan Brown and Warwick Edwards for their constant cooperation and many kindnesses, and to Unity Sherrington who had to disentangle the final text from some very foul papers before typing it. A number of other people have generously lent me photographic material and transcriptions: Richard Bethell, Alan Dickinson, David Fallows, John Langdon, Peter le Huray, David Mitchell, Jeremy Noble, Diana Poulton, Colin Slim, Colin Timms. Wherever I have worked – in London (University Library and Royal College of Music), Oxford (Bodleian Library and Christ Church), Cambridge (University Library, Fitzwilliam Museum and Pendlebury Library), Tenbury (St Michael's College) and Paris (Bibliothèque Nationale) – the librarians have given me every assistance, as have my colleagues in the Reference Division of the British Library.

O.W.N.

NOTE ON THE MUSIC EXAMPLES

Music examples from printed sources are used by kind permission of the following:

Stainer and Bell, for extracts from Vol. 17 of the *Byrd Edition* (restored to the original note-values) and Morley's *Keyboard Works*.

Stainer and Bell, for extracts from the volumes of *Musica Britannica* (© Musica Britannica Trust): Byrd's *Keyboard Music* (MB Vols. 27, 28), Bull's *Keyboard Music* (MB Vol. 19), *Music of Scotland 1500–1700* (MB Vol. 15).

Edition Wilhelm Hansen, Copenhagen, for extracts from K. Jeppesen, *Die italienische Orgelmusik am Anfang des Cinquecento*, Vol. 2, *Altitalienische Orgelmusik*, 2nd edition, 1960.

Key to Abbreviated Bibliographical References

The editions, books and articles referred to in this volume are treated in two ways. A certain number are quoted in abbreviated forms, the key to which is given below. Particulars of the remainder are given at the appropriate points, with index references under the names of composers, editors and authors.

BE   *The Byrd Edition*
              17. Consort Music, ed. K. Elliott
              (London, 1971). (This volume bears the
              general title 'The Collected Works of
              William Byrd', but is now to be
              considered part of the Byrd Edition.)

BK   *William Byrd: Keyboard Music*, ed. A.
              Brown, 2 vols. (London, 1969–71,
              2/1976). (= MB 27, 28.)

BW   *The Collected Works of William Byrd*, ed.
              E. H. Fellowes.
              8. Motets for three, four and five voices
              (recovered from manuscript) (London,
              1939).
              12. Psalmes, Sonets & Songs (1588), rev.
              P. Brett (London, 1965). (Also issued as
              Vol. 14 of *The English Madrigalists*.)
              13. Songs of Sundry Natures (1589), rev.
              P. Brett (London, 1962). (Also issued as
              Vol. 15 of *The English Madrigalists*.)
              14. Psalmes, Songs, and Sonnets (1611),
              rev. T. Dart (London, 1964). (Also
              issued as Vol. 16 of *The English
              Madrigalists*.)
              16. Additional madrigals, canons and
              rounds (London, 1948).

                                                     17. Chamber Music for Strings (London, 1948).
                                                     18–20. Keyboard Works (London, 1948).

Brown   H. M. Brown, *Instrumental Music printed before 1600: a bibliography* (Cambridge, Mass., 1965).

Chappell   W. Chappell, *Popular Music of Olden Time* (London, [1855–59]).

DVB   *The Dublin Virginal Book*, ed. J. Ward (Wellesley, 2/1964).

Dowland, *Collected Lute Music*   *The Collected Lute Music of John Dowland*, ed. D. Poulton and B. Lam (London, 1974).

EECM   Early English Church Music
                                                     1. *Early Tudor Masses I*, ed. J. D. Bergsagel (London, 1963).
                                                     6. *Early Tudor Organ Music I: Music for the Office*, ed. J. Caldwell (London, 1966).
                                                     10. *Early Tudor Organ Music II: Music for the Mass*, ed. D. Stevens (London, 1969).
                                                     18. *John Sheppard: II Masses*, ed. N. Sandon (London, 1976).

Edwards, *Sources*   W. A. Edwards, *The Sources of Elizabethan Consort Music* (unpublished dissertation, Cambridge, 1974).

Jacquot, *Musique instrumentale*   *La musique instrumentale de la renaissance*, ed. J. Jacquot (Paris, 1955).

JAMS   *Journal of the American Musicological Society* (Boston, 1948–).

MB   *Musica Britannica*
1. *The Mulliner Book*, ed. D. Stevens
(London, 1951, 2/1954).
5. *Thomas Tomkins: Keyboard Music*, ed.
S. D. Tuttle (London, 1955, 2/1964).
9. *Jacobean Consort Music*, ed. T. Dart
and W. Coates (London, 1955, 2/1962).
10. *The Eton Choirbook I*, ed. F. Ll.
Harrison (London, 1956, 2/1967).
14. *John Bull: Keyboard Music I*, ed.
J. Steele and F. Cameron (London,
1960, 2/1967).
15. *Music of Scotland 1500–1700*, ed.
K. Elliott (London, 1957, 2/1964).
18. *Music at the Court of Henry VIII*, ed.
J. Stevens (London, 1962, 2/1969).
19. *John Bull: Keyboard Music II*, ed.
T. Dart (London, 1963, 2/1970).
20. *Orlando Gibbons: Keyboard Music*,
ed. G. Hendrie (London, 1962, 2/1967).
22. *Consort Songs*, ed. P. Brett (London,
1967, 2/1974).
24. *Giles & Richard Farnaby: Keyboard
Music*, ed. R. Marlow (London, 1965).
27, 28. See BK, above.

MGG   *Die Musik in Geschichte und Gegenwart*
(Kassel, 1949–).

MME   *Monumentos de la Música Española*
2. *La Música en la Corte de Carlos V*,
ed. H. Anglés (Barcelona, 1944).
27–29. *Antonio de Cabezón: Obras de
Música para tecla, arpa y vihuela*, ed.
F. Pedrell, rev. H. Anglés (Barcelona,
1966).

Meyer, *Spielmusik*   E. H. Meyer, *Die mehrstimmige Spielmusik des 17. Jahrhunderts in Nord- und
Mitteleuropa* (Kassel, 1934).

Morley, *Introduction*	Thomas Morley, *A Plain and Easy Introduction to Practical Music*, ed. R. A. Harman (London, 1952).
Morley, *Keyboard Works*	Thomas Morley, *Keyboard Works*, ed. T. Dart, 2 vols. (London, 1959, 2/1964).
Neighbour	*Three Anonymous Keyboard Pieces attributed to William Byrd*, ed. O. Neighbour (London, 1973).
North	*William Byrd: Music for the Lute*, ed. N. J. North (London, 1976).
Simpson	C. M. Simpson, *The British Broadside Ballad and its Music* (New Brunswick, 1966).
TCM	*Tudor Church Music* 1. *John Taverner, Part I* (London, 1923). 5. *Robert White* (London, 1926). 7. *William Byrd: Gradualia* (London, 1927). 9. *William Byrd: Masses, Cantiones, and Motets* (London, 1928).
Tuttle	William Byrd, *Forty-five Pieces for Keyboard Instruments*, ed. S. D. Tuttle (Paris, 1939).
Tye, *Instrumental Music*	*Christopher Tye: The Instrumental Music*, ed. R. W. Weidner (New Haven, Conn., 1967).
Ward	J. Ward, 'Apropos "The British Broadside Ballad and its Music"', *JAMS*, xx (1967), 28ff.
White, *Instrumental Music*	*Robert White: The Instrumental Music*, ed. I. Spector (Madison, 1972).

Wooldridge   W. Chappell, *Old English Popular*
                              Music, new ed. by H. E. Wooldridge,
                              2 vols. (London, 1893).

Two *Musica Britannica* volumes of Elizabethan consort music are in course
of preparation by Paul Doe; they will include, among much else, the complete
consort works of Tallis, Tye, Parsons, White and the elder Ferrabosco.

A stroke and a number following the symbol for a particular volume indicate
a numbered piece within it, e.g. EECM 6/34, MB 19/129a, 1611/15 (the
dates 1588, 1589 and 1611 used in this way denote Byrd's vernacular
publications of those years; see BW 12–14 above). The class-marks Add.
(Additional), Egerton, Roy. App. (Royal Appendix) and R.M. (Royal
Music) followed by numbers refer to manuscripts in the Reference Division
of the British Library.

I

Introduction

Although Byrd wrote instrumental music throughout his life he published scarcely any of it. He included two consort fantasias in his last collection, the *Psalmes, Songs, and Sonnets* of 1611, and it was almost certainly he who a year or so later provided the engraver of the keyboard collection entitled *Parthenia* with the eight pieces that make up his contribution to it. But that is all. This might appear to suggest that he thought his instrumental music less important than his vocal – his Latin motets and masses, and his English songs, psalms and anthems. It is no doubt true that as man and musician Byrd gave first place to his religion, which he could serve most directly by setting sacred texts. Yet he brought the same intelligence, energy and certainty of purpose to his instrumental music as to the rest of his output; it shows the working of his genius no less clearly, and is no less remarkable for its qualities of personal expression. No composer, whether English or continental, working without the guidance of a sung text, had hitherto encompassed so wide a range of character or of structural invention. It is not a matter of his hand having been guided in moments of inspired in-attention by social pressures or the spirit of musical history. He recognized the problems of abstract musical construction that faced him, thought about them deeply, and never tired of devising new ways of meeting them. He built with endless resource upon the most diverse stylistic traditions and must certainly have known how to value his achievements.

His failure to publish is to be explained by external factors. Keyboard music presented special difficulties to the printer. Music publishing in England was too young and too insecure for the cost of setting up long keyboard pieces in type to be risked, and perhaps too inexperienced technic-ally, whilst engraving reached England too late for Byrd to profit from it to any great extent. Consort music would, of course, have been easy to print, but viol playing seems to have gone temporarily out of favour during the period of his main publishing ventures towards the end of the century, and he could not afford to ignore his market. He found it prudent to adapt his consort songs for fully vocal performance wherever possible in his vernacular collections of 1588 and 1589. Only in 1611, when viols were once again popular and his age and position enabled him to publish what he pleased

for anyone who still cared to perform it, could he bring out fantasias alongside choral pieces and undisguised consort songs.

No autograph manuscripts of Byrd's music survive. In the sphere of instrumental music the scarcity of sources approved by him gives rise to
innumerable problems of authenticity, textual criticism and chronology,
many of which can be tackled only through study of the music itself. Such
information as the existing sources provide will be taken into account as
appropriate in the following study; meanwhile some preliminary observa-
tions about their nature and limitations will be useful. The consort and
keyboard manuscripts containing music by Byrd number about thirty each.
As Byrd wrote three times as much music for keyboard as for consort the
equal tally of sources might be expected to favour the consort music. But
this part of his output has in fact fared badly. No comprehensive collection
survives; many of the sources contain only one or two pieces by him, and
many lack one or more of the constituent part-books. They do, however,
throw some light on the question of chronology. Although most were copied
long after the music was composed, there are exceptions from which the
approximate dates of certain pieces, including some important ones, may be
deduced.

The first pieces to appear in the manuscripts are In Nomines; one of them
is found in Tenbury 1464, which consists of music current in the 1560s. In
1575 Byrd published the 6-part fantasia in F in an adaptation as a motet;
the consort original was therefore composed earlier – probably considerably
earlier. The most extensive collection of textless polyphony of the period is
Add.31390,* which contains corrections dated 1578. As a source for Byrd
it is of limited importance: the In Nomine texts in the main body of the
manuscript, although the first to survive complete, are too late for dating
purposes. On the other hand the late addition of the popular *Browning* as
an afterthought strongly suggests that this piece was composed in the later
1570s. Of the 5-part canonic fantasia in C a keyboard transcription occurs in
My Ladye Nevells Booke, completed in 1591 (see p. 21 below). Bodleian
E.423, a part-book into which a large number of Byrd's compositions seem
to have been copied fairly promptly as they became available, contains both
the 6-part fantasias in G minor. The earlier appears to have been entered
during the 1580s, and the second a few years later, perhaps about 1590. The
latter was subsequently published in 1611.

*See J. Noble, 'Le Répertoire instrumental anglais (1550–1585)', in Jacquot, *Musique
instrumentale*, 91ff., and Edwards, *Sources*, i, 90ff., where it is suggested that the manuscript
was copied by Clement Woodcock in Chichester.

A number of the later consort sources come from the extensive collection of Edward Paston,* who was in direct touch with the composer. His manuscripts include five lute books in Italian tablature consisting of intabulations of polyphonic music intended to accompany full vocal or instrumental performances. Unfortunately they omit, in general, the top line of each piece, irrespective of the number of parts in the original. One of them (Add.29246), which gives singularly trustworthy ascriptions, contains a considerable number of consort pieces by White and Byrd which are otherwise unknown. Many of the plainchant settings discussed in Chapter 3 survive only in this source, so that the texts are unhappily incomplete.

The keyboard sources present a very different picture. They are dominated by four great manuscript collections which, taken together with *Parthenia*, contain all but half a dozen of Byrd's known keyboard works. These four will often be mentioned in later chapters; they will be called simply Nevell, Weelkes, Tregian and Forster – names which the following notes will clarify. My Ladye Nevells Booke† is not only the earliest of the four, but probably the earliest source altogether for Byrd's keyboard music except for Christ Church 371, a manuscript of the 1560s which contains his two settings of the *Miserere*. Nevell consists exclusively of music by Byrd. It was copied on the composer's behalf by John Baldwin, who completed it on 11 September 1591. The texts are nearly all excellent; with very few exceptions Baldwin must have worked from the autographs. Moreover the corrections in another hand which occur throughout the manuscript were almost certainly made by the composer.‡ Between 1588 and 1591 Byrd had published four large retrospective collections of his vocal music; Nevell is their keyboard equivalent.

Like the *Psalmes, Sonets & Songs* of 1588 it is arranged by genres. It divides into two parts, each introduced by pieces specially composed for Lady Nevell. In the first part the ground and *Chi passa* dedicated to her are followed by descriptive music and then dances, the first nine pavans and galliards forming a carefully ordered sequence of their own (see p. 179f).

---

*See P. Brett, *The Songs of William Byrd* (unpublished dissertation, Cambridge, 1965), i, 184ff., and 'Edward Paston (1550–1630): a Norfolk gentleman and his musical collection', in *Transactions of the Cambridge Bibliographical Society*, iv (1964), 51ff.

†The complete manuscript was edited with an introduction by H. Andrews (London, 1926). See also E. H. Fellowes, 'My Ladye Nevells Booke', *Music & Letters*, xxx (1949), 1ff., and A. Brown, ' "My Lady Nevell's Book" as a source for Byrd's keyboard music', *Proceedings of the Royal Musical Association*, 95 (1968–69), 29ff.

‡See M. Glyn, *About Elizabethan Virginal Music and its Composers* (London, 1924), 35ff., and A. Brown, *A Critical Edition of the Keyboard Music of William Byrd* (unpublished dissertation, Cambridge, 1969), i, 36ff.

The second part contains a mixture of fantasias, grounds and variations, headed by the 'Voluntary for My Lady Nevell.'* This scheme is broken only twice. The ground entitled *The Hunt's up* and the *Ut re mi* Fantasia precede the nine pavans and galliards; this is presumably a mistake. The tenth pavan and galliard pair occupies the third place from the end of the book, but it was clearly composed after the other nine and arrived late along with the D minor Fantasia which follows it. The great importance of the collection as a whole lies in its preservation of the composer's own choice of pieces from the 1570s and 1580s. It contains only three pieces likely to be earlier: the *Galliard Jig, The Hunt's up* and the fragment of a fantasia which is the last piece in the book and may have been tacked on by Baldwin (see p. 227).

The compiler of the second important manuscript, Add.30485, has been convincingly identified as Thomas Weelkes.† His texts are good, and there is only one apparently false attribution to Byrd. The manuscript contains the *Quadran* Pavan and Galliard, which were probably composed too late for inclusion in Nevell, and a slightly revised version of one of Nevell's late arrivals, the D minor Fantasia. Otherwise it covers the same period as Nevell, but is richer in early pieces. The selection of music by other composers is also rather backward-looking.

The publication of *Parthenia* in the winter of 1612–13 precedes the completion of the other two big anthologies. The engraver of the book, William Hole, brought together eight pieces by Byrd, seven by Bull and six by Gibbons. Everything points to Byrd's collaboration in the venture: the place of honour accorded him,‡ the accuracy of the texts, the high quality of the pieces chosen, their careful grouping, and the fact that apart from the two preludes they were all recent compositions or revisions which do not appear to have been in general circulation.

The famous Fitzwilliam Virginal Book§ was copied by the younger

---

*In the index the Fantasia C2 is described as 'for my ladye nevell', but these words have evidently been entered in the wrong place; they are missing from the 'Voluntary for My Lady Nevell', which is simply given as 'the voluntarie lesson'.

†By A. Brown in *A Critical Edition of the Keyboard Music of William Byrd* (unpublished dissertation, Cambridge, 1969), i, 42ff.; see also BK, ii, 192.

‡Compare Sir William Leighton's *Teares and Lamentacions of a Sorrowfull Soule* of 1614, in which Byrd's four pieces not only outnumber the contributions of any other composer except Leighton himself, but were evidently intended to open and close the second and third parts, although two more pieces were added at the end. (Byrd did not contribute to the first part because the accompaniments were for mixed consort, a combination for which he never wrote.)

§The complete manuscript was edited with an introduction by J. A. Fuller Maitland and W. Barclay Squire (Leipzig, 1894–99). See also E. Cole, 'In Search of Francis Tregian', *Music & Letters*, xxxiii (1952), 28ff.

Francis Tregian while he was a prisoner in the Fleet between 1609 and 1619. Not only is it by far the biggest of the virginal books, but it contains the largest collection of Byrd pieces – well over half his known output, as opposed to about a third in Nevell and Forster and under a quarter in Weelkes. Unfortunately Tregian, though a good copyist, was at the mercy of the sources that came his way, and these were plainly very variable in quality. Consequently he transmits a good many poor texts and false ascriptions. But as a Byrd source the book is valuable for the sheer quantity of pieces from all periods of his life, including many more unique texts than its nearest rivals.

Nothing is known of Will Forster, about half of whose virginal book is devoted to Byrd. He signed and dated the index 31 January 1624 (1625 in new style). Byrd had died in July 1623 and it has been suggested* that Forster had access to his papers. This theory would account for the good quality of his texts and the presence of several early pieces not recorded elsewhere – one of them (Pavan G8) in an apparently unfinished state. It is less easy to square, however, with Forster's incorrect attributions to Byrd and his failure to ascribe various genuine works. Whatever the truth of the matter, a curious pattern emerges in the Byrd pieces given anonymously, for all are in the composer's latest manner. They consist of four pieces (the revised version of *The Woods so wild*, Galliard F2, Pavan and Galliard C3 and the arrangement of Harding's galliard) ascribed to Byrd in other sources, a fifth (the Echo Pavan and Galliard G5) listed as his by Tomkins in a table of pieces, and three more (Alman C2 and the F major and G major Preludes) which can be ascribed to Byrd on internal evidence. On the other hand, only two of the pieces attributed to him by Forster (*Go from my window* and the arrangement of Dowland's *Lachrymae*) belong to the late period – an odd circumstance in the one collection to equal Tregian as a source for the late pieces.

After Byrd's death his consort music lay unnoticed until the present century. Its rediscovery was very largely the work of Edmund Fellowes, who eventually brought it together in Volume 17 of his Collected Works of Byrd (referred to here as BW 17).† This edition has since been entirely superseded by the corresponding volume of the Byrd Edition (BE 17), edited by Kenneth Elliott, which is both more complete and more accurate. The first collected

---

*By T. Dart; see BK, i, 169.

†For further details of this and all other editions mentioned up to the end of this chapter, see the Key to Abbreviated Bibliographical References (p. 13f).

edition of the keyboard works was also by Fellowes (BW 18–20), but here he was not first in the field. Not only had modern editions of *Parthenia*, Tregian and Nevell appeared, but Stephen Tuttle had published a volume containing all the pieces attributed to Byrd outside these three sources. As a result Fellowes felt free to adapt the keyboard textures to the piano in his edition, overlooking the fact that none of the previous editions was comparative, and only that of Nevell well edited according to its own lights. It remained for Alan Brown to do the job properly in two *Musica Britannica* volumes (27 and 28) entitled *William Byrd: Keyboard Music* (BK).

The only editions which it is safe to use, then, are BE 17 and BK. Their contents correspond with very few exceptions to the corpus of music treated as genuine in this book (three additional pieces given anonymously in Forster have been published by the present writer). Unfortunately they employ different editorial principles: BK preserves the original note-values whereas BE 17 halves them. When writing music of a particular character or in an established genre, sixteenth-century composers, like those of any other period, adopted the notation traditionally associated with it. The nature of a piece becomes hard to recognize if the notation has been falsified. The distinction between the treatment of cantus firmi in breves and in semibreves becomes blurred, and 3/2 measure takes on the appearance of black tripla in transcription. It has consequently been necessary to refer to the correct values throughout this study. This may cause some inconvenience to the reader when he turns to BE 17 and other current editions, some of which even quarter the note-values. A reminder of the values adopted in those which he is most likely to consult may prove useful:

Original values: TCM; Tregian; Tuttle; the collected keyboard music of Bull (vol. 2), Morley and Farnaby; BW 12–14.

Halved values: EECM 6 and 10; the Mulliner Book; the Dublin Virginal Book; the collected consort music of Tye and White.

Mixed values: the collected keyboard music of Bull (vol. 1), Gibbons and Tomkins.

Byrd never composed for lute, cittern or mixed consorts including plucked instruments. The abundant lute and cittern manuscripts compiled in his lifetime contain arrangements of the celebrated *Lullaby* (1588/32) and a handful of keyboard pieces, but only one piece attributed to him which is unknown elsewhere. This is a pavan; like the pair of galliards by 'W.B.' in a different manuscript it is unacceptable as his work for stylistic reasons (see p. 179).*

William Byrd: Music for the Lute, ed. N. North (London, 1976), contains all the arrangements and misattributed pieces, as well as some other pieces unconnected with Byrd.

Similarly the only Byrd piece in the mixed consort repertory is an arrangement of Pavan c2.*

*Edwards, *Sources*, ii, No. 705. S. Beck, in his edition of Morley's *First Book of Consort Lessons* of 1599 (New York, 1959), 190, suggested that the single settings of *Monsieur's Alman* and *My Lord of Oxenford's Maske* published in it might be by Byrd. There is, however, no reason to suppose that because Byrd composed keyboard variations on these tunes some years earlier he had anything to do with the consort versions.

2

In Nomines

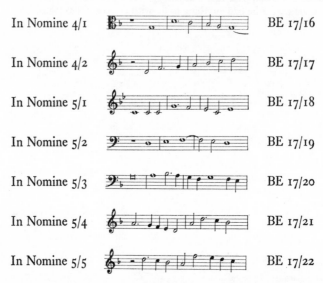

In Nomine 4/1		BE 17/16
In Nomine 4/2		BE 17/17
In Nomine 5/1		BE 17/18
In Nomine 5/2		BE 17/19
In Nomine 5/3		BE 17/20
In Nomine 5/4		BE 17/21
In Nomine 5/5		BE 17/22

The numeration of Byrd's In Nomines adopted here corresponds with that in BE 17. Each setting is denoted by the number of parts followed by the number of the piece; thus in the context of this chapter 'Byrd 4/2' means Byrd's second 4-part In Nomine, and 'Parsons 5/1' Parsons's single 5-part setting. The 7-part setting wrongly attributed to Byrd in Add.32377, and probably by Parsons, is discussed below. Of the 5-part In Nomines given to Byrd in Meyer, *Spielmusik*, No. 5 is his 5-part consort fantasia in C, and No. 6 is by John Baldwin.

The history of sacred vocal polyphony during the sixteenth century in England, as abroad, is that of an unbroken musical tradition, no matter what changes took place in response to drastic liturgical reform or the need for stylistic renewal. English consort music, so far as its history can be traced, shows no such continuity. It could not profit from the Church's stability, for it had no place there. At court, where the constant demand was rather for music to accompany dancing, ceremonial and spectacle, it was subject to fluctuating fashions. There was a growing feeling that textless polyphony offered a new range of possibilities to the composer, but the problems of building sizeable pieces without the aid of words were intensified by the difficulty of finding a pretext for tackling them. The more elaborate forms of instrumental music took root where they could, and owing to changes in social context and the impact of new developments in vocal music, the ground won by one generation was not always congenial to the next.

Apart from dances, the surviving English consort music of the sixteenth and early seventeenth centuries falls into several distinct phases. The first centred round the court in the early part of Henry VIII's reign. The next, which took little from the first, arose about the middle of the century and flourished until the 1570s, after which nothing of note was added except by Byrd, who continued to compose consort music till 1590 or so. This repertory remained popular in certain viol-playing circles till after the turn of the century and survives mostly in manuscripts compiled considerably later than its date of composition. Meanwhile other developments took place in which Byrd took no part. During the 1580s mixed consorts of string, wind and plucked instruments came into favour for lighter entertainment,* and after 1600 a vigorous revival of viol music was initiated by such composers as Thomas Lupo, the younger Ferrabosco, Coprario and Gibbons. Although this generation built on the earlier tradition in many respects, even adopting its most characteristic form, the In Nomine, the older pieces were seldom transcribed alongside the new and were soon forgotten.

The instrumental music of the mid-sixteenth century had strong links with the professional musician's schoolroom, although it may not have originated there and was certainly not confined to it. Morley's *Introduction*, published in 1597, provides a valuable guide to the methods of instruction already current half a century earlier, for Morley was thoroughly grounded in them by Byrd at a time when Byrd, his senior by only 14 years, would still have had fresh memories of his own education. Morley devotes the first part of his book to musical notation, which he teaches through singing at sight. His scholar starts by singing simple textless examples to solmization syllables and eventually graduates to a hair-raisingly difficult 3-part exercise in proportional notation entitled *Christes crosse*. Difficult cross-rhythms and proportions are frequently found in textless compositions of the mid-century, some of which were undoubtedly meant as exercises. Tye makes his intentions explicit in two pieces by calling them respectively *Sit fast* and *Howld fast*. This kind of writing became a persistent element in the repertory and sometimes did duty for more fruitful forms of elaboration. But the best composers recognized it for what it was and avoided it.

In the light of Morley's insistence on singing, the presence of sight-

*See Edwards, *Sources*, i, 28ff.

reading material suggests that the music may have been intended as much for singers as for players. This is confirmed by the title-page of one of the most important manuscript sources, Add.31390, which reads: 'A booke of In nomines and other solfainge songes of v, vi, vii and viii parts for voyces and instrumentes'. The wording echoes that of many contemporary Italian printed part-books, which offered the same choice of medium. In England a gradual transition from textless polyphony for general purposes to purely instrumental writing took place as the individual lines became ever more adventurous. Singers accustomed to the exceptional range and wide skips of English vocal writing would have been prepared to follow the composers quite a long way, if only for the sake of the exercise. But beyond a certain point instruments had the field to themselves. Through this transition the preparatory study, as so often happens in the development of musical forms, became the thing itself, demanding a new standard of performance and emerging from a limited sphere to claim a wider audience.

The great majority of compositions in the repertory were based, like much pre-Reformation church music, on plainsong cantus firmi. By far the most popular of these was the *Gloria tibi trinitas* chant, settings of which were called In Nomines because they originated in imitations of the *In nomine* section from Taverner's *Gloria tibi trinitas* mass.* It is hard to tell why such a tradition should have grown up, but the advantages of the chosen model are clear. It was a singularly beautiful piece by an acknowledged master, composed in an open 4-part texture that gave scope for elaboration, and based on a chant disposed in even breves. Monorhythmic cantus firmi were increasingly favoured at this time; and whereas textless pieces on other chants nearly always stated the cantus firmus in semibreves, following the common practice in their vocal counterparts, Taverner's breves allowed far more room for manoeuvre.

The composition of In Nomines was not primarily an exercise for beginners: the earlier In Nomine composers were already established by the time Taverner wrote his mass in the late 1520s, and Morley shows that the accepted basis for instruction in composition was discanting upon a plainsong in semibreves, not breves. But the genre became to some extent an arena for technical experiment or display, and by Byrd's time every young composer made a point of showing his paces in it. Byrd's own essays, which all belong to his early years, probably helped to establish his reputation before his recall to London in the early 1570s. Their originality, not least when they were based on particular models, would have been immediately

*See TCM 1, 148f.; also *In Nomine*, ed. D. Stevens (Kassel, 1955).

apparent to his contemporaries, who knew the background and acclaimed him on the basis of music that sometimes seems raw in the light of his later work. It is against that background that his swift rise to prominence can be seen in truest perspective.

Although many of the points of imitation and melodic figures used in In Nomines belong to families descended from phrases in Taverner's original,* the spirit of his music was quickly left behind. Taverner's main concern was with melody. His long lines move in slow note-values, with minims as the shortest except in the last phase of the piece, and cover very wide spans. The cantus firmus occupies the alto; the treble and tenor supply the main melodic strands, which develop freely in dialogue, connected only by approximate imitation in some of the phrases. The bass too sometimes discreetly echoes these phrases, but in general moves much more slowly than the other two parts and does nothing to distract attention from them. Some of the earlier In Nomine composers, notably Preston and Points, preserve this kind of texture to some extent in their 4-part pieces, though even here the melodies tend to move more quickly and the bass lays greater claim to equal status. In the typical In Nomines of the older composers these newer tendencies have entirely taken over as a result of the belated influence of continental imitative style. Thus the aggregate of the parts produces more or less constant minim movement, and more active participation by the bass frequently leads to harmonic change in minims such as Taverner had reserved for rare cadential passages.

The two most important In Nomine composers during this period were Tye and Tallis. Born early in the century, they grew up at a time when Taverner was setting the pace. When they came to write their In Nomines against the background of his work, probably not till the 1550s, they must have been fully conscious of the distance they had travelled from his style. But only Tallis showed himself aware of the loss in melodic freedom that the imitative style had entailed. He wrote only two In Nomines,† both in four parts with the cantus firmus in the alto, like Taverner's. His 4/2 begins with fairly straightforward imitations, but the treble assumes increasing independence, and in one passage pursues its own course while the main imitative point is allowed to degenerate into a purely accompanimental figure in the lower parts. In 4/1 the tenor and bass keep up a continuous free canon at the octave; the treble melody develops along its own lines, sometimes alluding to figures in the lower parts and sometimes referring back to

*For examples of the influence of his opening, see G. Reese, 'The Origin of the In Nomine', *JAMS*, ii (1949), 12.

†Neither has been published. Meyer's numbering is used here.

material unique to itself. But if Tallis pays homage to Taverner in his cultivation of melody, his melodic style, like the texture that throws it into relief, is entirely personal – so personal, indeed, as to discourage emulation.* Nevertheless, his pieces were quite widely circulated, and their thoughtful artistry was not lost on a Scot named Thomas Wood who copied them without realizing that both were by Tallis and commented (in Add.33933): 'Tuay sindry men upone ane plaine sang, and they bayth haue done uerray weill in this.'

Tye's output of In Nomines contrasts sharply with that of Tallis. As against Tallis's two quietly individual 4-part pieces he composed at least twenty-four (more than three times as many as any other composer), nearly all in five parts.† Yet although they display a wide variety of techniques and attracted imitators, they never quite reach the standard of the best examples of the genre. In the more traditional, and presumably earlier, pieces Tye shows excessive devotion to the imitative principle. His points of imitation are often only four minims long, beginning on the weak beat. This enables him to provide a new entry for nearly every breve of the plainsong, and he often pushes an extra one in at the half bar. In several pieces he increases the tedium by confining the first three minims to the same pitch, or by adopting monothematicism. One setting in which these features combine is entitled *Farwell, my good l. for ever* (most of Tye's pieces bear quaint titles, few of which have been satisfactorily explained); it is only forty-three breves long, but the point occurs over fifty times, sometimes immediately repeated in sequence in the same part. A comparison of this piece with Tallis's 4/2, with which it shares common material, emphasizes Tye's failure to plan his music in clear paragraphs or to achieve any overall sense of direction.

Nor did he escape these difficulties when he sought to heighten interest by other means. He shortened each note of the cantus firmus to three minims in *Howld fast*, lengthened it to five in *Trust*, indulged in the cross-rhythms of sight-reading exercises in *Howld fast* and *Seldom sene*, and tried out various kinds of tripla proportion. These features occur in In Nomines by other composers; there is no certainty that Tye introduced them to the genre, though in view of his seniority he may have done so in some cases. They are invariably accompanied by a good deal of crotchet movement or even faster divisions, and here Tye stands apart from the humdrum garrulity of William Mundy, Mallorie, Stonings, Woodcock and the like, for in the often quoted *Crye* and some of his triple-time pieces such as *Saye so* he

---

*The second half of Parsley 4/1 is perhaps an exception; see O. Parsley, *Three Consort Pieces*, ed. J. Morehen (London, 1974).

†The twenty-one that survive complete are printed in Tye, *Instrumental Music*.

starts off with really striking ideas quite outside the usual In Nomine vocabulary. Unfortunately even here his control over the development of line is poor and his imitations remain stiff. It is significant that he frequently cuts corners in the plainsong as though conscious of his inability to sustain his ideas for the full course.

Tye and Tallis were a generation older than their most important successors in the field of the In Nomine: Robert White, apparently born no earlier than 1537 or 38,* Robert Parsons, a slightly older man whose musical style is more forward looking than that of White, and Byrd, born almost certainly in 1543 – to whom may be added Alfonso Ferrabosco the elder, who was born in the same year as Byrd and visited England as early as 1562. However, the younger composers, as will emerge in the course of this chapter, produced their settings relatively early in their careers, so that the time-lag between the In Nomines of the two generations was much less than might have been expected. Tye's more adventurous pieces could even be later than those of his juniors, to judge from their poor dissemination in the sources. However widely White, Parsons, Byrd and Ferrabosco differed in style and aim, they shared a conservative approach to the externals of the In Nomine form. They kept to Taverner's breves and rarely changed the cantus firmus (when they did the changes were small and in many cases probably accidental). They avoided the cross-rhythms, tripla and continuous crotchets in which minor composers so often foundered, and such unpromising experiments as placing the plainchant in the bass, or setting the free parts in the major mode.† What they strove for, though in very different ways, was characteristic melody and formal discipline.

Some of the In Nomines by these composers bear conflicting attributions in the sources. Of the seven ascribed to Parsons, one also appears under White's name and two others under Byrd's. In order to sort them out it will be necessary to consider the authority of the manuscripts and the style of the composers in some detail. To facilitate comparison between different settings reference is made throughout, not to bar numbers, but to cantus firmus numbers derived from the fifty-four notes of the *Gloria tibi trinitas* chant as it appears in Taverner's In Nomine (Ex. 1). Thus the single B♭ remains CF 29 in all settings, whether or not the composer has omitted or reduplicated notes earlier in the cantus firmus, or brought in other parts in

*See D. Mateer, 'Further light on Preston and White', *Musical Times*, cxv (1974), 1074f.

†The first was done by Whytbroke and John Mundy, the second by Golder and Strogers – who, however, made something of it in his 5/2 (Meyer's numbering).

Ex. 1

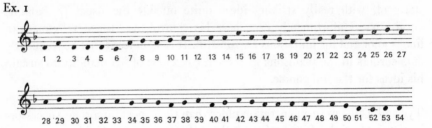

advance of it. Similarly, transpositions are ignored for this purpose: for instance the cadence, very common in early settings, on F at CF 30 is referred to as on F even when the cantus firmus is transposed up a fourth so that it is really on B♮.

Five In Nomines by White survive complete, four in four parts, and one in five.* Although they are thoroughly personal works, their involvement with the style of Tye's more closely imitative pieces, some of which they take as partial models, suggests that they are early ones. Moreover 4/1, which is one of the best, was already well enough known in the sixties for Mulliner to transcribe it in his organ book. Ex. 2 shows the approximate

Ex. 2

succession of points in this typical piece. The first is similar to that of Tye's only 6-part In Nomine; the pattern of entries only occasionally matches Tye's, but the occurrence of the admittedly common figure c later in his piece reinforces the impression that White had it in mind. At the end White quotes directly from a different Tye In Nomine, which itself contains a reference to Taverner's original. At the close of the latter a little figure is heard three times: in the tenor at CF 47–48, repeated an octave higher in the treble at CF 49–50, and then by the tenor a fifth lower at CF 51–52. In

---

*Printed in White, *Instrumental Music*, ed. I. Spector. Meyer omits 4/4; Spector reconstructs it incorrectly from the partial lute transcription in Add.29246 (for this MS. see p. 21). Spector's edition should be used with the greatest caution; except for the six fantasias and the settings of *Christe qui lux es* all the lute transcriptions should be ignored. For 4/1 see also *In Nomine*, ed. D. Stevens (Kassel, 1955).

Weepe no more, Rachell Tye imitates this procedure exactly, but substitutes a rather different figure at CF 35–36 in Taverner.* White takes over Tye's version precisely, except for a little decorative intensification of the phrase, together with features from his coda.

Issuing as it does from the inbreeding of the early In Nomine White's piece shares many of its characteristics. But there is a new sense of order. Each point is derived from the last clearly and easily, working towards the concluding quotation from Tye (Ex. 2f), which falls naturally into place. There is greater melodic breadth and rhythmic character than in Tye. The spacing of the entries is more varied and they are made to stand out by means of rests and slower movement in the other parts. Cadences are few but very emphatic, so that the piece falls into long, well defined paragraphs.

Of White's other In Nomines his 4/4 stands somewhat apart, because the plainsong is in the treble. But 4/3 and 5/1 are similar in style to 4/1, except that they are monothematic and perhaps a little less successful in consequence. In 4/3 the theme is slightly varied after each main cadence, but too little to prevent a feeling of anticlimax. In 5/1 this effect is avoided because the obsessive, if ingenious working of the point masks the cadences, but at some sacrifice to the sense of progression that White achieves elsewhere by marking out the paragraphs so firmly. Against the background of these pieces it is possible to establish the authenticity of 4/2, which was copied twice in Bodleian D.212–6 (see p. 34f), attributed once each to White and Parsons. The manuscript was written at least thirty years after the death of both, so that the contradiction merely shows that it was circulating under both names. It is a matter of chance that the only other surviving source (Add.22519) gives it to Parsons – immediately after an anonymous text of White 4/1. Internal evidence shows it to be by White. It shares all the general stylistic features of 4/1, 4/3 and 5/1, in particular the use of off-beat dotted minims to produce frequent suspensions, which help to give the entries prominence and the music momentum. The technique of thematic derivation, which includes adding and shedding prefixes, is close to that of 4/1; cadences are distributed much as in 4/1 and 3, three of the main ones exactly matching those in 4/1 (on F at CF 16, 22 and 30). As usual there are links with Tye: the first point recalls his instrumental piece *Lawdes deo*, and the plan of the first imitative exposition matches that of White's own 4/4, which is modelled on the opening of Tye's *Seldom sene* (see p. 42).

That this In Nomine can be confidently ascribed to White and withdrawn

*Tye quotes and elaborates on it in its original position in his *Blamles*, and Johnson does the same in his 4-part setting (printed in *In Nomine*, ed. D. Stevens, Kassel, 1955).

from Parsons is due entirely to the consistency of White's musical thought. Parsons's small surviving output is of such diversity that it would be very hard to attribute a piece to him without strong documentary evidence. Thus the authorship of Parsons 7/2 and Byrd 4/1, each of which also occurs under the name of the other composer, must be decided primarily by reference to Byrd's style. Five In Nomines appear to be the work of Parsons, one in five parts, and two each in four and seven.* Those in five and seven parts break entirely new ground. In his 5/1 he imports the brisk, dance-like homophony found in contemporary instrumental pieces in free style; it became the most popular of all In Nomines. In 7/1 he goes to the other extreme, adopting the long lines and rich texture typical of pre-Reformation church poly-phony. White was, of course, also a master of this style; he too wrote a 7-part In Nomine, but to judge from the single surviving part he kept to his usual manner. Parsons establishes the special character of his essay by allowing his singularly graceful melodies to expand for no less than sixteen breves before the plainsong enters and imposes some restraint.

As for the dubious 7/2 with the conflicting ascription to Byrd, though no less unusual than these two remarkable works, it cannot compare with them in quality. It is an exercise in thick textures and harmony so sluggish as often to move in breves (CF 30–39 are harmonized FFFFCFCFCF, with a 4–3 suspension on each C). The points are devised to maintain this pattern, and although inner parts stir into action from time to time their surroundings make them ineffective. Whether or not Parsons's marked tendency to think in harmonic terms and his liking for untried ways of treating the form provide sufficient reason for saddling him with such a stodgy work, one thing is certain: the attribution to Byrd can be ruled out, for the style is antipathetic to his musical mentality as it appears in even his earliest work.

Parsons 4/1 and 2 and Byrd 4/1 and 2 are all found in Bodleian D.212–6, an early seventeenth-century manuscript largely devoted to an extensive collection of In Nomines; it is the sole source for three of these four works, the exception being Byrd 4/1, ascribed to Parsons in Tenbury 354–8.† Despite his mistake in attributing White 4/2 to both White and Parsons (see p. 33), the compiler of D.212–6 was an In Nomine fancier whose ascriptions

---

*The numeration adopted here is that of Meyer, except that his 4/3 becomes 4/2, because he had White 4/2 in second place. Only 5/1 is published, in *Four In Nomines in 5 parts*, ed. H. T. David (New York, 1937).

†This manuscript is unreliable: it credits White with a stiff and repetitious 4-part In Nomine that no composer of his accomplishment could have written. D.212–6 gives it very plausibly to John Thorne, who is not known to have composed other In Nomines and is unlikely to have attracted false ascriptions.

are unusually trustworthy, and there are good reasons for believing his other ascriptions to Parsons and those to Byrd. Quite apart from questions of style, the cantus firmi provide evidence that Byrd 4/1 and 2 and Parsons 4/1 and 2 were written as pairs. It has already been mentioned that irregularities in the plainsong are common in some minor composers, and the rule in Tye, who follows no particular pattern. But they are sparse in Parsons and altogether absent from White, Ferrabosco, and Byrd in four of his 5-part pieces. When the irregularities in two settings match there is likely to be a connection (for instance there is a single omission – CF 33 – from Tallis's pair of In Nomines).

The fact that Byrd 4/1 and 2 both contain a reduplication in the cantus firmus at CF 24 is perhaps less revealing because this is the sole irregularity in various other settings,* but Parsons 4/1 and 2 share three irregularities: the reduplication of CF 24 and 42 and the omission of CF 46–47. The only other In Nomine to match this pattern is Johnson's well known example, and as all three pieces have the plainsong in the treble it seems clear that Parsons used the Johnson as a model, at least in externals. In these two presumably early In Nomines, Parsons shows nothing of the originality of his own 5/1 and 7/1, nor of White's control and sophistication. But his liking for sharper tonal definition than had been usual in English music is already evident in 4/1, in which successive perfect or interrupted cadences are approached by a pattern of parallel thirds more concerned with harmonic direction than contrapuntal elaboration.

The common authorship of the two Byrd 4-part In Nomines proclaims itself at every level. An entirely fresh voice makes itself felt here, eloquent, free of preconceptions and confident, despite some roughness of technical detail that betrays inexperience. The pieces are not special cases like Parsons 5/1 or 7/1: they stand not only within the central tradition of the genre, but closer to its origin than any settings since the very earliest. With the exception of Tallis, whose example he preferred to leave to one side, Byrd was the only composer who knew how to value Taverner's melodic breadth; he clearly studied him with care and composed under his direct impact. Like Taverner he places the centre of interest in the melodic dialogue between treble and tenor, and although he works with imitative points he does not treat imitation as an end in itself, as Tye and White were apt to do. In his 4/1–3 White makes constant use of stretto, and draws the bass into the imitative texture wherever possible, whereas Byrd is always ready to subordinate the bass to the interests of melodic development in other parts.

The very beginning of **In Nomine 4/1** provides a good example. The

*Parsons 7/2, Strogers's 6-part setting, and an anonymous 4-part piece in Add.30480.

bass makes only one short reference to the opening idea, as in Taverner's original on which the first paragraph up to CF 13 is closely modelled. Byrd replaces Taverner's unbroken treble and tenor melodies with two imitative entries each. The initial point itself, like that of many other In Nomines, is derived from Taverner – indeed, the second treble entry, at CF 9–13, adopts his melody for this segment, changing only the rhythm. Two of Byrd's characteristic procedures are already present: he brings the quasi-canonic exchanges between the two leading melodic parts into the closest possible relation by placing them at the octave, and he takes special care over melodic organization in the treble, allowing the first phrase to rise no higher than D (as opposed to Taverner's F), so that the Fs in the second phrase help to give shape to the whole passage. Byrd follows Taverner in rounding off the first section with a V–I cadence on D at CF 13, a feature not often taken up by other composers,* but habitually used, with only slight variations,† by Byrd as a springboard to launch the second stage. Here he invariably introduces a new, more compact point which quickens the pulse and leads to shorter periods, something scarcely to be met with in earlier settings; only in 5/1 and 2 is the treatment rather different. Byrd's thought is dynamic where his predecessors preserved uniformity.

In 4/1 the new point at CF 13 is a malleable little phrase (Ex. 3a) very typical of Byrd (Ex. 3c shows a similar idea from his In Nomine 5/3; the opening subject of a later work, the Canonic Fantasia 5/C, belongs to the same family). This has only a short run, to CF 19, where it gives way to an even shorter-lived variant (Ex. 3b). This little section illustrates two more

Ex. 3

characteristic features of Byrd's music. First his motivic skill: Ex. 3b may appear to derive from 3a, but the two figures are taken respectively from the last notes of the tenor and treble melodies heard simultaneously before the cadence at CF 13 (compare White's more literal example of the same

---

*It occurs in Points 4/1, Stonings 4/1, Brewster 5/1, Strogers 5/3 (Meyer's numbering) and White 4/1 (at CF 12) to herald a new point, and with less structural weight in Tye's *Blamles*, *Free from all* and No. 8 (Weidner's numbering), and in Strogers 6/1.

†In 5/1 and 3 it comes a breve later, at CF 14, and in 5/4 is replaced by a half close on A at CF 14, following a passing full close on D on the second half of CF 11.

process in Ex. 2c′ and d). Secondly, as the music moves away from the
foundation laid by the expository first paragraph, the cadences weaken:
following the V–I on D at CF 13 there is a II⁶–I on D at CF 19 and a half
close on A at CF 23. The succession was presumably suggested by Taverner,
who has a II⁶–I on D at CF 22; it recurs in Byrd 4/2 (II⁶–I on D at CF 22,
half close on A at CF 28), and although he does not use this cadence pattern
in his 5-part In Nomines he adopts a comparable one in various A minor
fantasias (see p. 238n).

It is also worth noting how Byrd enhances the liveliness of the new
section after CF 13 by overtopping the preceding high Fs with a G, and how
deftly he prepares for the lower tension of his third section by allowing the
half cadence that introduces it to trail for a breve and a half before the new
point enters at CF 24. Such spontaneous touches proclaim the born composer.

It has been remarked that 'subjects hinging on an expressive semitone
step are important in Byrd's work, and decidedly rare in earlier English
music'.* This holds good in the In Nomines of both Byrd and his elders.
The point that enters at CF 24 of Byrd 4/1 consists of nothing but a rise of a
semitone followed by a return and a free continuation. The cantus firmus is
thus able to supply one augmented entry at CF 28–30 (cf. Ex. 1); another is
shown in the bass of Ex. 4b. This passage quotes Taverner's treatment of
CF 19 (Ex. 4a), a moment that must have haunted Byrd, for his introduction

Ex. 4

a. Taverner

b. Byrd

of the same decorated resolution figure at twice the speed in both this piece
(see Ex. 3b) and his 4/2 is unparalleled elsewhere in the In Nomine repertory.
The version in Ex. 4b illustrates another aspect of Byrd's use of the semitone: his liking for dissonances involving a major seventh, which earlier
composers used rather sparingly.† It is scarcely accurate to speak of the
semitone figure in this passage as a point of imitation; it really only serves to
unify a piece of free composition (which incidentally alludes to the opening
point). Nor can the next section be called imitative: two consecutive state-

*See J. Kerman, 'Byrd, Tallis, and the Art of Imitation', in *Aspects of Medieval and
Renaissance Music*, ed. J. La Rue (New York, 1966), 532.
†Exceptional pieces in this respect include Tallis's organ hymns and antiphons.

ments of a 4-bar subject build an 8-bar period with a caesura (CF 33–41), rather like a strain of a pavan, beneath which the tenor contributes one statement and the bass none at all.

Byrd's propensity, shared by no other composer, to introduce symmetrical periods reminiscent of secular melody into contrapuntal contexts was to have a profound effect on his structural thinking. It comes to the fore at the very beginning of his **In Nomine** 4/2. This piece is not quite so close to Taverner as its companion. The bass plays a more active role and note-values are generally faster, so that the young composer finds himself not wholly at ease with his cantus firmus. He subjects it to decoration, either to provide the illusion of an imitative entry, or simply to make it fit in with the other parts, an expedient he no longer finds necessary in his 5-part settings. Even with modification he is pushed to an unorthodox, if effective resolution at CF 38, where the alto part represents G (Ex. 5).

Ex. 5

His first section appears to have been suggested by the opening of Parsons 4/1. Parsons allows his well shaped melody (Ex. 6a) to continue for three full breves before the second entry joins it – a first step towards the lyrical appeal

Ex. 6   *a.* Parsons

b. Byrd

of his 7/1 – but unfortunately he fails to sustain his initial inspiration. Byrd takes the same idea, transposes the second limb of the phrase up a fourth (Ex. 6b), and by delaying the next entry for a semibreve longer than Parsons, arrives at a 4-bar phrase. Then (at the cost of a brush with the plainsong at CF 6 and 9) he answers it with a 4-bar tenor entry. Although the last bar of this is overlapped by a new treble entry, it is underpinned by a cadential suspension at CF 8 so that the sense of symmetry is not lost before the music reaches Byrd's habitual close on D at CF 13. The next section falls into three more or less self-contained 3-bar periods separated by cadences. Symmetrical phraseology abounds throughout the rest of the piece, arising in part from the dangerously close relationship of the successive subjects. Monotony is avoided through the intervention of yet another of Byrd's highly original formal devices: his use of contrasting areas of tonal stability. Thus the music centres round the sonority of C major at CF 25–27, A major at CF 28–33 and E minor at CF 34–36, before returning to D minor at CF 40, from which it makes various short excursions before the close.

The final sections of the two 4-part In Nomines are constructed similarly. In both, the treble pauses before its last entry, a special effect for the conclusion such as Tallis might have devised – and executed with more skill than the young Byrd could muster. The last new subject in both pieces enters at CF 47. That in 4/2 is presumably Byrd's own, but the whole conclusion of 4/1 from here on is a 4-part adaptation of the corresponding passage in Tye's 5-part *Rachelle weeping*. The two sources for Byrd's piece give different versions of this section. The earlier, in the Tenbury manuscript that so implausibly attributes the work to Parsons, is very lame indeed,* and it is not surprising that Byrd should have revised it, decorating Tye's point a little and making other improvements. Neither version causes any stylistic inconsistency because Byrd transforms Tye's music by thinning it out drastically and adding melodic continuations of far greater character; that was no doubt the purpose of the borrowing.

At the same time he seems to have been in some sense competing with White. It can scarcely be coincidence that White arranged exactly the same portion of Tye's *Weepe no more, Rachell* to conclude his 4/1 (see pp. 32f), and that both White and Byrd took the opening of Tye's *Seldom sene* as the starting point for an In Nomine (see p. 42). It has already been argued that White's In Nomines are early works. Byrd would surely have known them, for he imitated hymn-settings by White at a very early stage in his composing career (see p. 53ff). However, the In Nomines had nothing to teach him. Although he may have appreciated White's thematic cogency and sound planning, his own methods were already far more subtle, varied and imaginative. The two composers' paths never coincide even in detail. For example, perhaps two-thirds of White's main articulating cadences are on F; Byrd is far from sharing this predilection, and rarely pauses at White's favourite cadential points.

Byrd's **In Nomine 5/1** raises an acute problem of authenticity. It is easily the least distinguished setting in the Byrd canon; its right to a place there

*It is printed in BE 17, p. 160.

can be defended but perhaps not conclusively proved. It is known in a single source, Add.31390 (see p. 20). The scribe first attributed it to Mundy, and then changed his mind. It has little in common with William Mundy's two characterless In Nomines, in which a standard opening point gives way to busy but essentially lifeless elaboration. In a general way the style suggests Parsons or Byrd, for instance in the very early appearance of E♭s,* which occurs in Parsons 4/1 and was apparently taken over by Byrd in his 4/2. The plainsong is in the treble, a very rare position in settings of more than four parts.† However, a subspecies of 4-part In Nomine with treble cantus firmus flourished for a time, especially among the composers Byrd studied. Six examples are known: Johnson's, Tye's only 4-part setting, an anonymous piece (in Add.30480–4), White 4/4 and Parsons 4/1 and 2. There are many signs that Byrd 5/1 started life as a 4-part setting too. At the beginning and in most of the tuttis the middle part has been pushed in as an afterthought.‡

It happens that the manuscript source contains only one 4-part text, and various 4-part In Nomines – Taverner's, Johnson's, Tallis 4/2 – provided with an intrusive extra part. The arranger, however, was probably not the one who worked on Byrd 5/1. He shows a more practised hand and a different approach. No doubt with the object of enlivening textures that seemed rather plain by the 1570s, he not only supplies additional imitative entries where possible but makes frequent use of quick notes. The result is an impertinence,§ but questions of taste apart he was reasonably skilful. It is significant that he left the original parts unchanged, whereas adjustments have been made in the Byrd. Ex. 7 shows the setting at CF 29–30.‖ The E♭ in the cantus firmus has been decorated (the only instance in the piece) in order to avoid near parallels (E♭–D) with the additional part. If this part is omitted a similar weakness (E♭–C) is uncovered between the plainsong and the alto. The arranger presumably altered the treble; and it follows that he may have made other changes, for instance in the distribution of the parts

---

*Actually A♮s in this piece (and Parsons 4/1), because the plainsong is transposed up a fourth.

†The only other examples are Parsons 7/1 and 5-part settings by Sadler, Woodcock, and an anonymous composer (in R.M.24.d.2).

‡It starts with a faked imitative entry without continuation, and produces wilful or downright clumsy part-writing at bars 23 (parallel sevenths), 25, 29, 33 and 46 (the last altered in BE 17 – see the commentary). However, some at least of these infelicities may be felt to presage the bold contrapuntal technique that was to emerge in 5/2.

§For this version of Johnson's piece see MB 15/75; the extra part is the fourth.

‖Note the 6–5 movement in the alto at CF 30, preceded by a rising fifth. The figure is common in Tye at this juncture, but is not used by White or Parsons. Byrd seems to have found it useful as a means of avoiding a too emphatic cadence on F here: see his 4/1 and 5/5.

in the 4-part texture at bars 10–13 and 16–20. Except perhaps in these passages the middle part is clearly a later insertion and can be omitted with benefit at least as far as bar 39. From here, however, it is on the whole much better integrated. There are two possible reasons for this state of affairs. The composer may have decided to increase the number of parts before he had fully worked out the later stages of the work, or it may simply be that the less linear character of the music here made the adaptation easier. In any case the final impression is that the composer and arranger were probably the same man.

Ex. 7

In its 4-part version the first paragraph of the piece, at least, looks more like Byrd than anyone else. Like Taverner's In Nomine and Byrd 4/1 and 2 it terminates in a full cadence on D without the third of the chord,* though at CF 14 instead of 13. The initial dialogue between alto and tenor, with shorter bass entries, is less original in plan than those in 4/1 and 2 (so far as uncertainty about the first version of bars 10–13 allows a judgement), but with all Byrd's usual interest in linear development. That interest continues to show itself throughout the middle reaches of the composition, but in a frustrated form that perhaps gives a clue as to how Byrd, if he was indeed the composer, came to write such an unsatisfactory piece. His ability to use the contour of his top lines as a formal agent already shows itself in his 4-part In Nomines, but in 5/1 the top free part could only run up and down within a limited range, constantly stopping short at B♭ for fear of bumping its head on the plainsong ceiling above. Moreover, as a result of his preference for exchanges at the octave between the tenor and the upper part, the tenor became infected with the same inhibition. And since the cantus firmus did not on this occasion stop the gap between the two parts, an uncomfortable rift appeared in the texture; the unhappy middle part probably originated in the need to fill this in. The style of the piece gave no opportunity for the symmetrical periods and differentiated tonal areas of 4/1 and 2, and it is understandable that the composer, in his haste to finish an uncongenial task, should most untypically have cut four breves of the chant (CF 40–43

*Note the uncharacteristic approach to the third in the additional part.

and ended with a section in tripla, somewhat in the manner of Tye's In Nomine *Rounde*.

Byrd's quotation from Tye in his 4/1, and the oblique reference to White that it implies, show that while still immersed in the study of Taverner he was already fully aware of the later, densely imitative approach to In Nomine composition. This offered a challenge that he proceeded to meet in his **In Nomine 5/2**. There is no faltering in this powerful work such as occurs occasionally in the 4-part settings, especially towards the close. But the part-writing is still rather headstrong, and the great stride forward that Byrd takes here probably indicates the speed at which he was learning rather than any great difference in the date of composition.* As in 4/1 he quotes from Tye apparently with White in mind, for like White in his 4/4 he starts by adapting the opening of one of Tye's least crowded imitative In Nomines, that of *Seldom sene*. Unlike White he does not decorate Tye's point. Both composers adjust some of the entries by octave transposition,† avoid Tye's modification of the entry at CF 7–9 by transposing it down a fourth, and then go their separate ways. Byrd may have been attracted to Tye's point by its pivotal semitone (see Ex. 8a),‡ but it is hard to escape the

Ex. 8

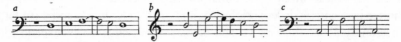

impression that his appropriation of the idea was less an act of homage than a piece of bravura. After CF 9 he makes for his usual cadence on D at CF 13 (actually A, because of cantus firmus transposition), leaving Tye to trudge stolidly on until, near the end of the piece, he breaks into unrelated cross-rhythms – or more strictly cross-durations – in a vain attempt to relieve the tedium. Meanwhile Byrd expands the technical and expressive scope of the music with astonishing rapidity, by means of diminution and free rhythmic variation of Tye's point and flowing extensions of a secondary motif of his own, previously worked into Tye's plain bass at CF 5–6 and now developed into a strenuous new point at CF 22 (Ex. 8b).

*Its presence in Tenbury 1464 suggests that it was in general circulation by the mid-1560s; see J. Kerman, 'Byrd's Motets: Chronology and Canon', *JAMS*, xiv (1961), 360.

†That is, in relation to the cantus firmus, which White transposes up a fourth (as is usual when it is placed in the treble) and Byrd down a fourth. The absence of B♭ in Byrd's setting led scribes to identify it as 'on the sharpe' (Add.32377) or simply '♯' (Tenbury 389).

‡Compare the emphasis on the flattened sixth in the points that he borrowed from Tye in 4/1, and probably from Parsons in 4/2.

After the gradual build-up of entries thus far, the new main section, the second of the three that make up the work, might have been expected to bring some relaxation. But Byrd starts straight away with entries in quick succession and reaches the closest possible stretto five breves later (at CF 27), a structural procedure that might have proved disastrous so early in the composition if imitation had been his only recourse. However, the section is brilliantly constructed on a plan of another kind, with techniques pioneered in the 4-part In Nomines: four breves centring on E minor sonority (CF 25–28), three more turning to A minor, and then eight governed by two 4-bar phrases in the treble and lifted into clear C major, with a final onset of crotchet movement to prepare a cadence on A.

Only the beginning of the third section brings a momentary truce to imitative activity. The new subject, Ex. 8c, combining a fifth drawn from Ex. 8b and the semitone figure from Ex. 8a, is heard only once in the first four bars, in the bass – to which the treble responds with a diminution of Ex. 8a, thereby emphasizing the connection between the two subjects and the recapitulatory element in the ensuing final section. Here entries at the semibreve soon become more persistent than ever; with one or two notable exceptions, which serve to punctuate the passage, they establish an ostinato-like pattern on a single degree, though in three octaves. The resulting harmonic stability in the tonic region of A minor gradually counteracts the imitative momentum, and after a telling melodic modification the alto and bass cease to compete seriously with the dominating partnership between treble and tenor, the answering phrases of which measure out the final bars. This In Nomine surely surpasses all previous contributions to the genre.

At first encounter the altogether quieter **In Nomine 5/3** may seem less impressive. But although a more relaxed and intimate work it is no less original. There are five successive points, of which only the first exceeds a couple of breves in length or gives rise to the kind of lyrical continuation so characteristic of the composer. Even here the crotchet movement is not allowed to culminate in a big cadence: the one on D at CF 14 is smoothed over and requires the support of another, three breves later, to effect the unobtrusive entry of the next point. The first point (Ex. 9) is adapted from

Ex. 9

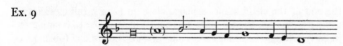

Alfonso Ferrabosco, who wrote three In Nomines, all in five parts. The third in Meyer's numbering must surely be the earliest, an unremarkable piece which Byrd evidently had by him when composing his 5/3. Ferrabosco, feeling his way in a genre that was new to him, starts with a point of a standard kind in which Byrd inserts an A (bracketed in Ex. 9) to produce his favourite rising and falling semitone figure. Like Ferrabosco he starts three breves before the entry of the cantus firmus, and ends the piece on a chord of G, instead of the much more usual D.*

These trivial resemblances are incidental to Byrd's real interest in the piece, which seems to have lain in the Italianate liking for clear major harmony. Ferrabosco uses a good deal of E♭ sonority, and the four Fs at CF 44–47 appear as a dominant pedal of B♭ instead of the traditional pivot between F and D minor, with plagal B♭. Byrd adopts Ferrabosco's harmonic field at this point for his immeasurably finer music, but elsewhere his quest for brighter harmonic regions takes him, in contrast to Ferrabosco, in the sharp direction (unfunctionally speaking), to an F major freed from D minor, and to C major. For the purpose of this harmonic exploration Byrd employs a special kind of subject. After the first the points all avoid crotchets and, except for the third (see Ex. 3c), include pairs of repeated minims that discourage fast harmonic change. No suspensions or passing notes arise from the nature of the points themselves; Byrd supplies them in free parts, but very sparingly so that nothing clouds the luminous major harmony. In the last nine bars he manages to introduce the major triad of every degree of the scale except the sixth. The new territory lay far beyond Ferrabosco, and perhaps only its discoverer could revisit it. He did not neglect to do so on at least one occasion many years later (see p. 253).

Byrd's two remaining In Nomines, 5/4 and 5, are his most elaborate and mature. In Nomine 5/4 is once again written against the background of Ferrabosco – this time his 5/1.† Ferrabosco 5/1 and 2, unlike his 5/3, are enterprising works, as independent of the tradition as Parsons's best pieces. If they lack the impact of Parsons it is because the music is oddly lacking in personality: the young Italian was able to achieve originality of a sort simply by employing standard techniques learnt at home in an alien context. His 5/2 is an unusual essay in triple measure that seems not to have been imitated. In 5/1 he handles a wealth of crotchet movement with a precision

---

*The held D at the end of the chant allows a plagal close on D or a full close on G. Taverner used both in his *Gloria tibi trinitas* mass. His choice of G in the In Nomine was not often followed in early settings. Examples are Tallis 4/1, an anonymous 6-part piece in Add.31390, Parsley 4/1 and 2 and a fragmentary 5-part setting, Golder 4/1, Stonings 5/1, all three by Ferrabosco, and Byrd 5/3 and 4, both imitated from Ferrabosco. The full close is naturally quite common in later settings.

†Printed in *Four In Nomines in 5 parts*, ed. H. T. David (New York, 1937).

that is certainly 'deeply skilled' in its detail by comparison with the diffuseness of many minor composers in the genre, and he closes with imitative
scale patterns in quavers* that entirely outpace Tye's halting efforts at
brilliance. Byrd was quick to recognize the novelty of the piece, and set
about clarifying his attitude to it. The last section, from CF 48, was all that
he needed to make his own, but his whole composition can be read as a
commentary.

Ferrabosco's opening shows a practised hand, but scarcely a supple one.
The movement of the music is hampered by repetition of the rhythm of the
main motive, and nothing happens to heighten interest before the next
idea takes over at CF 15. Byrd inverts this first motive whilst preserving the
rhythm, and continues each entry with a characteristic flexibility that
removes all possibility of rhythmic stagnation (see Ex. 10). Even his music
of this early period shows that the key to his extraordinary formal sense lies

Ex. 10

in his natural inclination to think in terms of expressive continuity rather
than of structural gambits. Here the treble leads off with a 4-bar phrase, a
basis from which the next sentence reaches in two spans, with no real point
of harmonic repose, to a break at CF 14. The keystone of this arch is a little
phrase derived from the second phrase of the main subject and marked X
in Ex. 10. Its function is to open the second period, which it effects in
various ways. It makes a harmonic break by introducing F♮, thus weakening
the connective force of the third entry, which runs across the division; it

*Comparable figures occur in duos by Licino (Brown 1545_2, 1546_{12}) and Lupachino
and Tasso (1559_6), and in 3-part pieces by Conforti (1558_1) and Ruffo (1564_8); see D.
Kämper, *Studien zur instrumentalen Ensemblemusik des 16. Jahrhunderts in Italien* (Vienna,
1970), 104ff., 132ff.

takes up the treble Bb not merely as an echo, but with a dissonant emphasis that announces comment and extension; and having modified its rhythm and contour in the following bar it migrates to the treble and stays there to act as a counterbalance to the persistent scale passages in the lower parts, and to carry the top line to its highest peak towards the end of the section.

At CF 14 both composers begin a new section. In Ferrabosco the crotchet movement becomes sturdier as a result of a quicker harmonic pulse which accommodates 4–3 suspensions and resolutions in the space of a minim (a feature that Byrd adopts). The texture is not really imitative: short phrases answer one another neatly, keeping the music going at an orderly jog-trot. Apart from a flurry of quavers at CF 40–41 there is little change of character till CF 48. The patterned style makes a welcome change from the usual aimless strings of crotchets, but runs into a difficulty of a different kind that is common in contemporary English organ music. This is illustrated by a bad moment where, after a complete little statement a breve long on the A at CF 33 has been answered in sequence a tone lower on the G of CF 34, the whole exchange is repeated almost unchanged on the A and G of CF 35 and 36.

Byrd is very wary of all this. His first move is a further section on material from the opening. He then (CF 24–31) increases harmonic density by imitative intensification – the opposite method from Ferrabosco's – and only reaches a texture comparable to his at CF 32–40. This section is diversified by reduction of the harmonic pulse to the minim until CF 36, whereupon a sudden crop of syncopations produces a quick succession of suspensions. At CF 41 Byrd anticipates Ferrabosco's ascending quaver figure by descending ones that recall those in crotchets at the beginning. At CF 48–49 he finally rejoins him, taking over his first set of four entries almost unchanged, except that by advancing three of them by one minim he is able to replace the feeble second entry with one that matches the rest (see Ex. 11). From here he carries the imitation through with greater consistency than Ferrabosco, but also with more variety and a finer sense of climax.

Byrd's **In Nomine** 5/5 was his most famous essay in the genre. It takes its inspiration from Parsons, whose celebrated 5/1 it rivalled in popularity. The originality of Parsons's piece lies in its predominantly chordal texture, at first in minim beats and later in crotchets. As in the case of Ferrabosco 5/1 it was the handling of the faster pulse that caught Byrd's interest, and he turned to this aspect of Parsons's writing in the later sections of his own setting. He begins quite differently, with a beautiful *Lachrymae*-like subject perhaps suggested by the opening of Parsons's 7/1 (see Ex. 12): the rising

Ex. 11

sixth is very distinctive and the challenge of encompassing within a single piece the sharply contrasting qualities of Parsons's two finest settings may well have appealed to Byrd. In any case, one of his aims in adopting Parsons's homophony was evidently to incorporate it in a broader stylistic context, instead of isolating it as Parsons had done. The five almost equal sections of his marvellously constructed composition are very subtly integrated. The first subject is worked out in terms of Byrd's highly individual polyphony, compounded in equal measure of the English tradition behind Parsons 7/1 and continental imitative style, but closely allied to no other music, vocal or instrumental, English or foreign, antiquated or contemporary.

Ex. 12

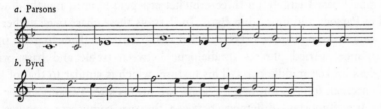

Yet alongside such typical traits as the initial phrase of eight (4 + 4) bars in the treble, there is one striking peculiarity: most of the entries of the point, including the very first, are doubled at the third, sixth or tenth. This feature is absent from the second section (CF 13–24 – a typical example of Byrd's second sections, with a shorter point, more closely spaced cadences and a higher melodic peak), but reappears at the beginning of the third (CF

24–35). Here the new subject begins with three repeated minims inducing a tonal stability that carries the strongly vertical treatment of the first section a step further, and prepares for the eventual arrival of homophony (see Ex. 14b) in the last section. In the intervening fourth section (CF 35–45), where the first passing reference to Parsons's 5/1 occurs (see Ex. 13), Byrd uses

Ex. 13

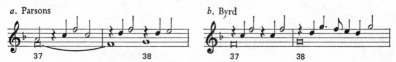

crotchet movement to increase the rate of harmonic change, so that Ex. 14b exercises the same kind of stabilizing influence as the beginning of the third section does after the more fluid second.

The debt to Parsons illustrated in Ex. 14 is more apparent than real, for

Ex. 14

Byrd characteristically makes his borrowed material serve entirely different ends. Where Parsons uses crotchets effectively enough to increase the momentum of his homophony, Byrd devises special harmonic schemes to counteract their forward drive. Each composer follows his version of Ex. 14 with music based largely on three-crotchet arpeggio figures, mostly downward in Parsons and upward in Byrd. In Parsons these chase one another in close canon through three octaves, whereas Byrd allows them to grow into longer, more varied phrases in dialogue between treble and bass, with freer, less broken middle parts. This texture, which is similar to that of the fourth section, follows through for some two breves after Parsons's close.

The first important difference between the two composers emerges in Ex. 14 itself. Parsons's version is the more forceful because he places the local V chords on the strong beats, Byrd's the more static for the contrary reason. Byrd maintains this distinction in the sequel. In this kind of writing every chord must, of course, be a root position or inversion of local I, IV or, more rarely, VI in relation to whatever note is sounding in the cantus firmus. Parsons uses local I and IV in about equal proportions on strong crotchet beats; Byrd by contrast uses local IV on the strong beats throughout CF 47 and 48, and I only once in that position during each breve at CF 49–51. At the same time he banishes quasi-cadential formulae such as those in the fourth section (CF 36 and 41), and admits fewer passing notes than there. Consequently the insistent crotchets are virtually deprived of harmonic extinguished his interest altogether, especially as composition of a plain-impetus; up to CF 53 the cantus firmus groups them in eights, but once it has stopped moving there is nothing left to define their progress.

Byrd uses the only dissonant suspension in the whole section to mask the arrival of the plainsong's final D (see Ex. 15), and from CF 52 removes the

Ex. 15

last vestiges of harmonic control, letting the figures run on as they will. These continue to observe the strong crotchet beats, but by the time they come to a standstill the cantus firmus has been stationary for over three breves, so that any sense of strong and weak minim beats has been lost. Thus the final harmony, and the cessation of movement a semibreve later, can fall without impropriety on what in ordinary circumstances would have been weak minim beats. That at least seems to have been Byrd's view,* but contemporary copyists evidently concerned themselves less with ideas about the interdependence of melodic periods and graduated harmony than with counting four in a bar; most of them tampered half-heartedly with one part or another in an attempt to square the circle, and versions exist with a complete minim beat added or subtracted.†

---

*For a subtler subversion of the strong minim beat in a much later work, see p. 253.

†The latter, surely unauthentic form, found in the Paston manuscripts, is printed in BE 17. For further details see Edwards, *Sources*, i, 183.

It is a long way back from this piece to Byrd's 4-part In Nomines, but it is extraordinary how clearly even they exhibit the main characteristics of his musical thought and sensibility. As the only sizeable instrumental works that can be placed with certainty at the beginning of his career they are of special interest. They show that sensitivity to tonal regions, and to the formal potentialities of treble contour, was natural to him; its mere presence is no guide to chronology. The same is true of his feeling for symmetrical periods: the interplay between the open melodic lines associated with an earlier English tradition (or in a rather different way with imitation), and the closed ones belonging most obviously to the dance, was to remain a source of structural vitality at every period of his life. There will also be further opportunities in this study to observe his sympathy for the music of Taverner's generation, and his critical approach to the modern ideal of thoroughgoing imitation. Early or late he keeps imitation to heel; it carries his thought rather than engendering it.

An approximate relative chronology can be deduced on internal evidence for Byrd's In Nomines, as for other categories of his instrumental music, for he travelled a long way between the earliest and latest, but as usual there is little documentary evidence for dating the journey or determining its duration. However, it is possible to speculate. The 4-part In Nomines, at least, suggest student works and may well antedate Byrd's appointment as organist at Lincoln early in 1563. At the other extreme 5/5 can scarcely have been composed later than 1570, when Parsons died, for it seems improbable that his celebrated 5/1 would have become known only posthumously, or that Byrd would have lingered over his response to it. In any case, 1570 seems too late. The impression is that new pieces circulated rapidly in professional circles, and that action and reaction followed in quick succession. It is difficult to picture White, Parsons, Byrd and Ferrabosco composing their In Nomines at rare intervals over a long period. Although Byrd's pieces are undoubtedly the finest in the genre, he never turned to it without the stimulus of other men's work; a long interval would probably have extinguished his interest altogether, especially as composition on a plainsong was soon to drop out of his work entirely. Thus the In Nomines of these composers are most easily seen as occupying a relatively brief period of fairly intense activity, from the late fifties for White and Parsons, or early sixties for Byrd and Ferrabosco, until the mid-sixties.

3
Consort Hymns and Misereres

The sources of these works are very confused. The grouping in the above list corresponds with that in BE 17. The settings in each group belong together, but some groups may be incomplete or in the wrong sequence; the twelve *Te lucis* verses may constitute a single set. No fewer than nineteen of the thirty-two pieces survive only in Add.29246, a lute intabulation that omits the top part of every piece (see p. 21). Seven of these pieces have the cantus firmus in the treble and so can be reconstructed after a fashion; they are the second 3-part *Sermone blando*, *Christe qui lux es* I/2 and 3, the 4-part *Sermone blando* I/1–3, and *Te lucis* I/5. The other twelve remain fragmentary: *Salvator mundi* 1 and 2, and *Te lucis* I/1–4, 6–8 and II/1, 3 and 4. The second main manuscript, Tenbury 354–8, contains a random selection of only ten pieces, yet six are not in Add.29246, and the fact that it provides one more *Christe redemptor* verse than Add.29246 shows that the latter source cannot be relied on to transmit the groups complete. *Sermone blando* II is anonymous in the Tenbury manuscript, which is the only source, but there can be no doubt that it is by Byrd, like the rest of the hymns that surround it in the manuscript – and *Miserere* 2 which, though given anonymously there, is twice ascribed to Byrd elsewhere.

The consort works discussed in this chapter occupy a curiously isolated position in the music of the time. Unlike Byrd's antiphons and hymns for organ, they cannot be shown to have had antecedents in a pre-Reformation liturgical repertory, for a single 4-part setting of the melody for the 8-verse hymn *A solis ortus cardine** is the only piece of the kind to survive from pre-Elizabethan times. One thing seems clear, however: neither Byrd's pieces, nor such models for them as can be traced, were intended for liturgical use. It was common liturgical practice in the unreformed Church for the verses of hymns sung to plainchant to alternate with settings for choral polyphony or organ solo. Thus *Christe qui lux es*, a hymn of seven verses, would require three elaborated settings for the even-numbered verses; Byrd's first two groups of settings of this melody, as will be seen, were indirectly influenced by liturgical tradition and so contain three verses each. On the other hand his numerous settings of the *Te lucis* melody, which belongs to a 3-verse hymn, can have no connection with the liturgy, and the same is true of his two consecutive settings of the *Miserere* antiphon. Consequently it is impossible to use the number of verses in a hymn as a test of completeness in Byrd's groups of settings. For what it is worth it may be noted that the pair of *Salvator mundi* settings fit the 5-verse hymn (Byrd also composed a pair of organ settings), as do the three in the first 4-part *Sermone blando* (a 6-verse hymn). But the other four groups all fall short: the 3-part and second 4-part *Sermone blando*, *Christe qui lux es* III and *Christe redemptor* (a 7-verse hymn).

This repertory, which Byrd probably composed over approximately the same period as his In Nomines, may never have been intended for wide distribution;† some of the earlier pieces suggest composition exercises. The two 3-part settings of **Sermone blando** must be among the earliest. In England textless 3-part composition was regarded mainly as a vehicle for technical exercise, taking the form of studies in rhythm and proportion for sight-reading practice,‡ or 2-part canons at various intervals upon a cantus firmus, such as composition students were required to construct.§ Byrd's *Sermone blando* 2 belongs to the latter class: it is slightly uncom-

---

*Printed in EECM 6, p. 181.

†The two main sources are Paston manuscripts (see p. 21). The same is probably true of Add.18936–9 (see MB 22, p. 174); if so, the whole repertory is confined to Paston sources except for *Christe qui lux es* II.

‡For example Preston's *O lux*, Tye's *Sit fast* (*Instrumental Works*, 105ff.) and Morley's *Christes crosse* (*Introduction*, 78ff.). For Baldwin's *Browning*, a 3-part study in transposition, see p. 73n.

§Morley gives instructions in Part 2 of his *Introduction*, with examples. Apart from many scattered examples in various sources there are larger collections in William Bathe's *A brief introduction to the skill of song*, Thomas Woodson's forty canons on the *Miserere*, and the collection of canons by 'Wm B.' incautiously printed as Byrd's by Fellowes in BW 16 (see P. Brett, 'Did Byrd write "Non nobis Domine"?' *Musical Times*, cxiii (1972), 855ff.). In 1603 a book of canons on the *Miserere* by Byrd and Alfonso Ferrabosco in an arrangement by Thomas Robinson was licensed for publication under the title *Medulla musicke*, but it almost certainly never appeared.

fortable canon at the seventh. Yet the well controlled increase in activity in its adventurous lines places it right outside the normal range of such pieces, while its more freely imitative companion, despite some rather pinched sonorities, displays a feeling for shape and climax that betrays the exceptional quality of the tyro.

The same precociousness distinguishes the **Misereres**. The chant for this antiphon was one of the most popular in non-liturgical textless music: it provided the basis for canonic exercises, as described above, for more elaborate single settings akin to the In Nomine, and for sets of variations.* The fact that two pairs of settings by Byrd survive, one each for consort and for organ, suggests that each may be complete as it stands. The consort settings may be no later than the organ pair, which is very early, for the first of them contains some very unorthodox dissonance treatment (on the last beat of bar 4 and the second of bar 6), and an unusual feature at the close which it shares with only one piece among the hymn settings, the undoubtedly early *Christe qui lux es* I/2: in both pieces the final is harmonized as the fifth of the last chord, instead of the root, although the chant is untransposed. So it is all the more remarkable that the young composer, having adopted *cambiata* figures in the first setting and run into the rhythmic impasse that they so often induce, should have found his way out again in the second through varied and telling melodic continuations. And the cadence scheme, which he may soon have come to regard as ill balanced, is undeniably effective: three cadences on F and a final one on C in the first setting, followed by G, D and final G in the second.

Of the various groups of 4-part hymn settings, two at least seem to claim a place among Byrd's earliest efforts – **Christe qui lux es I and II**. They are heavily indebted to White, who composed no fewer than five sets of verses on this melody. The first four of these each comprise 5-part vocal settings of the three even-numbered verses of the hymn in accordance with *alternatim* practice; the fifth consists of two 4-part settings for instruments.† White was not writing for the liturgy; he merely set one hymn melody repeatedly, as an exercise. Byrd followed his lead, making settings both for voices and for consort, and perhaps for organ too. His imitation of White's purely chordal set I shows how little he had liturgical needs in mind, for he

*For instance the single 5-part setting by Mallorie, in which each note of the cantus firmus is beaten out in five minims and a crotchet (as described by Morley, *Introduction*, 169), and Stonings's set of continuous variations (see p. 66).

†The four vocal sets are printed in TCM 5, 168ff. Only the second verse of the fifth set is printed there (p. 191); the first verse is given in White, *Instrumental Music*, 61f., without the plainsong, which should be supplied in the treble.

composed not only verses 2, 4 and 6, but filled in 3 and 5 as well; since the work is meant to be sung it falls outside the scope of this volume. An anonymous organ verse closely related to some of his consort settings is discussed later (p. 101). Whether or not it is by Byrd its presence in the earliest source to contain instrumental music by him provides additional evidence of the early date of the consort verses.

White's sets II, III and IV all display his characteristic love of order. Whereas Tallis and Sheppard apply various rhythmic patterns to the plainsong in many of their hymn settings, White confines himself to the undifferentiated succession of semibreves. When Tallis adopts this plan he often leaves it to the rhythm alone to produce a semblance of imitation between the other parts, two or three of which may enter together in chordal movement. Sometimes he will preserve the same figure for more than one line of the text, and monothematic verses occur in Sheppard. White, however, insists on a new point for every line and endeavours to work in at least one complete exposition of four entries between the four free parts every time. The two verses of set V are quite different. Both are monothematic, and the lines are unsuited to verbal underlay.

Byrd selected verses from White's sets II and V as the basis for his set I. He borrowed the first line of White's II/2 (a setting, of course, of verse 4 of the text) for that of his own I/1, introducing more suspensions and placing White's alto and tenor entries successively in the tenor because he was working with four parts instead of five (Ex. 16). The first line of his I/2 is

Ex. 16

a. White II/2 (omitting words)

b. Byrd I/1

similarly taken from White's V/2, whilst that of his I/3 is another version of the same idea. White's set V is the precedent for Byrd's 4-part texture, but

Byrd usually allots a new point to every line in the manner of White's II–IV. It seems clear that Byrd's I is an instrumental set: even in I/1 where the model is vocal Byrd irons out White's rhythm for the words 'Oculi somnum capiant' without making it fit those of the second verse ('Precamur sancte domine').

The question of medium is less easily resolved in the case of set II. Here Byrd looks less often to White for his material, but there are frequent· correspondences with his own set I. The opening verses of each set end with virtually the same close, and show some kinship at the beginning as well. Verse II/1 is monothematic, and Byrd took advantage of the identity of the first and last lines of the plainsong to make a repeat (whereas White in the two monothematic verses of V was careful to prevent the inevitable similarity from becoming too obvious). On the same principle Byrd used almost the same music for the first line of I/3 and the last of II/3, and a decorated version of it for the first line of II/3. The connections between his I/2 and II/2, though present, are more remote.

But if Byrd quotes White less in set II than in I, in other respects he draws nearer to him. He not only imitates the general layout of his vocal sets, with an exposition of entries for each line (as he does fairly consistently in set I), but takes over the rhythms devised by White to fit the words. It happens that in the second and sixth verses of the text every line begins with an unaccented syllable, so that White and Byrd (in his II/1 and 3) begin every point with ♩ ♩ ♩ ♩ or with ♩ ♩ ♩ ♩ . But in verse 4 the first syllable of each line is accentuated, inviting ♩· ♩ ♩ except in line 2, where the rather heavy 'Cor ad te' suggests three minims. These rhythms are White's in nearly every case, and Byrd follows him in II/2 (even though his music at 'Cor ad te' is adapted from White's setting of the words 'In gravi isto corpore' in his II/3). It therefore seems likely that Byrd had vocal performance in mind at least as an alternative to instrumental for his set II,* though for no other of his consort hymns. (Some of the consort songs published with verbal underlay throughout in 1588 and 1589 may have been composed in the same spirit.) A difference of medium between *Christe qui lux es* I and II would explain the existence of two such

---

*In one of the sources (Tenbury 354–8) II/1 and 3 are associated with other consort hymns by Byrd; in the other (Add.30480–4) the complete set II appears in a typical mixed group of instrumental and vocal pieces (including White's vocal set III) transcribed without text for instrumental performance. In both contexts the work is entitled *Precamur*, which is the first word of the second verse and therefore implies a vocal setting. In Add.29246 set I is called *Christe qui lux* because it is simply based on that melody. The same distinction is correctly drawn in the textless sources of White's II and III on the one hand (*Precamur*) and V on the other (*Christe*).

closely related sets apparently written at much the same time – perhaps even concurrently.*

In I/2 Byrd's continuation after his initial quotation from White is far more spirited than White's original. In general, however, Byrd treats his slightly older contemporary with greater respect than he does Tye or Ferrabosco in his In Nomines. At this very early stage he has less of his own to offer. White uses more dissonance in his instrumental settings than in his vocal ones; Byrd takes his cue from the former, and allows one harmony to stand for the length of a semibreve much more rarely than White (see Ex. 16). The gain is questionable. There are tedious passages where every semibreve of the chant is accompanied by a dissonant suspension and its resolution, or by a consonant sixth falling to a fifth. This difficulty is avoided in the isolated setting of **Christe qui lux es III**, where harmony is very much simplified to give free play to conjunct crotchet figures. The piece is purely instrumental in style, presumably the sole survivor of a third set. The cantus firmus is in the tenor, as it is in White's set IV. Since White also makes use of some striking crotchet figures in this set, which is his finest, Byrd may have turned to it as a model. If so this setting, though superior in every way to sets I and II, was probably not composed much later.

How many more of Byrd's consort hymns may have been student pieces it is hard to tell, for the fragmentary and jumbled sources make his aims difficult to decipher. To judge from the available evidence **Te lucis I** and **II** did not differ much in style from the pieces already considered. But whereas *Christe qui lux es* I and II lack the sense of aesthetic purpose nearly always perceptible in even his earliest works, the *Te lucis* settings, only two of which survive complete, at least suggest his growing ambition through their unliturgical abundance.

The two groups into which the manuscript divides the total of twelve verses are separated by only one intervening item (*Christe qui lux es* I). The second group cannot constitute a self-contained set because in the last two of its four verses (as in group I/6 and 7) the plainsong migrates to the alto and is transposed up a fifth to suit the range of the part.† Even though the

---

*Fellowes assumed that the four verses that he found complete were vocal and printed them with words in BW 8, 34ff. He set II/1 and 2 correctly to verses 2 and 4, but II/3 and I/1 incorrectly to verses 3 and 6.

†This is not the only unliturgical feature, quite apart from the number of verses. In five other verses he modifies the chant at the final cadence, changing AGG to AGAG so that he can end with a full close on the tonic G. He does not need to make this change in I/6 and 7 or II/3 and 4, because the transposed plainsong ends on the dominant, nor in

same final chord closes transposed and untransposed verses alike, there is no example of cantus firmus transposition (except at the octave) in the last variation of any English set. Both in England and abroad, however, variations were often composed in sets of twelve (several of Byrd's earlier grounds were either composed or drafted on this pattern), and it seems likely that the two *Te lucis* sets belong together, with the second preceding the first.* Placed in this order the sequence shows some affinity with that in Byrd's grounds. These invariably increase in pace up to var. 6, which employs extensive quaver runs, and then explore more diverse musical characters in the later variations, usually starting with tripla in var. 7.† The composite *Te lucis* set would gradually increase crotchet movement in vars. 1–3 (II/1–3), drop back in 4–5 (II/4 and I/1), reach even more continuous crotchets in 6 (I/2), turn to triple measure (the only example in Byrd's consort hymns) in 7 (I/3), introduce its only verse with treble cantus firmus in ninth place (I/5) and close with a long crotchet coda on a held final in 12 (I/8).

In his development of the In Nomine, as has been seen, Byrd assigned an important role to the top part, and the relatively rare disposition of the plainsong in the treble did not appeal to him. To place the chant of a consort hymn in a middle part was to invite treatment of the genre as a kind of small-scale In Nomine, and that was in fact how most composers who took it up thought of it.‡ It is most unlucky that the top parts of only three of Byrd's pieces written on this pattern should have survived – those of *Miserere* 2, *Christe qui lux es* III and *Te lucis* II/2.

As they stand the *Te lucis* variations give the impression that the composer did not yet command a wide enough variety of character for so long a work. The one verse with treble cantus firmus§ makes no advance on *Christe qui*

I/8 or II/1 and 2, because they have lengthy codas on a held final, which are necessarily plagal. The same modification is made in both verses of *Salvator mundi*, despite plagal extensions; the difference is that the note before the two final tonics is the flat seventh F, so that an additional A is still required between the two Gs if there is to be any dominant harmony.

*The scribe may have misread his source as he apparently did in the case of the two *Salvator mundi* settings. Here he transcribed the second first, immediately realized his mistake, and followed it with 1 and 2 as a pair (without repeating the ascription to Byrd).

†Cf. *The Hunt's up* (var. 6, revised version), the *Second Ground* and *Hugh Aston's Ground*.

‡William Mundy, for instance, composed a pair of widely circulated 5-part settings of *Sermone blando* altogether in the spirit of his In Nomines. The first has the cantus firmus in semibreves and the second in dotted semibreves, just as his two In Nomines employ breves and dotted breves respectively. The second is full of the broken crotchet figures that had become a cliché in Parsons's lesser imitators.

§A tenor entry can be reconstructed in bar 90 (BE 17, p. 138) by adding a minim C on the second beat and retaining the quavers on the fourth (see the Commentary).

lux es I and II, but some of the fragmentary settings were clearly on a different level: I/2, for example, was a study in crotchet movement comparable in style, and no doubt in quality, to *Christe qui lux es* III. The latter piece is admirably constructed from two successive points, the second of which, being shorter, enables the entries to answer one another more rapidly and increase tension towards the close. In *Te lucis* II/2 Byrd starts right from the beginning with a subject capable of more eventful exchanges. It is based on a *cambiata* figure, like that of the much shorter *Miserere* 2. This device has the merit of giving the counterpoints a more individual cut than steady minims or crotchets can provide, but it tends to establish the rhythm   ♩ ♩ ♩   too insistently for comfort. In the present piece Byrd skilfully builds this characteristic rhythm into the phrase structure and maintains it even after he has dropped the *cambiata*. Although he does not entirely avoid rhythmic stiffness, he is able to devise within the limited space available a series of symmetrical periods which he supports with a varied cadence scheme and a clear progression from A minor through F to G. All this allies the piece with the probably roughly contemporaneous 4-part In Nomines, where he uses similar procedures to expand the life of the form. However, although *Te lucis* II/2 and *Christe qui lux es* III stand up to this comparison quite well, the faster-moving cantus firmi in the hymns, and the consequent brevity of the pieces based on them, both in their different ways obstructed any wide-ranging development of the genre along these lines.

For Byrd these difficulties apparently came to a head with the composition of his **Salvator mundi** settings and the first 4-part **Sermone blando** group. His earlier cultivation of the genre culminates in these two sets. Their greater maturity is evident in their clear tonal organization and elaborate melodic style. It is most regrettable that the top part is missing in both sets. The *Salvator mundi* pair, like most of *Te lucis*, defies reconstruction because the plainsong is in the tenor, but the treble plainsong of *Sermone blando* I can be supplied fairly satisfactorily, even though it does not fit quite so easily as in other pieces surviving in the same state, so that the suspicion lingers that the small adjustments necessary to satisfy the demands of grammar are not enough. The three verses of this set are very well planned, the first the most strongly characterized rhythmically, the second based on two concurrent subjects in slower values, the third in crotchet movement similar to *Christe qui lux es* III and *Te lucis* I/2. As in In Nomine 5/3 there is a new preference for firm major harmony. This was not prompted by any quality in the melody; unlike the popular tunes used for variations, the even notes of the cantus firmus did not make individual demands, and Byrd's earlier 3-part settings of the same melody still display an older harmonic sense.

At first sight it might seem that the main difference between the style of these more developed hymns and that of the In Nomines lay purely in the notation, and would vanish if the note-values of the hymns were doubled. But there is an important distinction. At this time convention seems to have forbidden the use of quavers in this kind of composition except for occasional passing notes (Byrd employs them extensively only in In Nomine 5/4, in imitation of Ferrabosco). Since the growing intricacy of the subjects in Byrd's consort hymns had to be expressed primarily in crotchets and quavers against the semibreves of the cantus firmus, the range of note-values became proportionately limited. There was, for instance, no way of increasing speed at the approach to important cadences, as he so often did in the In Nomines by means of crotchet runs. Thus he had reached a point in his development of the consort hymn with free treble beyond which the qualities it favoured could only be taken further in the wider context of the In Nomine. In his subsequent essays the two forms diverged sharply. In the In Nomines he adopted 5-part texture as the standard and continued to stress the treble line as a formal agent; in the hymns he retained 4-part texture, returned the plainsong to the treble once and for all, and avoided heavy cadential or rhythmic punctuation – just as he had in the early *Christe qui lux es* I and II.

However, the last two pairs of verses, *Sermone blando* II and *Christe redemptor*, stand apart from all previous hymn settings, and also from one another. In **Sermone blando II*** Byrd has moved a long way from his earlier 4-part set on the same melody. The confident harmonic language of the latter has cleared the path for a far subtler style, with more inversions and a greater variety of suspensions over a freer range of bass notes. The composer is now concerned less to work imitations below his cantus firmus, though he still does so, than simply to let the parts move in response to each other. Another feature, one that he had tried out only tentatively in earlier hymns, comes into prominence here: he fashions the first point of each verse from the opening notes of the chant, starting with an anticipatory prelude in the free parts, and draws on later sections of it as well.

In the **Christe redemptor** pair he takes this idea a step further. Verse 2

*In this set the *Sermone blando* plainsong takes the usual form. In both his earlier sets Byrd inserts an extra note between the 15th and 16th notes: a B between two Cs when the final is G. This irregularity is not found elsewhere in vocal, consort or organ settings of *Sermone blando* or *Aurora lucis rutilat* (the same melody), though Mundy inserts a third C at this point in his two consort verses.

has an even longer prelude based on the chant, and in both verses he elaborates the plainsong for imitative or purely melodic purposes, though without obscuring its identity with the wealth of decoration common in organ settings. The harmony is as varied as in *Sermone blando* II, but more severe. As though to compensate for subdividing many of the semibreves of the cantus firmus into minims, he admits crotchet motion in the other parts very sparingly. The resulting even harmonic tread moves with greater certainty of aim, and in verse 2 encompasses a wider cadential field, than ever before. Moreover, since all the parts now speak in the same terms, these pieces, instead of being merely accompanied settings of the chant or independent compositions incorporating a neutral cantus firmus, acquire a new force as meditations centred upon the hymn melody itself. This may seem the natural territory for compositions of this kind, but there is nothing in the earlier hymns to suggest that Byrd originally thought so. His change of approach endows his last two sets, and especially *Christe redemptor*, with his characteristic certainty of artistic purpose, and places them among his wholly personal and independent consort works.

4

Consort Music in Five and Six Parts:
Fantasias, Variations, Pavans and Galliard

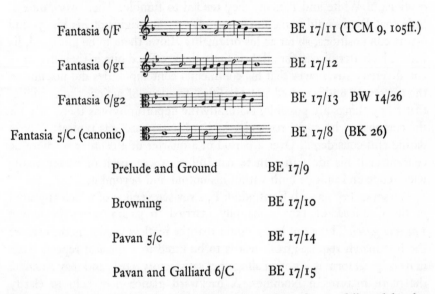

Fantasia 6/F	BE 17/11 (TCM 9, 105ff.)
Fantasia 6/g1	BE 17/12
Fantasia 6/g2	BE 17/13 BW 14/26
Fantasia 5/C (canonic)	BE 17/8 (BK 26)
Prelude and Ground	BE 17/9
Browning	BE 17/10
Pavan 5/c	BE 17/14
Pavan and Galliard 6/C	BE 17/15

The fantasias and pavans are denoted by the number of parts followed by the final; major modes are indicated by capital letters, minor by lower case. The fragment listed by Meyer as 6-part fantasia No. 3, and by Fellowes as 'Fantasy Sextet No. 4', is the later part of Fantasia 5/C. Since the publication of Pavan 5/c with one reconstructed part in BE 17, a complete set of five parts has been discovered by Warwick Edwards in the Murhardsche Bibliothek der Stadt Kassel und Landesbibliothek (4° Ms. mus. 125).

In mid-sixteenth-century England the In Nomine was far more popular than any other form of consort music, apart from dances. Only a score or so of textless pieces not based on a plainsong survive complete, and few of them match the best In Nomines in musical quality. Nearly all are in five parts and were composed between the 1550s, at the earliest, and the 1570s. As a group they provide evidence of English isolation from continental developments. The forms are either entirely different from those cultivated abroad or, where they are analogous, different in treatment. There are four main types: pieces based on a constructed cantus firmus such as the hexachord; variations or grounds; predominantly imitative pieces; and dance-like compositions tending towards homophony. The last two types, the characteristics of which alternate in certain pieces, show some features respectively of the ricercare and chanson.

It is an oddly heterogeneous repertory, and not at first sight an inspiring one. The composers lacked a guiding tradition; with the predictable exceptions of White and Parsons they tended to fumble. Their work offered little that Byrd could make direct use of, yet the origins of his big 5- and 6-part compositions, so far as his originality allows them to be glimpsed, lie here. The better pieces, for all their limitations, offered him in their liveliness and diversity advantages that his continental contemporaries did not find in the ricercare: undiscovered potentialities, freedom of action, the reminder that many things are possible. Naturally the opportunity was there only for the composer who could recognize it. Byrd's response was typical: at once daring and considered. Over a period of a quarter of a century or more he concentrated his ideas in a mere handful of works, each of exceptionally wide scope and unique both within his output and beyond it.

The series begins with **Fantasia 6/F**, a revised version of which appeared in the *Cantiones* of 1575 unhappily married to psalm verses beginning *Laudate pueri*. There can be no doubt that the textless version is the earlier: the bad match requires fresh words to be fitted to a musical repeat. Even in its original form it is not an altogether satisfactory work, and may antedate the more mature In Nomines. A backward glance may help to clarify Byrd's intentions in this early essay in imitative style. Only two long English instrumental compositions survive complete from the early part of the century, both in a similar 3-part style: Robert Cowper's *Me fa me* and William Cornysh's more considerable *Fa la soll* (MB 18/6). Cornysh was a contributor to the Eton Choir Book, and his piece has much in common with reduced-voice sections of votive antiphons of the time such as his own *Salve regina* (MB 10/12). The music turns for the most part on short motives that are not primarily subjects for imitation, but are treated in imitation or sequence, echoed between the parts, incorporated as elements in freer melodic strands and otherwise manipulated to produce the richness of detail but slight uncertainty of direction that characterizes so much English music of the time.

Old habits of mind die hard. When the imitative principle became acclimatized in England composers saw it as a means not only of uniting the texture but of stamping each passage with a particular character – hence the perpetual stretto found in the In Nomines of Tye and White. The same characteristics appear in a 5-part *Song* by White (*Instrumental Music*, 102ff.), a close-knit piece on the usual pattern of a series of related points of imitation (Ex. 17). The substance of the music is in the frequency of the entries and

Ex. 17

the cogency of the progress from one subject to the next, contrasting strongly with the principles underlying the Italian ricercare from the *Musica nova* of 1540 onwards, where lengthy melodic continuations were favoured, and new subjects were often introduced almost surreptitiously.

What pieces such as White's fine composition lacked to Byrd's way of thinking as it appears in his In Nomines, was a framework capable of relieving the imitative work of some of the structural load, and thereby admitting a measure of relaxation and textural variety. In his In Nomines he had solved this problem with great subtlety, deriving order from the very element that threatened to stand in its way: the arbitrary cantus firmus. Freed from the obstacle's perverse guidance he was obliged to seek some other way to the clear paragraphing he instinctively preferred. The means he chose in Fantasia 6/F were as characteristic as the aim: that of pushing a principle to extremes, in this case the principle of symmetry. One of Byrd's great strengths was to lie in his capacity to follow up an idea while remaining the least doctrinaire of composers. In this early piece his consistency of thought leads to inflexibility.

There are four sections, all but the first repeated without variation except for some exchange between parts of equal pitch. The first section takes the form of a rigorous double exposition (see Vol. 1 of this study). The six parts enter in stretto, each a breve behind the last, alternately with subject and tonal answer. Two further breves bring a cadence, thus establishing an 8-bar period. The first entry of the second exposition coincides with the eighth breve, so that the whole section consists of 15 instead of 16 breves. The second section, like those in Byrd's In Nomines, is made up of shorter phrases. A threefold imitation leads to a cadence at the end of four breves; the entries are then exactly repeated by the other three parts, and follow a third time with an exchange of the upper two in double counterpoint as the sole variant. Each of the 4-bar phrases overlaps the last by a semibreve, giving a total of 11 breves for the section. As this is immediately repeated, the same short imitative exposition followed by the same tonic cadence is heard six times in quick succession. The third section (12½ breves) is slightly less rigid, as the second exposition has a freer continuation. Moreover the harmony, hitherto confined to tonic and dominant in the first section with the addition of little more than subdominant in the second, now opens out a little. Even so the tonic cadence again occurs three times.

The last and longest section is rather different. The subject is quieter in contour (Ex. 18), bringing respite from the insistent tonic cadences. In-

Ex. 18

sistence of another kind steps in: the section is constructed on a melodic ostinato.* The subject is repeated five times in the treble, sometimes with the addition of two or three terminal notes and with slight rhythmic variations, but always at the same pitch. Byrd was evidently trying out an established technique, for the same treble ostinato had been used by Alwood as the basis of a keyboard piece. Alwood treats the subject as a kind of cantus firmus† above sporadic imitation only partly related to it. Byrd integrates it as part of the imitative texture. The scheme was a curious choice for Byrd. It prevented him from using the top line to help shape the form as he did so effectively in his In Nomines, and the coda is too brief to restore the balance after the section has been heard twice. When he adapted the piece as a motet he showed himself conscious of the weakness. Although there was nothing to be done with the ostinato itself he did his best to compensate. His two main revisions were concerned with maintaining melodic tension at

*Treble ostinatos are uncommon, but are by no means confined to England. Examples of various kinds are found in Tye (*Instrumental Music*, 105ff.), Cabezón (MME 2, ii/44), Bull (MB 14/32), Frescobaldi (*Orgel- und Klavierwerke*, ed. P. Pidoux (Kassel, 1949), ii, 8off.).

†He did, in fact, use this subject as the cantus firmus for a mass. The keyboard piece is called 'In nomine' in the Mulliner Book (see MB 1/23), and J. D. Bergsagel has pointed out a very slight resemblance to the *In nomine* section of the mass, which he feels may explain the title (see EECM 1, p. xii); the matter is further discussed in a correspondence in the *Musical Times*, cxvii (1976), 489, 739, 997. However, there is a simpler explanation: Mulliner's title is probably a mistake.

the end of the first section (bars 12–13), and devising a melodic climax at the end of the third (bars 39–40 and 43; the second section needed no change).

Despite a more liberal use of passing notes, Byrd adopts in this work a melodic style close to that of White's *Song*, with similar contours and the same habit of splitting semibreves into two minims or a dotted minim and crotchet – to rhythmic rather than contrapuntal advantage. This makes the *Song* a useful point of comparison. It is White who is on home ground, which is one reason why Byrd's piece is unusually impersonal in feeling. White's dense texture, untouched by Byrd's chanson-like cadences, allows kinds of subtlety that Byrd has to sacrifice; for instance in telling melodic and harmonic sequences arising from a close stretto on his third point (Ex. 17c). On the other hand Byrd's gain is perceptible immediately in the bold stride, the harmonic clarity and, at least in the short run, the certainty of purpose. The gentle undertones of mid-century English style are brushed aside at a blow. The clean-cut paragraphs tell the player or listener exactly where he is going at any given moment; if he has any doubt there will be a repetition to reassure him. However, the use of extreme imitative symmetry, though initially effective enough, sets the music in a straiter jacket than ever White devised. By comparison with Byrd's later methods the present essay in paragraphing, which imprisons imitation instead of liberating it, appears self-defeating.

One solution to the problem lay to hand in variation form. Byrd adopted it in two works, a prelude and eleven variations on a ground, and twenty variations on the tune known as *Browning*. The earliest known English sets of variations are the three curious masses by Taverner, Tye and Sheppard, based on the *Western Wind*.* The tune is used as a cantus firmus, but without the interruptions and rhythmic distortion to which the *L'homme armé* melody is subjected in continental masses. Each statement follows immediately upon the last, though not necessarily in the same part, and is the signal for a change of texture or contrapuntal treatment. The pattern invited schematic planning of one kind or another: for example Taverner and Tye (except in his *Agnus Dei*) used the same number of variations for each section of their masses. In consort variations composers developed as a constructive principle the rotation of the melody between the various parts.

---

*For the Taverner see TCM 1, 3ff.; also the separate edition ed. P. Brett (London, 1962). For the Tye see *Christopher Tye, the Latin Church Music*, Part 1, ed. J. Satterfield (Madison, 1972), 69ff.; also the separate edition ed. N. Davison (London, 1970). For the Sheppard see EECM 18/2.

Thus in Johnson's *Knell** a short descending bell-like scale, which operates like a very short variation melody, continually passes through the parts in a fixed order; this is reshuffled only once, after which the new order is maintained to the end.

No strict order of this kind is observed in the consort variations on *Browning my dear*, but the principle of rotation governs the number of variations in each of the three earliest sets, by Stonings, Woodcock and Byrd. Each set is composed for five instruments. Stonings wrote five variations with the melody once in each part, a pattern that he also adopted for his composition based on the *Miserere*. Woodcock doubled the number, having presumably intended to give the melody twice to each part, though in the event he broke the symmetry: the tenor has it three times, the bass only once. Finally Byrd doubled the number again, so that each part has the melody four times.†

In Byrd's other set of variations, the **Prelude and Ground**, schematic planning is rather less evident than is usual in the over-all design, but rather more so within the individual variations. The work seems never to have been popular, for it occurs in only two sources.‡ Internal evidence suggests a date of composition between the Fantasia 6/F and the *Browning*. In some respects it is still close to the fantasia. The fourteen-breve prelude is very similar: although in five parts, it opens with six entries, each a breve apart, reaching a tonic cadence after eight breves, and continuing no less symmetrically to the close. The variations themselves show the same preoccupation with extreme formal clarity, but a greatly expanded range of technical and imaginative resource. Byrd's wider structural grasp, which is evident as early as the In Nomine 5/2 but had failed him in the fantasia, reasserts itself here. It is clear that the experience of the piece, especially in relation to melodic transposition, was still alive in Byrd's mind when he wrote the *Browning*.

Some English grounds, like continental ones, imply a series of chords in root position. They have no melodic value and can only serve as a bass line. The ground Byrd chose for his consort piece, and also for the *Second Ground*

---

*Printed edition edited by P. Warlock and A. Mangeot (London, 1930). An anonymous source entitled *The Belles* in Add.22597 was misattributed to Tallis by Hughes-Hughes in his *Catalogue of Manuscript Music in the British Museum*, iii (London, 1909), 219.

†William Inglott composed a *Browning* for keyboard (Tregian No. [251]) in which the melody rotates four times in regular sequence through bass, middle part and treble.

‡The attribution to Byrd is beyond question, although it rests on the authority of the unreliable Add.32377, a single part-book of the mid-1580s. The piece occurs anonymously but complete in the much later and highly inaccurate Add.17792-6. The text is by far the worst of all Byrd's complete consort works, and makes assessment difficult here and there.

for keyboard in My Lady Nevell's Book (see p. 126f), is of a different kind. It is a bass melody with conjunct motion which therefore entails chordal inversions. As many as eleven other settings for various instruments are known (see DVB, p. 44). At a purely technical level these differ from Byrd's in two respects: none contains the little reprises* at the end of each half of the tune (see Ex. 19a), and rather surprisingly only one† uses the melody

Ex. 19

·a. Ground

b. Browning

in any part but the bass. In both Byrd's sets the reprises play a very important role. In the first eight variations of the consort work they are confined to the bass part, which is otherwise virtually silent. They are the basis for little episodes that stand apart and punctuate the music, characterized not only by the different instrumental texture but by a rhythmic break, a sudden irruption of quaver movement or tripla, or some treatment that foreshadows the next variation. They give great weight to the supertonic and tonic cadences, respectively half-way through and at the end of each variation. Later, in vars. 8, 9 and 11, the musical lines are allowed to run across and absorb the subdivisions, which are now too firmly impressed upon the hearer to lose their force.

During the first four variations the melody is used as a true ground, for when the tenor has it the bass is silent. But thereafter the work becomes a set of variations in the same sense as those on the *Browning*, or the *Western Wind* masses. The melody appears twice in each of the four upper voices,‡

*This term is used on the analogy of the *ripresa* sometimes found at the end of Italian grounds (see p. 133). It is not, of course, intended to imply a repeat.

†An anonymous keyboard set in the National Library of Scotland, Panmure MS.10, which has it in the treble in one variation. The melody is also heard as such when it is played unadorned in the set of divisions for solo gamba in Cambridge University Library Dd.5.20.

‡Byrd also uses the melody in the treble in the last six variations of his keyboard set. He comes near to quoting it in *I thought that love* (1589/32), at the words 'like tales of fairies', merely substituting his own descant for the first half (see var. 1 of the keyboard set). In the anonymous *My little sweet darling* (MB 22/25) the first two appearances of the words 'Sing lullaby lulla' closely resemble the reprises in Byrd's version of the ground melody, and the instrumental accompaniment opens rather like the keyboard version of the ground in Paris, Bibliothèque Nationale, Rés. 1186 (DVB, p. 44).

in no fixed order. Two of them have to share the last variation to complete the scheme, which shows that Byrd originally allowed for the usual twelve variations, but for some reason changed his mind. At the same time, he developed a technique that had hitherto played little part in the form: that of melodic transposition.* The melody of the Ground is transposed to C when it is given to the first (treble) or third part (i.e. in vars. 7–9 and the first half of the final var. 11), and remains in F in the second and fourth (tenor) parts. The reprises, however, are never transposed, so that a kind of dominant relation tends to emerge between main section and reprise, strengthening the stabilizing force of the latter.

The variations are paired, though 5 and 6 only by contrast. The style is primarily non-imitative, rather galliard-like in the early variations but capable of carrying imitation with ease, whether incidental (var. 3 and 4) or more thoroughgoing (vars. 6–8, based on the subject of the ground itself,† and 11). It also allows for very fast divisions of four or six notes to the minim which, to judge from the anonymous three-stave variations on this ground (DVB/10), were part of the tradition. Byrd's setting is the most brilliant of his consort works. Perhaps it was inevitable that it should have been overshadowed by the more complex *Browning*, yet it seems likely that its special subtleties would in any case have been less readily understood by contemporaries, despite Byrd's evident concern to ensure comprehensibility. In the first variation the two main sections answer one another fairly precisely, as do the two reprises. The second variation likewise insists on regularity, emphasizing the norm against which the succeeding variations will play. The first sign of what is to come appears with the beautiful third variation where, quite apart from the sharp contrasts introduced in the reprises, the rhythmic factors in the first four bars of the treble melody are neatly rearranged in the second half to form a perfect answer (roughly XX′YY answered by XYXY). As the work progresses the sophisticated interplay of emphasis, caesura and enjambement within the four-line stanza presented by each variation increases, and demands a good deal of the listener if he is to grasp the patterns complete. It is very unlucky that the

---

*It was not unknown. Stonings had transposed the plainsong up a fourth in the treble variation of his set on the *Miserere*. Byrd himself had used the idea as a matter of convenience in his vocal setting in chordal style of the hymn *Christe qui lux es*. He wished to give the melody to each of the five voices in turn. The top, middle and bottom voices could each sing it at the same pitch, though in different octaves, but to accommodate the intermediate second and fourth parts he transposed it up a fifth. This did not disturb the fundamental cadence structure. The same feature appears in the instrumental variations on *Te lucis ante terminum* (see p. 56f).

†This is a common enough tag, cf. Ex. 18, not to mention the spurious *Non nobis domine* (BW 16, 106ff.).

text is so corrupt as to put passages in the elaborate ninth and intricate eleventh variations beyond accurate reconstruction, for their finer balance is inevitably impaired.

The melody of Byrd's second set of variations, **Browning my dear,** or *The leaves be green,** has certain features in common with that of the Ground (see Ex. 19). The most important is the implied supertonic cadence halfway through. Although the reprises in the Ground emphasize the melodic relationship between the two tunes, their presence is responsible for the difference of Byrd's approach in the works that he based on them. Whereas the more complex melody of the Ground led him to concentrate on contrasts within the individual variations, in setting the shorter *Browning* tune his interest turned to the construction of groups of variations. His first decision in planning his *Browning* must have been to outdo the five variations of Stonings and the ten of Woodcock by increasing the number to twenty. There is additional evidence, both internal and external, to suggest that Byrd's set was the last to be composed. The internal evidence is provided by the opening variations. None of the composers uses all five parts in his first variation; Stonings uses four, Woodcock and Byrd only three. In Stonings and Woodcock the melody is first heard in the tenor, while the bass is silent, and the second variation is a tutti with the melody in the bass. Thereafter all the parts are kept in play.

This is exactly what happens in Byrd, except that it is his second and third variations that correspond to the first two of the other composers. His first variation is very like his second; the melody is in the bass instead of the tenor, and the two upper voices are simply changed over in double counterpoint. A clue to the origin of this variation is to be found in the layout of the whole work. It looks as though Byrd originally planned it in four groups of five variations, in each of which the melody was to occur once in each part, though not in the same order. In the work as it stands there are three such groups: vars. 2–6, 7–11 and 16–20. It seems fairly clear that he began with what is now var. 2. At an early stage during composition he realized that in a work of this length it would be an advantage to delay the tutti until the third variation. He therefore borrowed a potential variation from some point where he felt he could still spare it, which happened to be the third quarter, and tacked it on to the front. As a result the original vars. 1–10, whether composed or only partly worked out, all moved up one. Vars. 2 and 3 show that Byrd knew the settings of Stonings and Woodcock (or others just like them); if he took nothing else from them it was because they had nothing to

*See Wooldridge, i, 154; Edwards, *Sources*, i, 8.

give him. On the other hand it is difficult to believe that the minor composers could have escaped the impact of Byrd's setting, had they known it.

The sources tend to confirm this chronology, and also suggest an approximate date of composition for Byrd's piece. It is found in all the main manuscripts containing instrumental music of the time, but in the earliest (Add.31390), in which corrections were made in 1578, it was added after the main work of copying had been completed.* Its widespread and lasting popularity argues an early success, so the compiler of this very comprehensive collection, which contains both the Stonings and Woodcock settings, would hardly have overlooked Byrd's until later had it been available. It was, however, available to the copyist of Add.32377 in the early or mid-1580s, and was therefore probably composed towards the end of the 1570s.

Although Byrd planned the equal distribution of the *Browning* melody between the five parts very early on, he obviously did not expect the scheme to tell as a structural element; in the finished composition it coincides with only the last of the three groups of variations that determine the design. However, his original view of the work as a sequence of 4×5 variations persisted. Its three sections comprise variations 1–10, 11–15 and 16–20. They are built up with the aid of a variety of techniques which it is of some interest to compare with those found in earlier variations. English variation form dates back to the time of differentiated style and is well adapted to it. In the *Western Wind* masses it is Taverner, the composer least concerned with imitation, who shows himself most at ease. The imitative style accommodates itself more easily to a cantus firmus in long notes than to a tune that retains its own independent rhythm and melodic life. Although Tye, whilst making some use of differentiated style for contrast's sake, manages to base the majority of his variations on imitation, his subjects are restricted in character by the requirements of the unchanging melody, so that the contrapuntal texture becomes rather monotonous.

It was no doubt this difficulty that led Tye and White, who in maturity thought primarily in imitative terms, to fight shy of consort variations, leaving them to composers like Stonings and Woodcock who were content to dispense with imitation altogether; indeed, the texture of Woodcock's *Browning* is largely homophonic. Byrd, on the other hand, who had allotted a subordinate role to imitation in his Ground, gave it an important one in the *Browning*. As his In Nomines show, he entertained no fixed notions of the forms that imitation should take. Since he was not writing for voices he was not obliged to restrict his counterpoints to rhythmic values similar

*Apparently by the original compiler using a finer pen and a narrower stave. For this manuscript, see p. 20.

to, instead of faster than those of the song melody that served as cantus firmus. He therefore re-established the more flexible relationship between the two by using very lively points predominantly in crotchets.

The situation was none the less new. For one thing the song melody remained a voice that demanded attention. Byrd adopted a slightly more decorated version at bars 3 and 7 than his predecessors had done (see Ex. 19b), so that its moments of animation match the quieter phrases in the surrounding parts and unite the texture; no doubt one reason for the piece's popularity lay in Byrd's flattery of the unpretentious melody, directly by harmonic touches, and indirectly by allowing its spirit the occasional free flight in purely lyrical counterpoints. Imitation itself shades into something rather different. The points move so fast that at times they have established their identity and run their course before a second voice has entered. The result is a technique that is no longer imitative in the accepted sense, and may perhaps be called 'figural'. Short figures in which the constants are the rhythm and general shape rather an exact sequence of intervals pass freely from part to part, now in succession, now overlapping, now doubled in thirds or sixths. Byrd makes a general distinction between the two techniques, but not a hard and fast one. His figural work is new-minted but not unprecedented. In the context of variations something analogous occurs in the first *Osanna* of Taverner's *Western Wind*,* and it flourished over a long period in organ music.

The first section (vars. 1–10) of Byrd's *Browning* is the province of imitation proper. It is not much in evidence in the first two variations, but increases in the related third and dominates the next five. Vars. 4 and 5 are paired by inversion, and so are 6 and 7; var. 8 is a transposed variant of 7; vars. 9 and 10 are again a pair in which shorter subjects begin to break the strong forward pull of their forerunners. Var. 11 marks the beginning of the second section (vars. 11–15) with a contrast. It is the quietest in the set and, although the texture embodies imitation derived from the melody, broadly harmonic in effect. The whole section is planned as respite from close imitative work. Vars. 12 and 13 gradually regain speed; again there is just enough imitation present to keep the part-writing astir, but it is not allowed to obtrude until the brisk approach to var. 14. Vars. 14 and 15 rely less on any kind of countersubject than on elaborate cross-rhythms. The technique is in essence that of old-fashioned sight-reading games such as Tye's *Sit fast*, but the result is brilliant.

---

*The figure that Taverner uses here remained very popular. For example, it crops up in Woodcock's *Browning*, though not in Byrd's, and in var. 5 of Byrd's Consort Ground. It is also the basis of the second half of Parsons's famous 5-part *In Nomine*, which many composers, including Byrd, imitated (see p. 46ff).

Vars. 16–19, like the previous group, steadily build up activity, but at greater intensity. Var. 16 does not drop back to the calm of 11, and 18 and 19 employ tripla. It is in this section that figural writing comes into its own. Byrd builds upon the idea by combining it with a speeded-up version of the kind of motivic development familiar in imitative pieces. In the course of vars. 16 and 17 he develops a chain of figures from an initial three-note motive. Ex. 20 shows various stages in the series, though it cannot convey its full subtlety: for instance, the bass does not forget its initial open fifth,

Ex. 20

so that when the exuberant tripla figures arrive at the end of the line their origin is not lost to view. The passage is an excellent example of Byrd's capacity to create something entirely new by fusing different techniques. After the climax of the work the marvellous final variation returns to the more lyrical style of the early ones, where the influence of the variation melody was stronger. The main melodic idea is borrowed from var. 3, but a succession of acute false relations brings about an astonishing intensification of feeling. This highly charged music makes the greater impact for following so quickly upon the torrent of tripla in vars. 18 and 19, and leaves an indelible impression.

The foregoing outline shows that Byrd relies upon two agents to control the form of the work: pace and technical affinity. The first moulds the sections, the second gives each its character. In addition he introduces a third factor, that of melodic transposition, to support the structure in one important particular. The technique is used with greater freedom than in the Ground. It is no longer confined to transposition to the fifth above or to certain instrumental parts. There is double transposition, and each part has the melody at two different levels, in three cases a fifth apart. As in the Ground the transposed melody takes its typical cadences along with it; more often than not the harmony touches the local supertonic and tonic respectively at the end of each half of the melody. The melody is stated in the following keys: F in vars. 1–4; C in 5–7; G in 8–9; C in 10–11; F in 12–14; C in 15; F in 16–20. There is, of course, no question of modulation: vars. 8 and 9 are at the furthest remove, yet in 8 the halfway A is harmonized by a transient F chord, and the final G by a plagal alternation of C and G, so that the harmonic regions merely reverse the typical ones of G followed by F in untransposed variations.

On the other hand no contemporary listener hearing the melodic transpositions, at times sharply stressed by local major supertonic chords (D major in vars. 5 and 15, A major in 9), would expect the piece to come to an end until the balance had been restored, and to that extent transposition prefigures modulation. Evidently with this in mind Byrd transposed the melody in var. 15, which closes his second group, to forestall any impression of finality in this complex passage. Transposition is used more elaborately to support the sense of continuity in the long first section. Here the original pitch is not reached with the opening of the new section in var. 11, but one variation later, presumably because the original scheme for transpositions in the first ten variations, like that for the distribution of the variation melody among the parts, was shifted along by the late addition of the first variation. Byrd saw no need for revision: there is no sense of homecoming on reaching the original pitch as there is on regaining the tonic in later music. But if instead the change of plan had brought the return one variation too soon, he might, to judge by his careful placing of the transposition in var. 15, have made some readjustment.*

Although there were certain instrumental forms that Byrd especially favoured, he composed a number of ambitious pieces, both for consort and keyboard, which remained unique in his output simply because in each he had explored an idea so thoroughly that he had no need to return to it. The *Browning* is a case in point. He never again cared to attempt the kind of accumulation of expressive detail that he achieved in this extraordinary composition. It is the work that owes most to the early schooling of his musical sensibility in a tradition that goes back beyond Taverner to the time of Cornysh's *Fa la soll*. If the unregulated repetition of short phrases in the earlier style led some composers of the next generation towards stretto in their use of imitation, it was the element of freedom that lodged in Byrd's consciousness. The quality that impresses most in the dense textures of the *Browning* is his quick-witted flexibility of mind; nothing is routine, everything invention. Indeed, virtuosity of invention was in a sense his central idea for the work. The impression is strong that the structure, for all the

*Later Bevin (MB 9/15) and Baldwin wrote 3-part *Brownings* in which they concentrated on transposition, though for no compelling structural purpose. They both added B♭ to Byrd's F, C and G; Baldwin uses D as well, and predictably provides a would-be verse about hexachord changes: 'These flatts & sharps here shall: you teach your notes to call:- & change sowle in to fa: against the gam vt la:- & so, fa in to me: as heare you may it see:-'.

thought he put into it, took second place to his vision of a texture of composition. In the three great fantasias that followed he adopted the opposite approach. There is no less flexibility, expressiveness or invention, but his point of departure is the structure.

In **Fantasia** 5/C the two top parts are in strict canon at the fourth above from beginning to end. This work is absent from the earlier consort manuscripts, but since a keyboard transcription occurs in My Lady Nevell's Book, completed in 1591, it was probably written in the 1580s. It survives in two versions. The earlier is represented only by the transcription found in Nevell. The consort original is lost; but it certainly existed. In the keyboard transcription the polyphonic structure is often necessarily incomplete or so densely entangled as to become ineffective. Byrd never employs such textures in his original keyboard fantasias; on the contrary, their style is native to the instrument – and this in its turn entails a quite different approach to formal questions. Later Byrd revised the consort work, introducing an additional entry of the point in bar 7, lengthening the coda, and making various smaller improvements in between. This version too circulated in keyboard transcription.*

As a group Fantasias 5/C and 6/g1 and 2 show fewer connections with mid-century consort music than the two sets of variations, which for all their originality are built upon old foundations. Nevertheless, the canonic fantasia may perhaps owe something to the opening of a short imitative 5-part *Song* by Parsons (Add.31390, f. 60), though there is no thematic resemblance. Parsons brings in his first five entries regularly at a distance of three semibreves. The lower three parts continue more or less freely while

---

*The sources are as follows. Version 1: consort, none; keyboard transcription, Nevell and Lübbenau Ly. A2. Version 2: consort, Add.17786–91 and Paris Bibliothèque Nationale Rés. 1122 (keyboard intabulation by Tomkins); keyboard transcription, Add.29996 and Christ Church 1113 (both fragmentary). The keyboard transcription of the first version (BK 26) does not provide an adequate basis for a reconstruction of the consort original because it simplifies many passages and, more rarely, substitutes inner parts of its own. However, it gives enough information to put the relative chronology of the two versions beyond question, as a few examples will show. The entry in bar 7 disturbs the normal imitative pattern of one entry to a part, thus increasing tension before the first appearance of the canon in the upper parts; Byrd must have added this – it is inconceivable that he should have taken it out. Bar 41 seems to have contained fifths between treble and alto, or octaves between treble and tenor, or both, scarcely obscured by the passing D in the treble; the revision puts the matter right (cf. the similar revision in Fantasy 6/g2, mentioned on p. 86n.). The new subject at bar 60 (Ex. 23) originally had even crotchets at every appearance; in the revision the livelier dotted rhythm was substituted for the first two crotchets. The melody in bars 74 and 76 is improved in the revision (bars 75 and 76) by an octave drop after the respective D and G.

the upper two, which enter last, have two short, closed entries each, making two exchanges of almost strict canonic dialogue at the octave; meanwhile the bass and tenor introduce a new point beneath. This is exactly how Byrd begins (the additional entry in the revised version slightly disturbs the resemblance). His melodic lines are much longer, but he preserves the distance of three semibreves between the first two entries, and between the canonic entries at the outset and throughout the composition. Although the closed canonic phrases are not initially as short as Parsons's, they are soon reduced. In many cases they total only about three semibreves, so that the second phrase sometimes fails to overlap the first. The resulting dialogue sounds like a series of couplets of varying length in a song setting, with the emphasis thrown on the answering second line in each case by the upward transposition.*

As is usual in English consort music the points or, where the imitation goes no further, the canonic couplets, are thematically related. There are passages where each couplet arises directly from the last, rather like the successive points in a piece by White. But Byrd takes the principle of motivic development further in this piece than in any other consort work except the 3-part fantasias (see p. 99). Apart from one extraneous element that will be discussed later, there is nothing that cannot be traced directly or indirectly to the somewhat neutral opening melody (Ex. 21). Any feeling of neutrality,

Ex. 21

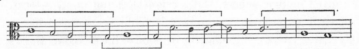

however, quickly vanishes; as the work grows and the range of its material

*Naturally Byrd never set words in such an unvarying pattern. The difference may be seen by comparison with *Christ rising again* (1589/46), particularly from the words 'for in that he died' to 'he liveth unto God'. Even so, Parsons and Byrd were drawing on a long vocal tradition in their use of closed imitative phrases. In continental church music of the Josquin period, short self-contained musical phrases matching a phrase of the text were common. The next generation of composers preferred a less broken imitative texture, but in England the short phrase continued to find favour for its declamatory force. Taverner exploited it in his Meane Mass, Tallis coupled it with more regular imitation to curiously urgent effect, for instance in *Absterge domine*, and it was naturally found useful in hymn settings. The reason may lie in the value the English placed on speech-like directness in secular song. During the early years of the century song-style was often very simple, a matter of syllabic homophony with a pause at the end of each line; some of the songs transcribed by Mulliner half a century later are not very different, and from the rhetorical point of view neither are the simpler consort songs, though here each line of verse is separated from the next by the instrumental surround (see MB 18, MB 1 and MB 22).

expands it establishes an identity as distinct as any in Byrd's music. The main motives are marked with brackets in Ex. 21. The second point is also important; it derives from the first by way of the bass, as Ex. 22 shows.

Ex. 22

Since many couplets in the canonic dialogue are variants of their immediate predecessors they are apt to stray beyond the direct influence of the source material, but it is never long before they are pulled back into line by fresh reference to it.

Byrd thus organizes his fantasia round a canon that evolves continuously within a given motivic sphere. But a canon does not imply a form: in the hands of such a resourceful composer it could go on renewing itself indefinitely. Other factors determine the division of the piece into three sections in roughly the same proportion as those of the *Browning*, the first being a little longer than the other two put together. The work opens with a series of imitative points in the manner of a ricercare, if the term may be used in connection with a piece so un-Italian in melody and part-writing. The three lower voices sometimes anticipate the canon, are sometimes led by it, and in various ways diversify the effect of the unchanging canonic relationship. Cadences are few. Not until Byrd wishes to rein in the contrapuntal movement in preparation for the next section of the work does he look to the short entries in the canonic parts to give the structural cue.

In certain circumstances the end of a short entry may imply a cadence. In this respect such entries resemble the halves of the two melodies that Byrd used for his consort variations. It will be remembered that in each there is an implied supertonic close at the end of the first half, and also that when the melody of the Ground is transposed, a potential dominant relationship develops between its cadences and those of the untransposed reprises.

This relationship is also latent in the couplets of Fantasia 5/C, since the answering entries lie a fourth higher, and every chromatic inflexion is exactly imitated in the answer.

At the point illustrated in Ex. 23 Byrd drops the fully imitative texture.

Ex. 23

The lower parts provide free accompaniments, guided by a stronger harmonic current. In the upper part in the example, that is to say in the second and fourth lines of the quatrain, the implied cadences are supertonic and tonic, but with the canonic anticipations the sequence is amplified to a circle of fifths: A, D, G, C (cf. vars. 7-9 of the Ground). This is the widest of three diminishing circles by which Byrd approaches the final tonic cadence of the whole first section. His treatment of the cadences may be seen in the bracketed bass notes. He interrupts the first and third in order to run on, rounds off the first couplet with a local II⁶-I, but cheats the last line of its rhyme in order to carry through to the last stage of the section. This consists of two tercets (bars 65-70, 70-74),* each made up of a normal couplet followed by repetition of the second line an octave lower in the top accompanying part. The implied cadences† are therefore G, C, C in each tercet. The reason for the repeat of the tercet pattern lies in the graduated treatment of the cadences; in the first tercet all are interrupted, in the second they are local II⁶-I, II⁶-I, V-I. On the final chord the melody of the second section enters.

Byrd's remarkable use of harmony as a means of formal control somewhat alters the character of the composition. Regular imitation does not return; even in the recapitulatory third section the lower parts go their own way, sporadically lending a hand in the canonic proceedings, but not bound to them. This allows Byrd freedom to break in a surprising way the mono-

---

*The bar numbers given here are those in BE 17. Those in the keyboard transcription of the original version (BK 26) are half a bar behind throughout because it lacks the entry in bar 7.

†Implied, that is, by the last note before the next entry; the last notes are covered by the overlap.

tony that commonly threatens imitative pieces: at the beginning of the second section he jogs the listener's attention by quoting a popular tune. Sharp contrast is not his aim: the general character of the tune has already been anticipated here and there in the first section. Indeed, it fits in as easily with the song-like couplets of the first section as the couplets themselves into Byrd's imitative texture. This perhaps reflects, beyond his skill in the particular case, a quality that pervades his melodic style in general. All the same, a contemporary would certainly have felt, if not surprise, at least a twitch of recognition at the entry of the tune. It is one of the two known as *Sick* (Ex. 24a).* Byrd divides it into two halves for canonic purposes. The

Ex. 24

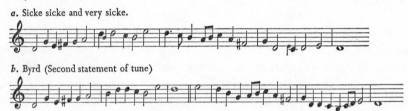

a. Sicke sicke and very sicke.

b. Byrd (Second statement of tune)

first phrase is related to the opening of the fantasia by diminution and the identity through crab motion of the first five notes (a glance at Exx. 21 and 24b will show how this strikes the ear). But the tune is an entity in itself and brings with it, and in a pedantic sense justifies, motivic shapes that are new to the fantasia, though not foreign to it. With their aid Byrd builds a lively episode in tripla which completes the trio-like second section.

Although formal recapitulation was not unknown in England,† Byrd showed little interest in the idea. The third section of the canonic fantasia is perhaps his nearest approach to it. He starts with a quatrain (bars 103–109) on precisely the same pattern as the one in Ex. 23. The implied cadences and the treatment of each are the same, and in the context the new melodic lines, which follow on from the foregoing tripla section, sound like variants of the old. Further reminiscences, including one of the *Sick* tune, lead to one more

---

*See Chappell, 226; Wooldridge, i, 73; Simpson, 660; Ward, 73, 75. Quoted here from Holborne's *Cittharn Schoole* (1597), with variants from Cambridge University Library Dd. 4.23, fol. 6.

†There are literal examples in a fantasia by Tye, also known as *Rubum quem* and *Sol mi ut* (*Instrumental Music*, 85ff.), and William Mundy's *O mater mundi* (Add.31390). The feature is clearly adopted from Netherlandish chansons, which appear in considerable numbers without text in English manuscripts. A third example is the solfaing song attributed, probably correctly, to Tallis in the unreliable Add.32377 (it occurs anonymously under the title 'Je nilli croyss' in Add.31390, but bears no relation to the famous *Je ne la croy* by Sandrin).

quatrain on the circle of fifths (bars 119–125), this time treated very forcefully: the first cadence is local II⁶–I, the remainder all V–I (compare the second tercet at the end of the first section). There follows a coda consisting of a brisk quatrain (D, G, G, C; bars 125–131) and a broader close.

Recapitulations, like everything else in music, must be judged by their effect. The mood of Byrd's canonic fantasia hovers between tranquillity and gaiety, with the latter tending to predominate as time goes on, particularly in the second section and at the beginning of the coda. Yet despite its recapitulary features the third section sounds a new note of uneasiness. The two circles of fifths in close proximity, the increase in crotchet movement and so in harmonic change – such technical intensifications are no doubt to be expected as the work draws to a close. But they bring restless shifts of feeling that cannot be ignored, above all at the last circle of fifths (bars 119–125) where doubt insists for a moment and is then wonderfully assuaged just before the coda sweeps all before it. In the original version that is the end, but the slightly lengthened coda of the revision changes the emphasis. Byrd slows the music down to a minim pulse and in the process introduces false relations and simultaneous sharp and flat sevenths – features that have hitherto been absent from the serene course of the work and echo in a less acute form the astonishing close of the *Browning*. They unexpectedly bring the undercurrent that had made itself felt before the coda to the surface – an ambiguous twist that painfully deepens the meaning of the work and imposes retrospective reinterpretation.

In most of his consort fantasias Byrd cultivates the unity of mood that textless polyphony encourages; the equable flow of the greater part of 5/C provides one example. But in his keyboard fantasias the flexibility of the medium leads to far greater restlessness, above all in the early A minor work of the 1560s, where he set out to encompass the widest possible range of character (see p. 235ff.). Many years later, during the 1580s, he evidently decided to attempt something comparable in consort music, and composed **Fantasia 6/g1**.* Neither his keyboard style nor the formal procedures appropriate to it could have any relevance to a consort work; once again he seems to have turned to Parsons for a texture of composition capable of carrying his conception – in this case to a pair of 5-part fantasias with the unexplained title of *De la court*, and another in six parts called *Trumpets*.†

*The earliest source is the single part-book Bodleian E.423. The compiler, an assiduous collector of Byrd who seems to have acquired his new pieces fairly promptly, transcribed the fantasia sometime in the 1580s; see Edwards, *Sources*, i, 111.

†Also called *Lusti gallant*, *Cante cantate* or simply *Song*. Published by Partita Edition (London, 1966).

De la court was one of the most popular pieces of the time, rivalling the same composer's In Nomine 5/1 and Byrd's 5/5. The two halves are exactly the same length (64 breves) and follow a very similar course, starting with well spaced but not particularly distinctive imitations, and moving on to livelier sections to which the pieces no doubt owed their success. Parsons bases his faster music primarily on a succession of short phrases, each of which is immediately repeated with the same harmony but some interchange between the parts. The idea is apparently an outgrowth of the echo effects between pairs of treble or bass parts that were popular at the time and survived in the Italian vocal duets and trio sonatas of the next century. In *Trumpets* the 6-part texture enables this antiphony to emerge even more clearly. It takes control sooner because the piece begins with chanson-like homophony instead of imitation. Indeed, Parsons is so anxious not to deflect attention from the antiphonal interplay of varying phrase-lengths that he reduces harmonic interest to the level of monotony.

Byrd adopted antiphonal technique for the first time in Fantasia 6/g1. His practice is so varied, both in itself and in the ends it serves, that the connection with Parsons may seem tenuous. Moreover his repetitions are not always exact, because he does not allow the technique supremacy. Nevertheless, there are signs that *De la court*, at least, was at the back of his mind. Although he works in the more favourable six parts of *Trumpets* the mode is that of *De la court*, and at the point when antiphony first takes over from imitation he adopts a figure which recalls the corresponding point in *De la court* Part 1 (see Ex. 25). Other little resemblances catch the ear, for

Ex. 25

a. Parsons

b. Byrd

instance Ex. 26, where the Parsons quotation is from Part 2.* But, as always

Ex. 26

a. Parsons

b. Byrd

with Byrd, to trace his creditor is to understand how little he owed.

The contrasts that Byrd explores in this fantasia do not depend on divisions, like those that were to become popular in the madrigalian fantasias

*But see also *Constant Penelope* (1588/23) at the words 'Oh that he had when he first took shipping'.

of the next generation (and that Byrd himself had made use of in his own terms in the Ground); they are more fundamental because they involve technique at a deeper level. The first of the two main sections passes through half a dozen phases, some of which resemble nothing else in instrumental music of the time. The total effect is still bolder. The first two phases introduce two controlling factors, one of mood and one of procedure. The short opening imitation consists of a single exposition of seven entries divided into 3 + 1 + 3 in such a way that the two groups of three form matching periods. This strengthens the purely melodic force of the passage. Nothing in the subsidiary counterpoint is allowed to disturb the primacy of the eloquent subject. Its elegiac quality, though often modified or contradicted, plays a unifying role in the work. The second phase (bars 12–32), announced by Ex. 25b, is in the same vein, but here antiphony initially takes precedence over imitation. The technique provides Byrd with a means of measuring and establishing the progress of the music such as he had striven for in the early Fantasia 6/F, and had found in variation form: the canonic couplets of Fantasia 5/C serve the same purpose. Antiphony is in its nature more repetitious than these devices, an advantage in a long composition without recapitulation: each idea must make a very firm mark if it is to stay in the mind and contribute to the balance of the complete work.

The third phase of the first section (bars 32–50) brings the first sharp contrast in the form of syncopated homophony such as Byrd employed to punctuate some of his smaller fantasies (see p. 94). Here again antiphony precedes imitation. The extraordinarily choppy texture of this passage is smoothed away by the fourth phase (bars 50–65): a triple antiphonal statement of a most beautiful melodic line with more or less homophonic accompaniment. The antiphony here is very much longer than in the second or third phase, whereas in the next (bars 65–83) it becomes shorter, tightening the harmonic pace in anticipation of the closing phase.* This springs a surprise in the form of *Greensleeves* (at bar 84),† first of all the tune set to thumping chords on the customary *Romanesca* bass, and then a repeat of the bass supporting a free variation that contains the first high E♭ and the only high F in the work.

The popular tune represents a triumph for a new strain of feeling that first stirs in the syncopated episode but takes time to emerge from the shadow of the solemn opening. As the contrasts between the successive phases become more extreme Byrd secures their coherence through two

---

*Compare the first of the two sections on the words 'So by Christ all men shall be restored to life' in *Christ is risen again* (1589/47).

†See Chappell, 227; Wooldridge, i, 239; Simpson, 268; Ward, 44.

sequences of cross-references. In the first place he connects each phase
loosely to the last with an answering rhythm or motive. Thus the melody
in phase 4 closes with syncopations echoing phase 3, and is itself recalled by
a sudden outcrop of fauxbourdon in phase 5 (bar 81), whilst melodic fragments in phase 5 prepare for *Greensleeves* and its free continuation in phase 6.
At the same time he evidently planned phases 1–3 and 4–6 as parallel cycles,
on the principle that he often employed in variation works. The flowing
conjunct crotchets of phase 4 relate to phase 1, the antiphony of phase 5
echoes that of phase 2 (see Ex. 27), and phases 3 and 6, though unrelated,

Ex. 27

each bring an unexpected turn of events. And just as in the *Browning* he
guards against a possible break between variations 11–15 and 16–20 by
transposing the melody in var. 15 (see p. 73), he closes phase 3 of the
fantasia, not in the tonic like all the others, but in the subdominant.

The second main section of the fantasia consists of a galliard in the usual
three strains with repeats, only the third of which is varied.* There follows
an elaborate coda in duple time. This recalls the mood but not the material

---

*Fellowes, who spotted the quotation of *Greensleeves*, also saw a reference to *Walsingham*, presumably in the third strain of the galliard (see his *William Byrd*, 2nd edition
(London, 1948), 190). This seems wide of the mark: Byrd's quotations of tunes are
usually quite explicit. It would be equally possible to read *Callino casturame* into the
second strain, which in fact relates much more plausibly to the corresponding strain of
his own early keyboard galliard G4.

of the opening, to which its strongly plagal character is especially foreign. It was almost certainly an afterthought. It does not occur in all the sources, and in Add.17786–91 it has been added later on slips pasted into the part-books. Byrd obviously felt that something was needed to stop the galliard from coming adrift from the rest of the work, and decided to add a sufficiently weighty coda to tie it in. In one manuscript, Tenbury 379–84, the galliard itself is missing along with the coda,* so it seems possible that the work originally ended with *Greensleeves*. There are really two questions to be asked, neither of which can be answered with any certainty: whether a galliard section formed any part of Byrd's original conception; and whether the existing galliard was composed specially for the fantasia or incorporated ready made.

To take the second question first: two points might appear to dissociate the galliard from the fantasia. It is in only five parts, and it makes no use of antiphony; indeed, the texture of the first strain can be compared to that of vars. 1, 2, 7 and 8 in the Ground, though the part-writing is now much smoother. The varied repeat of the third strain, which adds the sixth part and introduces echo effects between the two trebles, could well be a revision to help the galliard fit the fantasia. Against all this it may be said that Byrd had no compelling structural reason to carry antiphony through to the galliard (and did so only to a very limited degree in the corresponding section of Fantasia 6/g2), and that it is present anyway to the extent that the melody changes position from the first to the second treble in the repeats of the first two strains.† Moreover, although the galliard lacks close links with the first section of the fantasia it sounds perfectly appropriate.

The question whether the galliard formed part of the original conception is equally thorny. It appears to be bound up with the relation of the piece to Fantasia 5/C. The length of Fantasia 6/g1 up to the end of *Greensleeves* is 89 breves, which is about average for the longer English consort pieces of the time. The last note of the *Sick* tune in 5/C also falls on the eighty-ninth breve,‡ though the composition can never have been intended to end there. Since English composers still sometimes worked to predetermined measure-

---

*The second treble has a held G on the last chord of *Greensleeves* (bar 92), without the falling phrase F E♭ D.

†The reduction in the number of parts has parallels in the 4-part choruses to two 6-part pieces in the *Songs of Sundrie Natures*, *From Virgin's womb* (1589/35, 24) and *An earthly tree* (1589/40, 25). In the context of the galliard itself the increase to six parts at the end is like that in *Have mercy upon me, O God* (1611/25).

‡More precisely, at the beginning of breve 89 in the first version, and on its second semibreve beat in the revision. The last chord of *Greensleeves* takes the latter position, but since Byrd provided Baldwin with a transcription of the earlier version of 5/C for inclusion in Nevell, the revision would appear to be later than 1591 – unless Byrd simply neglected to bring the transcription up to date.

ments (the equal length of the two parts of *De la court* provides an example
to hand), Byrd may have taken the proportions of one fantasia as a guide
when planning the other. If 6/g1 preceded 5/C it may have started life
without the galliard. In this case Byrd would have found the ending too
abrupt and responded in two ways: by adding a galliard, and also by composing 5/C, which absorbed its quotation of a popular tune into a longer
continuous movement. If 5/C preceded 6/g1, however, the galliard would
have been planned from the beginning, for it is inconceivable that Byrd
should have considered working out the ambitious ideas of this fantasia
within dimensions taken from only a portion of 5/C.

Whatever the history of the work one thing is certain: Byrd did not feel
entirely satisfied with it and determined to improve upon it. If he wrote it
piecemeal he would inevitably have been more conscious of the effect on the
finished design than his listeners, either then or now. He accordingly
composed **Fantasia 6/g2** on a similar plan, even incorporating some of the
same material, but avoiding the diffuseness he seems to have found in the
earlier piece. The fundamental change lies in the handling of contrast. The
first main section and the one in galliard style contain less internal contrast
than the corresponding parts of 6/g1, but the first section is shortened to
make way for an entirely new one in tripla, so that contrast between three
very firmly differentiated sections takes the foreground. At the same time
Byrd is careful to make clearer motivic connections between the sections,
and to shape these with more regard to the whole.

He starts with an imitation about twice as long as before on a remarkable
subject which, despite a wealth of crotchet movement, induces a very slow
harmonic pulse, mostly in semibreves or even in breves. The harmony itself
is restricted, continually circling round i and iv. Yet in the expressive
texture created by the almost unbroken succession of passing notes there is a
new refinement of technique and feeling that is typical of the whole work. A
brief bridge passage, the bass of which is borrowed from the melody of Ex.
27a, shades into a reworking of the opening imitation from the earlier fantasia.
This takes a relatively modest place in its new context, not merely because
it is shorter than the first imitation, but because Byrd, with his acute formal
sense, has introduced it in such a way that its quicker harmonic pulse
marks it out as the subordinate second phase in the composition. The subject,
however, kept its hold on his imagination; it is more important as a motivic
source than the opening point, which is one of its remoter derivations.* He

---

*By rhythm and crab motion, cf. the relation of the *Sick* tune to the opening of Fantasia
5/C (p. 78).

treats it at the same length as before, but moves the entries a little closer together so that he has room for two more at the end in the dominant minor. The beautiful dominant close strengthens the transition to variants of Exx. 25b and 27a, which as before open an antiphonal phase. The chief technical features that distinguish this from its predecessor in 6/g1 are an almost complete absence of imitation and a considerable excursion in the relative major.* The whole passage is remarkable for perfect balance between the successive antiphonal phrases and for great harmonic sensitivity – above all in the two answering versions of the final cadence.

At this point the syncopated imitation of the earlier work is replaced by a sizeable section in tripla. Although there is a similar widening of the harmonic field and element of caprice here, the two pieces no longer run parallel. The general character of the new section is imported from Byrd's keyboard music.† The structure is individual and wayward, the interest linear and the treatment unpredictable. The opening imitation, closely modelled on the passage in the first section taken over from the opening of 6/g1, gives way to an echo at the fourth in the manner of the canonic fantasia, further antiphony, figural work in the manner of the *Browning* and finally a fivefold ostinato on the dominant minor (an important region in this work, though not in 6/g1).

Stability returns with the third section. This begins as a regular galliard with an 8-bar strain‡ and varied repeat. In one respect, however, it differs from Byrd's usual practice: every phrase until the coda begins with an upbeat. This opens the way for a subtle stroke in the second strain, which is four bars long, again with varied repeat. From the last chord of the first strain Byrd adopts hemiola rhythm for harmonic change, so that the accent is thrown on to the upbeat throughout the second strain. The altered balance of the phrases makes an excellent foil to the succession of 2-bar phrases that prepare for the coda, four based on subdominant and tonic harmony, followed by four on tonic and dominant. The latter pattern is reversed in the 8-bar coda in duple time, which grows straight out of the preceding section and brings the total number of bars up to the 48 of a normal galliard.§ This succinct conclusion makes a more decisive effect than the expansive coda of Fantasia 6/g1. Two telling details among many may be

---

*At bar 49f. there is a near-quotation from Fantasia 5/C (bar 111f.).

†But see also the chorus *Pari jugo dulcis tractus* in *The match that's made* (1588/26).

‡Counting a dotted semibreve as a bar, as in the edition of this piece in BW 14 (and also throughout Chapter 10 of the present study). A different barring is adopted in BE 17.

§Once again the three sections of the piece are in the approximate proportion 2 : 1 : 1 (to be precise, 56 : 23 : 24, measured in breves and taking two dotted semibreves in ₵/3 as equal to a breve in C).

mentioned: the two consecutive bars on the dominant caused by the change of harmonic scheme at the beginning of the coda, and the absence of dissonant suspensions from the coda until the two just before the final close.

Byrd published Fantasia 6/g2 in 1611, but manuscript sources show that he composed it some twenty years earlier, and also that he made a few small improvements before publication.* It cannot have followed closely on 6/g1, for although there is no reason why he should not have seen how to achieve the greater formal co-ordination of 6/g2 soon after completing the earlier piece, the finesse with which the scheme is carried through and the perfection of detail speak for a lapse of time and still greater maturity. Whether or not Byrd thought of the later work as replacing the earlier, some of his contemporaries did not, for two of them transcribed both in close proximity. They were surely right. Fantasia 6/g1, like 5/C, is an extraordinarily original and individual composition, enshrining an experience that could not be superseded. Something of its boldness and prodigality of invention is sacrificed in the deeper and even finer work.

When Byrd first turned his attention to pavans and galliards, perhaps after his return to London in the early 1570s, he composed a number of pieces for 5-part consort which he subsequently transcribed for keyboard. The only one to survive in its original form is Pavan 5/c, but others can be detected behind the keyboard Pavan a4 and the Pavan and Galliard in B♭. Byrd probably regarded the keyboard versions as definitive, for in transcribing them he considerably elaborated the texture and added decorated repeats. They are discussed in Chapter 10.

The isolated **Pavan and Galliard 6/C** belong to a much later period, when Byrd's consort and keyboard writing had long passed the point where any interchange was possible – indeed, they may constitute his last known consort work. English composers do not seem to have written 6-part dances till Jacobean times. That does not mean that Byrd's could not be an exception, for he had already developed a 6-part antiphonal style in his Fantasias 6/g1 and 2. Nor does his work show the influence of his juniors. The less

---

*The earliest source for this work, as for 6/g1, is Bodleian E. 423 (see p. 79n.). The bulk of its contents was copied in the 1580s; Fantasia 6/g2 was added rather later than the rest, though the handwriting shows no change. The first version of the piece survives complete in Add.37402–6. The most significant revisions are in bar 42, where the fourth part was changed to avoid near-consecutives with the second part, and bar 97 (see BE 17 Commentary for both points). BE 17 adopts some readings from this manuscript in bars 74–75 (see the Commentary, or the 1611 text in BW 14). The pencil date 1603 has been written alongside the keyboard transcription of the piece in Add.29996, but the handwriting appears to date from at least 150 years later.

enterprising ones had nothing to teach him, and his interests did not coincide with those of such men as Philips and Gibbons: theirs lay in the proliferation of decorative patterns,* his in the melodic value of counterpoint and the interplay of phrase length and cadence structure. Nevertheless, there are other stylistic features that point to a date in the new century. All his life Byrd had rejected earlier tradition in avoiding any obvious thematic resemblance between the two dances in his pavan and galliard pairs. But in 6/C he not only starts both with the same fairly widely used tag,† but bases every strain on some facet of it. There are other cross-references too, including inversions, and rhymes between the closes of various strains. Among the keyboard dances comparable motivic density occurs only in a group of late pieces: the Echo Pavan and Galliard, which work out the antiphony of 6/C in keyboard terms, and the Mary Brownlow and Earl of Salisbury pieces, composed not long before their publication in *Parthenia* in 1612–13 (see Chapter 10). The consort work is unlikely to have been composed much earlier.

The opening of Pavan 6/C recalls a passage in Fantasia 4/G. Byrd adapted this piece to the text *In manus tuas* for his 1605 *Gradualia* (see p. 92), and perhaps had it in mind when he composed the pavan. The exchange of phrases in double counterpoint in the first half of strain I resembles the beginning of the last section of the fantasia, where the words 'Sancta Maria,

Ex. 28

a. Fantasia 4/G

b. Pavan 6/C

*Cf. Philips's Passamezzo Pavan (MB 9/90) and Gibbons's 6-part pavan and galliard, published separately by Fellowes (London, 1925).

†However, the example that opens Richard Dering's 5-part pavan (MB 9/61) is surely a direct quotation from Byrd.

mater dei' enter in the motet version (see Ex. 28). The pavan may originally have been composed a fourth lower at the pitch of the fantasia, for the transposed Mixolydian is very unusual, and at the lower pitch the instrumental tessitura matches that of Fantasias 6/g1 and 2. However, another fleeting reminiscence of Fantasia 4/G (at the words 'Deus veritatis') in the second half of strain II of the pavan corresponds as it stands to the pitch of the fantasia. Strain II of the galliard contains a different kind of reference, perhaps intended for the listener. Its eight dotted minim bars are constructed rather like a setting of *The Woods so wild* (see p. 156), starting with two bars on an internal F pedal, and two on G. After a momentary return to F in bar 5 the pattern is broken for a time to allow for an excursion in D, but the final cadence is on the expected G. At the same time the antiphonal phrases in both the melody and the bass of the first four bars are related not only to phrases in the preceding strain, but to the *Woods so wild* melody as well. The last strain of the galliard, like those of the late keyboard Galliards F2 and C3, strips the music down to its essentials – in this case its motivic essentials.

Both the pavan and the galliard display extraordinary refinement of workmanship throughout. Except at the end of the strains and in two passages in the pavan (the opening, shown in Ex. 28b, and the second half of strain II), the music progresses entirely in antiphony of two bars in the pavan, and of one bar in the galliard. Yet phrase lengths are so finely calculated, and the antiphonal repeats varied by such subtle changes in part-writing and harmonic definition, that a plan that might appear unpromising in the abstract yields a work of quite exceptional grace and distinction.

5

Consort Fantasias in Three and Four Parts

Fantasia 4/a		BE 17/5
Fantasia 4/G		BE 17/34 (TCM 7, 163ff.)
Fantasia 4/g		BE 17/4 BW 14/15
Fantasia 3/C1		BE 17/1
Fantasia 3/C2		BE 17/2
Fantasia 3/C3		BE 17/3

Each fantasia is denoted here, as in the preceding chapter, by the number of parts followed by the mode.

Two more 4-part pieces, both in D minor, were published by Thurston Dart in 1958 as Fantasy Quartets Nos. 4 and 5, and taken up in BE 17 (Nos. 6 and 7). The sole source is a manuscript set of part-books, lacking the treble, from the Paston collection (Folger Shakespeare Library V.a.405, formerly 460328). The ascription to Byrd has been added later and is hard to credit. The two pieces are uninteresting in both material and construction. No. 4 is really a set of seven variations on a cantus firmus of eight semibreves, with the last two statements overlapping (the texture can be completed in the two variations where the cantus firmus is in the treble). No. 5 treats a series of four points, the first and last related; near the end there is a long madrigalian dominant pedal that Byrd could only have written, if at all, in a late work (cf. the last repetition of the words 'it pleaseth her to stay' in *In crystal towers*, 1611/8).

An argument that a hastily executed commission for the Paston circle might result in routine work can fortunately be dismissed with its biographical and psychological assumptions untested, for the part-writing abounds in untypical usages – for example: two parts approaching an octave from the same direction (No. 4/bar 13); two parts leaving a unison in the same direction (5/15–16; 5/18–19, the unison being a fourth from the bass in the latter case, and the resolution upward); a decoration involving parallel seconds (4/26); hidden fifths (5/23); uncomfortable crossing of parts (5/5; 5/7); series of parallel thirds in untypical contexts

(4/28; 5/2). Byrd was no doubt occasionally prepared to admit one or other of these for some special reason, especially in less exposed textures, but they form no part of his normal style, either early or late. The second point of imitation in No. 5 (Ex. 29a) is worth noting. Parsons and Byrd had used similar figures to this

Ex. 29

for melodic purposes (see Ex. 25), but as a subject for imitation it is singularly feeble, as it depends for its character upon a group of notes that could be replaced at every appearance by a plain semibreve (Ex. 29b) without affecting the essence of the part-writing. In short, whoever supplied Byrd's name seems to have made a mistake; perhaps he was misled by a superficial resemblance between the openings of No. 4 and Fantasia 4/g.

The Fantasy Trio No. 3 in BW 17 is an arrangement by Fellowes of the Keyboard Fantasia C3. He was evidently led to postulate a lost consort original by two features in the keyboard piece: the predominantly 3-part texture and the presence of a couple of uncomfortably wide stretches for the hand. Neither supports his assumption, for there are three short passages of 4-part texture (two of them essential to the part-writing), and English organ composers were sometimes prepared to write wide stretches when pushed (e.g. EECM 6/25, bar 23). In any case the piece has no links with any known tradition of consort composition, but grows straight out of pre-Reformation organ music (see p. 225ff.).

The single part-book Add.32377 contains the cantus firmus of a piece constructed on *Ut my re* and attributed to Byrd. Fellowes printed the complete part in BW 17, 119, as Fantasy for Quintet, though the number of parts is unspecified in the source. Its rigid plan is exactly the same as that of an immediately preceding *Ut re my* by Parsons. The latter attribution is corroborated in Add.30480–4, where the piece survives complete in four parts. The two pieces are undoubtedly meant as a pair: Byrd himself composed comparable works for keyboard (see Chapter 11). It is possible that at an early date he wrote the *Ut my re* as a sequel, presumably in four parts, to Parsons's composition, but as the manuscript contains one mis-attribution to Byrd of a work by Parsons (his In Nomine 7/2, see p. 34), it seems quite likely that this was another.

In the volume of lute transcriptions (Add.29246) which contains the only text of so many of Byrd's consort hymns, there are six 4-part fantasias by White (*Instrumental Music*, 34ff.). Like everything else in the manuscript they lack the top part (see p. 21), but they provide useful information about English 4-part consort music without cantus firmus in Byrd's earlier years. As in White's 5-part *Song* the imitations are closely worked and short-lived, and there are clear cadences between sections like those in his 4-part In Nomines. In addition some of the fantasias contain short passages of homophony. They are more concise than contemporary Italian ricercares, but also rather stiff, so far as may be judged in the absence of the treble line.

In this sphere at least the distance between Italy and England was the width of Europe. In France, as in Spain, Italian influence was strong. Two long, intermittently impressive 4-part fantasias by Claude Lejeune* illustrate the point. The impact of Willaert and his circle is responsible for the general cast of these pieces, their length and the predominance of ample imitative sections. At the same time certain features point to another tradition, less remote from England: concern for the characterization of the different sections, and the admission of passages of non-imitative counterpoint, though Lejeune stops short of White's homophony. Like the English he concludes his sections with punctuating cadences, a practice that returned to Italy only with the cultivation of the canzona in the last thirty years of the century. Whether its earlier use in the north is to be linked with the chanson it is difficult to say, since the context is so different. Indeed Lejeune, for whom the chanson was home ground, approaches his cadences by way of sequences and pedal points quite beyond the scope of the chanson. Such passages, which show him at his best, naturally find no place in White or Byrd, who work in much smaller spans.†

Most of Byrd's fantasias are short by continental standards, not through lack of enterprise on his part, but as the result of a radically different approach to form and texture, deriving from earlier English practice. The flow of imitative counterpoint favoured on the continent, whether in four parts or three, could be prolonged almost indefinitely. Byrd preferred firmer modelling based on a balance of contrasts. The larger the structure, the more boldly its proportions needed to be thrown into relief. Since the strongest contrasts required textural variety he employed five or six parts for all his longer pieces. In his 4-part fantasias he made no attempt to introduce antiphony or dance-like sections, or to overstep in any fundamental way the vocabulary represented by White. As a result they are on a smaller scale – though not necessarily less original for that. Each one offers a different solution to the problem of investing imitation, as the technique of composition best suited to a restricted number of parts, with the kind of

---

*See Lejeune, *Trois fantaisies instrumentales*, transcribed for organ by J. Bonfils (Paris, 1956).

†G. Sutherland, in his informative article 'The Ricercari of Jacques Buus', *Musical Quarterly*, xxxi (1945), 448ff., points out that Buus showed greater interest in thematic character and the shaping of sections than his Italian contemporaries. Although as organist at St Mark's in Venice he was naturally less independent of Italian example than Lejeune, his preferences may perhaps be put down to his Flemish origin.

definition necessary to Byrd's conception of abstract form. The same is true of his even shorter 3-part fantasias.

No textless composition of Byrd takes so much from his motet style as **Fantasia 4/G**. Not only does it start with two well developed imitative periods, but their related subjects both divide into two phrases which can be used separately or in conjunction – a favourite device in his motets. It is not surprising that he should have arranged the piece as a motet for the *Gradualia* of 1605, to the text *In manus tuas*. The one surviving part of the original textless version shows that in adapting it Byrd made a good many changes of detail, not all required by the underlay, but left the larger structure unaltered (except for extending the approach to the final cadence by a semibreve).

It is only after the second imitation that a procedure less typical of his vocal music makes its appearance. The new section is built on three melodious phrases well attuned to the general spirit of the work. They are heard simultaneously, and constantly change position in triple counterpoint (see Ex. 28a), giving rise to a series of 4- and 6-bar periods. These continue, with some overlapping, until stretto and augmentation lead into a final section on the same subjects (at 'ora pro nobis'). The regular phraseology recalls the middle reaches of the Mixolydian keyboard fantasias G2 and G3 (for instance the passages represented by Exx. 68d and 73e), and also parts of the rather later Fantasia C2 (at Ex. 75c and e) where the parts change places in double counterpoint very much in the manner of those in the consort piece – though there is no closer relationship. Since Byrd was in the habit of transferring technical features from his consort to his keyboard music, rather than in the reverse direction, Fantasia 4/G is likely to antedate C2, a work of the later 1580s (see Chapter 11). A relatively early date is in any case suggested by its unidiomatic structural elements.

Unfortunately **Fantasia 4/a** cannot be assessed properly because it lacks the whole of the top part after the first thirteen breves. But the structural outline is reasonably clear. Of the five sections (beginning at bars 1, 18, 29, 34, 40), only the first, third and last are fully imitative. The more freely composed second and fourth employ a rising tetrachord to unify the texture; this is echoed in inversion in the related subjects of the third and fifth sections. The rather staid opening section of seventeen breves is designed as a foil to its less stable successors, and so sets the scale of the whole piece, which is correspondingly short.

Though published in 1611, **Fantasia 4/g** can be dated with some certainty about 1590 or a little before, along with the Keyboard Fantasias C2, G1 and dı, with which it has links of various kinds.* Tomkins made a keyboard intabulation of it which contains not only changes for the convenience of the player (and some mistakes), but differences from the 1611 text which show that Byrd revised the work before publication (see Ex. 30, and the small

Ex. 30

a. First version
Bars 53-4, 58

b. 1611 text

notes in Ex. 31a†). The structure of this fantasia combines features found in the other two 4-part pieces. It begins like 4/G with two imitative periods on related subjects, but only the first of these divides into two separable phrases, and the whole section is more compact than in the relatively relaxed Mixolydian work. The main cadences differ significantly. In 4/G the two imitations end respectively in the tonic and dominant; in 4/g both close in the tonic, though only the second conclusively. Thus the entry of the next section of 4/G in the tonic is felt as a reversion, and prepares for the level course of the rest of the piece, whereas the movement away from the tonic at the corresponding juncture in 4/g arouses contrary expectations, which are not disappointed.

In its wider formal layout 4/g resembles 4/a and, as the more boldly characterized and highly developed work of the two, was presumably modelled on it. Both consist of three imitative sections separated by two interludes. The proportions, however, are different. Naturally the two opening imitative periods of 4/g form a bigger first section than the single one of 4/a, and the imitations of the middle and last sections are also far more substantial. But the interludes are shorter, and distinguished from the main sections not so much by diminished imitative activity as by note-

---

*For its relation to Fantasia dı, see p. 248ff. Compare also bar 46ff. with Gı, 41ff.; and 34ff. with C2, 68ff. and Gı, 43ff. The latter section (from bar 34) may contain a reminiscence of a 4-part fantasia by Ferrabosco (at breve 30ff.; in Add.32377, fol. 4 and Weelkes, fol. 43′), but in general Byrd's lack of interest in Ferrabosco's Italianate fantasias contrasts strongly with his close study of the same composer's In Nomines.

†Other examples: bar 13, alto, first two notes, E♭, D, instead of C, A; bar 41, the alto is missing here, and the tenor has E♭ in place of its rest before the final D. There are also interesting differences in bars 48-49, but the text is unfortunately too faulty at this point to be relied on.

against-note part-writing. Ex. 31 shows most of the first interlude and the whole of the second. The entire composition hinges on them. They serve

Ex. 31

simultaneously to separate and connect the panels of the triptych, bringing the whole structure into focus. The alternating minims and crotchets of the first interlude were probably suggested by those at the corresponding point in 4/a (bar 18), but Byrd insists on them here and uses their disruptive rhythm, emphasized by quasi-homophony and coupled with a move to the dominant, to turn the music in a new direction.* The beautiful imitative section that emerges soon settles into the relative major, and stays there until the second interlude (which arises out of the same melodic idea) leads back to the dominant. The closing section declares its function in two ways: it is firmly based in the tonic, and like that of 4/a it is repeated, though in a subtle manner that takes the hearer unawares.† At the same time the imitative point makes its own contribution to the symmetry of the over-all

---

*Morley gives a description of this technique (*Introduction*, 168) to which two non-imitative, sequential transitions in Lejeune's first fantasia correspond more closely than any example by Byrd. A curious parallel to the present passage occurs at the words 'Non est qui consoletur eam' in the much earlier motet *Aspice Domine quia facta est*, published in 1575, and an entirely different usage in bars 32–50 of Fantasia 6/g1 (see p. 81).

†It is unclear whether the omission of the repeat in one of the two sources for this part of 4/a represents an earlier version or a scribal error. The repeat in 4/g may be seen in two ways. The first phrase of 1½ breves (bars 50–51) may be regarded as omitted the second time; but as the upper part in this phrase occurs an octave higher immediately before the repeat (bars 54–55), it may here be heard simultaneously as the close of the first statement and the beginning of the repeat. The section can thus be interpreted as 6 breves repeated with an overlap of 1½ breves. What counts, of course, is the ingeniously asymmetrical effect.

design by referring back (by inversion and diminution) to the opening subject of the work.

The formality that characterizes the whole fantasia is further illustrated by a comparison of the central imitation and the second interlude with cognate passages in the keyboard fantasias C2 and G1. In the latter the successive episodes claim less for themselves, taking their place in a more continuous train of events, whereas in the consort work even the transitional interlude of four breves (Ex. 31b) contains exposition, intensification and close. The rather austere tone of the music matches the work's measured periods. Its quiet inflections are indebted to mid-century sobriety (the second point occurs, on a different degree of the scale, in White's third 4-part fantasia). Beyond questions of form Byrd turns his interest here to a mode of feeling that he had long ago put behind him. Now that it was too remote to threaten his freedom he could find in it the way to a very personal vein of reserved and intimate expression.

The absence of any direct influence of Italian instrumental music in so mature an imitative piece as this raises an interesting question. Was Byrd ignorant of the ricercare, or did he reject it as a model? An answer can be found in one of his 3-part fantasias. All three must belong, like the 4-part work, to his maturity. The fact that they are confined to late sources, all but one of them from Paston's collection, is by no means conclusive, but their close motivic work and perfection of detail suggest a date no earlier than the 1580s, and would allow them a place in the period of the *Gradualia*. A late date would not be surprising. During the height of his fame Byrd had composed with a wide public in view, but as time went on and new musical fashions came to the fore he increasingly devoted what energies he could spare from his work on the Roman rite to providing music for private circles, where small consort pieces would have been welcome. As a rule, Byrd liked to build on an established tradition. It happened that the English tradition of 3-part textless composition was too unattractive to offer him a lead (see p. 52). His own vocal music did not help him, for however vocal in character his instrumental music may appear by comparison with that of the next century, the absence of a text always fundamentally affected his approach to structural questions. In the absence of an acceptable native tradition he turned his attention to the Italian ricercare.

Half a century earlier, during the 1540s and 1550s, Willaert had published a number of 3-part ricercares which proved so popular that the last reprint did not appear till 1593. They are excellent examples of their problematical genre, entirely contrapuntal, beautifully written for player or singer, and somewhat low in temperature. As late as 1585 Giovanni Bassano published examples which, though more closely imitative than Willaert's and only about half the length (even allowing for *note nere*), still conform essentially to the same pattern.* It is impossible to tell whether Byrd studied Willaert himself or a later follower, since the features he adopted were common to all, but the impact of the style on his **Fantasia 3/C3** is unmistakable.† The piece is set a little apart from its 3-part companions by its extreme brevity, and also by the higher tessitura of the parts. There are three points of imitation. The opening resembles that of several of Willaert's ricercares; the second point employs the ubiquitous Italian upward run of four quick notes filling in the interval of a fifth. But the influence reaches far beyond details of this kind to the whole contrapuntal style.

Ex. 32

a. Fantasia 3/C 3

b. Fantasia 3 / C 2

*See Willaert, *IX ricercari per sonar con tre stromenti*, ed. H. Zenck (Mainz, 1933), and various examples by Bassano in *Hortus musicus* 16 and 64, ed. respectively E. Kiwi and J. Bacher (Kassel, 1933 and 1939).

†The influence is too clear to need documentation, but it is worth noting that Byrd's patron Lord Lumley possessed a copy of the *Motetta trium vocum* (Brown 1543₃), which contains ricercares by Willaert. It is listed as No. 2586 in *The Lumley Library, The Catalogue of 1609*, ed. S. Jayne and F. R. Johnson (London, 1956). This copy is now in the British Library, along with similar publications that seem to have been added to the collections in the eighteenth or early nineteenth century, when acquisitions were drawn largely from English sources. Among them is another Willaert edition: Giuliano Tiburtino's *Fantasie et ricercari a tre voci* (Brown 1549₇).

Ex. 32 (Cont.)

The borrowed language is illustrated in Ex. 32a, which shows the greater part of the third section. To the attentive ear Byrd's distinctive voice is perceptible, but in the nature of things the tone is less personal than in the other two 3-part fantasias, where he speaks more freely. The contrapuntal style that Byrd had inherited from the instrumental music of his elders was rather solid, no doubt as a legacy of the note-against-cantus-firmus-note habit of mind, and hence closely harmonic. At the same time memory of the earlier differentiated style lingered on, so that at any given moment certain voices might dominate the others, usually through quicker movement, and the feeling of melody and accompaniment was never far away. In Byrd's hands the style is still recognizable, though he refined the dross out of it. It persisted not only in his 5- and 6-part music, but even in the strictly imitative Fantasia 4/g; the harmonic aspect is fundamental to the deeply personal quality of Byrd's polyphony.

In 3-part writing there is, of course, less room to vary the relative importance of the voices. It would thus have been all the more natural for Byrd to wish to study the equality of Italian part-writing before proceeding to his two more typical fantasias. The style of these may be seen in the extract from 3/C2 in Ex. 32b. The two passages are built on similar figures but have little else in common. In Ex. 32a the flexible alternation of different note-values, designed to promote smooth independence between the parts rather than salient melodic features, is thoroughly Italian. The second and more important phrase of the subject (ECDE in the treble, and so on), does not make a strong mark, but flows into a free melodic continuation (in this case less free than it might be because Byrd characteristically ties it in with further imitation, and with motivic references to other sections of the piece). In Ex. 32b the subject is the same, but its distinguishing features are

intensified by repetition so that it imprints its character on the new phase of
the composition. The quotation shows clearly enough how this is carried
through. In the treble the subject rises at each appearance, throwing out a
contrasting limb in minims which is taken up from the opening section (see
Ex. 34a). In the remarkable bass line it takes an even more striking course.
The middle part, however, though imitative, plays a subordinate role: its
primary function is to support the other parts and enrich the harmony.

One feature of 3/C3 is very far from Italian – its small scale. Byrd answers
his long models with the shortest of all his fantasias, only a third of the
length of most of Bassano's, and minute by comparison with Willaert's. It
might be thought that he was merely trying out a style and was not interested
in prolonging the experiment. However, since the piece is constructed with
the greatest care and was presumably circulated with the composer's consent
it is not to be dismissed as a mere exercise. Other reasons for its brevity
suggest themselves.

By the 1580s Byrd commanded means of structural control undreamt of
in Italy. His mastery of harmonic nuance in Fantasia 5/C and contrasting
character in 6/g1 would have inclined him to view the ricercare with an
independent eye. His little fantasia would appear to contain his commentary:
not only his interest in the polyphonic style, but his disbelief in the capacity
of subtle variations in texture and refined melodic prolongations to shape a
lengthy composition effectively. He denies himself the cadential schemes and
syncopated or homophonic transitions that play such an important part in
most of his fantasias. But in accepting the limits imposed upon material by
his models he makes it clear that in his opinion other limitations are entailed.
He takes the English view of imitation as a means of establishing character.
The Italian convention favours rather weakly characterized points that
further the wider contrapuntal flow without calling too much attention to
themselves. Byrd takes three such points and asks no more of them than he
feels their slender resources can bear, which is very little indeed. Each
yields a tiny section. To add another section would present a difficult formal
problem, for the series would cease to cohere. Short as it is, the piece is as
long as Byrd's attitude to the style would allow. To have given short measure
or fallen in any way below his best level would have spoiled his critical point.

The other two fantasias may be a pair. They appear as such in two of the
manuscripts, and for all their differences draw on similar source motives.
The three subjects of **Fantasia 3/C1** are built round a pair of ascending or
descending interlocking fourths; they are shown in Ex. 33 in the versions
which reveal the relationship most clearly. The piece consists entirely of

Ex. 33

imitative counterpoint. Only two other fantasias by Byrd are comparable in this respect, and both are special cases: the Italianate 3/C3, and the 3-part Keyboard Fantasia C3 (see p. 225). Fantasia 3/C1 is not an essay in a special style. It is a leisurely piece, deriving its individual character from a gentle, even flow that Byrd is careful not to disturb by breaking the texture, as he almost invariably does in order to articulate a form. Although it is longer than 3/C2, events are less densely packed, and the careful shaping of the first two imitations allows the last to be approached without additional formal clarification. The second half is entirely based on the more animated Ex. 33c,* but the calm is not disrupted, for the sense of momentum is counteracted by an altogether unusual degree of near-repetition. The music turns slowly on its own axis, shifting only slightly with each revolution, and finally runs quietly to a halt. It is as though the composer had left the whole responsibility for shaping this beautiful piece to its own unhurried eloquence.

The first subject of **Fantasia 3/C2** is shown in Ex. 34a. It is closely

Ex. 34

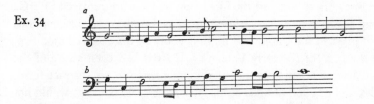

related to those of 3/C1, and the material of the two works shares the same warmth and gentleness. But whereas 3/C1 is primarily static, 3/C2 is a study in continuous development. It is scarcely possible to set the subjects side by side for comparison like those of 3/C1, because they are always changing. The motivic work is correspondingly intense, perhaps more so than in any other piece by Byrd; even in Fantasia 5/C, where it plays an equally important part, it is under less pressure than in the swift activity of the compact 3-part work.

*This figure is made up of various well worn contrapuntal tags. What Byrd makes of the rising crotchet scale followed by the falling third and second is brought home by comparison with Tye's use of it in *Sit fast* (*Instrumental Music*, 106), or Andrea Gabrieli's in his third *Ricercar arioso* (*Canzonen und Ricercari ariosi*, ed. P. Pidoux (Kassel, 1961), 41).

Like the other shorter fantasias, 3/C2 is in three sections. The first consists of three phases: an exposition on Ex. 34a, a second set of entries on a very considerably varied version of the same subject, and a syncopated stretto on the descending tailpiece, in which imitation contracts to a mere contrapuntal pattern. The start of the second section (Ex. 32b) brings the most marked thematic break, though the new figure grows out of the preceding stretto pattern with the help of inversion. The climax of the piece is the second phase of this section. It is built on the subject in the bass at the end of Ex. 32b. It will be seen that when the treble takes this up in the last notes of the quotation, the A and G minims are so placed following the C and B that they contrive to echo not only the first A and G in Ex. 34a, but the second as well. Such touches abound in this work. The last section immediately announces its function as a coda by restricting harmonic movement with pedal points: two breves of tonic followed by nearly as much dominant. The two lower parts use figural technique purely as an accompaniment to the treble melody, which is built out of elements from Ex. 34a. A shorter figure eventually detaches itself and allows the other parts to join in a final imitation for the perfectly judged conclusion. The middle part's first entry here is almost a quotation from the opening (see Ex. 34b and a).

Byrd's shorter fantasias illustrate his exceptional sensitivity in matters of form no less clearly than his large consort works, and they differ from each other almost as widely. Each is planned on an entirely different principle. The firm framework of 4/g and the loose rein of 3/C1 are replaced in 3/C2 by modelling so sharp that every phrase in the composition seems conscious of the part it plays in the whole, and nothing could be displaced or modified. Ever since the time of the early Fantasia 6/F Byrd had been aware of the need for a sense of orientation at every moment within an abstract form. The complex and original designs of his later large-scale fantasias would not in themselves have solved the problem. They live by an intuitive quality which runs in every fibre of this small 3-part masterpiece.

6

Organ Antiphons and Hymns

Clarifica me pater: 3 settings	BK 47–49
Gloria tibi trinitas	BK 50
Miserere: 2 settings	BK 66, 67
Salvator mundi: 2 settings	BK 68, 69

The first of the *Miserere* settings bears no ascription in the only source (Christ Church 371), but as the two are written in sequence the attribution to Byrd clearly applies to both, not merely to the second (as was first pointed out by J. Steele in his unpublished dissertation 'English Organs and Organ Music from 1500 to 1650' (Cambridge, 1958), 143). The same manuscript contains an anonymous setting of *Christe qui lux es* (EECM 6/34; listed in BK, second edition, 121) closely allied to two of Byrd's consort settings of the same melody. The opening resembles that of his setting II/1 and the close those of both I/1 and II/1. It was probably composed either by Byrd himself or by White, whom Byrd imitated in several of his consort settings (White, like Byrd, is represented in the manuscript – by a short hexachord piece). It employs two points of imitation, the first in conjunction with the first line of the hymn melody, and the second with the remaining three. White works more schematically than this in his known settings, either confining himself to a single point or adopting a fresh one for each line of the melody. In contrast Byrd allows himself greater latitude, at least in his set I, and therefore seems the more likely claimant of the two. The piece is a modest effort in which the two free parts behave rather like those in Byrd's *Miserere* 2, but move predominantly in minims instead of crotchets. (For further discussion of this piece, as well as the others dealt with in the present chapter, see A. Brown, 'Keyboard Music by Byrd "Upon a plain-song" ', *Organ Yearbook*, v (1974), 30ff. Ex. 35 owes its presence on p. 107 below to this article.)

When as a young man of about twenty Byrd took up his duties as organist at Lincoln in February 1563, the Elizabethan prayer-book had been in use for less than four years. Its requirements had finally silenced the organ as a solo voice in the liturgy. Until the Act of Uniformity of 1549, and again under Mary I, the organ might alternate with the choir in mass sections and canticles, replacing parts of the sung chant with interludes employing the appropriate sections of the plainsong as cantus firmus. It could likewise play alternate verses in hymns, the complete offertory (except, usually, for the intonation) and antiphons. Having seen the Edwardian reforms so soon revoked, organists probably hesitated to regard Elizabeth's as permanent. As there was no firmly established tradition of organ composition outside the liturgical framework to fall back on, they continued to base their music on those Sarum melodies which had offered scope for more or less independent pieces within it, namely hymns and antiphons. Thus whereas the vocal music of the church had to be refashioned to play its new and relatively restricted part, organ music pursued its old course, affected only by the removal of liturgical restraints.

Of the considerable surviving body of English keyboard music based on plainsong melodies rather more than half seems to have been written for the liturgy,* and so before the Act of Uniformity of 1559. This is the organ repertory that Byrd would have played and studied during his formative years. Its influence on his keyboard music stretches far beyond his plainsong settings, for his early impressions gave rise to inalienable habits of mind. What he chose consciously to develop or ignore, whether in the work of predecessors or contemporaries, is no less revealing; however remote his organ pieces with cantus firmus may appear from their consort counterparts, the same characteristic preferences can be seen to underlie both.

Throughout the period the cantus firmus, in keyboard as in consort music, was almost invariably disposed in equal note-values. But whereas it was left largely or wholly undecorated in consort and in later keyboard pieces, composers of liturgical organ music frequently elaborated it in accordance with principles current in the previous century, often to the point where the chant became all but unrecognizable. The styles involving this procedure are best represented by John Redford, who died in 1547 when Byrd was only four. Although older composers such as Avery Burton and younger ones such as Philip ap Rhys used the same techniques, none did so with such assurance and imagination.

The heart of Redford's musical thought lies in his sensitivity to the possibilities of unfettered melodic line. His 2-part hymn verses show this particularly clearly. The decorated cantus firmus here becomes a real part, largely subservient to the right-hand melody but intermittently elevated through imitation to the status of equal partner. The free upper melodies are not continuous but fall into periods or phrases, each marked off from the next by a rest, a skip or an appreciably longer note. These periods vary in length from a mere three or four notes to passages of several breves' duration, and in pace from predominantly minim and semibreve values to crotchets with quaver ornaments. Redford works his highly flexible material to fine

*All the music of this earlier period has been printed in three publications: MB 1 and EECM 6 and 10. Most of the later pieces have also been published. For details see J. Caldwell's invaluable guide to the whole repertory, 'Keyboard Plainsong Settings in England, 1500–1660', *Musica disciplina*, xix (1965), 129ff.

effect, deriving each phrase from the last by varied sequence, fragmentation, extension or brusque contrast and yet encompassing by this seemingly point-to-point method a complete piece in a single perfectly balanced paragraph.*

The primacy of melody is no less marked in his 3-part music. In many pieces the phrase structure differs from that of the 2-part music only through the absence of extended crotchet movement. There is naturally more harmonic weight, which sometimes carries with it a degree of quasi-cadential articulation surprising in so linear a style. Three main techniques may be distinguished: occasionally the lower parts do little more than support a melody; more often phrases are imitated in dialogue, or they may be echoed between all three parts, usually at the same degree but in three octaves. These techniques are drawn on freely;† imitation usually plays a secondary role in the sense that it is less a structural necessity than a means of reflecting the melody at different levels in the transparent texture, in a more formal manner than in the motivic play of Cornysh's *Fa la soll* (see p. 62) but in much the same spirit. The music remains linear in structure; it progresses by the accumulation of phrases to which all the parts, but especially the treble, contribute, and so permits swift turns of feeling and fluctuations in tension beyond the reach of a more fully imitative style.

An appreciable shift of interest declares itself in the music of Redford's younger contemporary Thomas Preston, who was still active in the early years of Elizabeth's reign. Most of his music survives in a single manuscript (Add.29996) which also contains an important group of anonymous hymn settings. It has been suggested‡ that these may also be by Preston; the style is certainly similar to his, and for convenience the composer will be referred to here as 'Preston', in quotes. In these hymns 'Preston', like Preston in much of his organ mass, shows himself a close student of Redford. He follows him in increasing the number of parts in successive verses of hymns from two to three, but often continues the sequence to four parts and may conclude with a verse of keyboard figuration. Redford's essays in the last two styles are rare, so 'Preston's' imitation of him is restricted to the 2- and 3-part verses, where he shows the concern for fuller sonority that was to be expected at this late date even in England. He allows fewer pauses in his 2-part writing and works out runs and sequential figures with greater persistence. In his 3-part writing he achieves a closer texture by preserving

*See e.g. EECM 6/36I, 52, 60, 61II.

†By exception they can be seen more or less isolated respectively in EECM 6/40III, 42II, 49.

‡By D. Stevens in his article on Preston in MGG.

a more even flow in all parts and tends to work in more regular imitation. In both styles his lines fail to hold the listener as Redford's do by their eventfulness and singular poise. 'Preston's' 4-part hymn style is an extension of his 3-part; the texture is dense, the sense of direction a trifle uncertain, and the connection with Redford rarely perceptible.

In some respects the longer pieces, mostly offertories and antiphons, show a parallel development. Redford expands his hymn style in his sometimes wayward but always imaginative offertories; Preston, when employing a cantus firmus in semibreves (the usual procedure in hymns), keeps close to the more stolid 3- and 4-part hymn styles of 'Preston'. But another tradition of composition, which had not held much attraction for Redford, now came to the fore. There exists a group of four anonymous pieces,* probably transcribed in the 1530s, in which the chant is disposed in long note-values without decoration. In two of them (EECM 10/10, 29) the free parts alternate between fairly consistent imitation and keyboard figuration. Preston and his contemporaries developed both styles, but in separate pieces. The studies in figuration, by Preston, Richard Wynslate and Richard Farrant, all have cantus firmi in dotted semibreves, and as this was the usual measure in grounds and hornpipes they may owe something to secular keyboard music. The imitative pieces, by Preston and Thorne, have cantus firmi in breves, and approximate to the all too sober style of the early imitative In Nomine. It is perhaps worth noting that in Redford's three known examples of 4-part writing, which embody his nearest approach to this style,† his characteristic feeling for phrase structure still makes itself felt. All three pieces begin strikingly with a fourfold repetition, once in each part, of a rhythmically enclosed subject, after which the more flowing movement that ensues derives unusual impetus through the sense of rhythmic release. This kind of effect was not sought, and perhaps not understood, by Preston's generation.

Nevertheless, Redford found posthumous admirers, among them Thomas Mulliner, who compiled a personal anthology of keyboard music almost

---

*EECM 10/2, 10, 11, 29. They occur in Roy. App. 56, and are followed by popular French chansons published about 1530.

†MB 1/37, 39, 54. The last two are in standard In Nomine notation, but the first, though in exactly the same style, is written in halved values so that the cantus firmus is in semibreves and harmonic change occurs here and there in crotchets. By the middle of the century each type of keyboard piece was linked to and fostered by its own notational convention. Redford's deviation is unusual but not unique: his O lux on the faburden (MB 1/28) is a simple example of the style associated with dotted semibreve cantus firmus, but is written in black notation against semibreves. This suggests that in Redford's time the conventions were not yet firmly established.

certainly in the 1560s,* when Byrd was organist at Lincoln. Although there are dangers in taking Mulliner's tastes as representative of the time, because so much of the extant music survives only in the manuscript that reflects them, the subsequent development of keyboard writing confirms the general picture given there. His attitudes to Redford and to the Marian developments in both figuration and the imitative In Nomine style are therefore of considerable interest. The last of these styles did not interest Mulliner: he transcribed Taverner's original In Nomine and two consort examples of the genre, but no imitative organ pieces comparable to those of Preston; in England consort and keyboard music never shared common cause for long. Of Redford, he copied a large number of 3- and 4-part pieces, but to Mulliner (or to the copyists on whom he was dependent) any music, whether in two parts or three, strongly dominated by a treble melody evidently seemed too old-fashioned for transcription; thus from three sets of verses by Redford which are known complete elsewhere he selected only the final ones in three more or less imitative parts.†

Other single verses in this manuscript, not all of them by Redford, must originally have belonged to sets that are now lost. Tallis, for instance, whose organ hymns are unhappily almost confined to this source, is represented by nine hymns and antiphons in four parts as opposed to one each in three and two; yet his two known 2-part antiphons, in contrasting styles, show a practised hand. It is therefore likely that some at least of his 4-part verses are extracted from sets planned on similar lines to those of 'Preston'. Be that as it may, the survival of the existing pieces is fortunate, for their enclosed perfection sets them apart from all others. Each is a meditation on a single subject, to which extraordinarily dissonant harmony imparts the quiet intensity peculiar to so much of Tallis's music.‡

*See especially J. Ward, 'Les sources de la musique pour le clavier en Angleterre', in Jacquot, *Musique instrumentale*, 225ff.

†Compare EECM 6/36, 61, 63 respectively with MB 1/31, 47, 66; also the *Te deum* EECM 6/2 with the four sections from it in MB 1/59–62.

‡In the preface to the New Issue (1934) of her book *About Elizabethan Virginal Music and its Composers* Margaret Glyn pointed out that one of these hymns occurs under Bull's name in Messaus's manuscript (Add.23623), and suggested that other hymns of apparently similar date in the same source might also be by Tallis. Several writers have adopted her argument since. The music, however, gives no support to Tallis's authorship. Quite apart from questions of musical quality, three characteristics of the pieces in the Mulliner book will serve as mechanical tests: (1) their monothematicism, (2) their dissonant harmony, (3) the special care expended on the close of each piece (cf. Tallis's *Gloria tibi trinitas*, his short *Point*, and his untitled 3-part organ piece). Of the pieces attributed questionably to Bull by Messaus none answers to (1), only the antiphon *Alleluia: Post partum* to (2) (except where recalcitrant canons are being forced into place), and only one or two to (3). The harmonic style in any case suggests a somewhat younger man. All the pieces are printed in MB 14.

It was not, however, by these wonderful pieces that Tallis was remembered as a keyboard composer during the next sixty years, but by two enormous settings of *Felix namque*, the offertory in the Lady Mass. Neither is in Mulliner's book, but both occur in Tregian (Nos. [109, 110]), where they are dated, with an exactitude that inspires confidence, 1562 and 1564; the second and superior work occurs in no fewer than five late sources. Although Tallis sets out the plainsong in breves the music is not in the short-lived In Nomine style, but is almost entirely given over to elaborate figuration of a kind hitherto largely associated with cantus firmi in dotted semibreves. Tallis fills out his breves in both pieces with ever smaller divisions in which the number of crotchets (in modern transcription) increases by proportional notation from eight to twelve and finally to eighteen, with copious quaver movement in the first two stages. The figuration, though remarkably inventive, is uncontrolled by any structural factor capable of giving the pieces unity and shape.* That did not stand in the way of their success, for keyboard composers now began to cultivate figuration at the expense of other considerations, as Mulliner's anthology shows, and later men were to follow suit, notably Bull.

Figuration is prominent in the music of the most important of the younger composers to appear in Mulliner, John Blitheman. Mulliner may have known him in Oxford and perhaps for this reason paid him the compliment of not censoring the 2-part sections of his thoroughly traditional *Te Deum* or of his hymn *Aeterne verum*, a set of four verses laid out exactly like 'Preston's' sets. These must be early works written under Queen Mary. The 4-part verse of *Aeterne verum* is apparently indebted to Tallis's hymns, but although Blitheman misses the older composer's intensity he shows a lightness of touch that enables him to handle complex figuration very stylishly in his six ambitious settings of *Gloria tibi trinitas*, which are presumably later works. In his best passages he keeps the figures moving from one part to another in a manner all his own. It is a pity that in this respect Bull was to show himself more Tallis's pupil than Blitheman's.

*This state of affairs is altogether unexpected in the work of a composer whose concern for aesthetic propriety invariably triumphs even where, as for instance in *Spem in alium*, he is in some special way out to impress. It suggests that the offertories were required for a particular purpose, a possible clue to which is provided by the well known account of the queen taking communion thirty years later at Easter 1593 (see *The Old Cheque Book of the Chapel Royal*, ed. E. F. Rimbault (London, 1882), 150f.). On that occasion Bull played the offertory, which must have been a very long one as the queen needed time to play her appointed part in the service with due ceremony. Bull probably played music of no special liturgical significance, but if Tallis had been called on to provide a very long piece for such an occasion the *Felix namque*, which had been used regularly in its liturgical context until very recently, would have been a natural choice of chant, and perhaps not unacceptable in the queen's chapel.

Byrd's plainsong settings for organ must all date from the earlier 1560s. So few of them survive that no comprehensive pattern of development can be traced, but even so these few suffice to demonstrate his extraordinary independence of mind. Whereas his contemporaries regarded the old Redfordian melodic style as dead, he turned to it as a primary source of inspiration; by contrast their enthusiasm for figuration left him cold. His only consistent studies in figuration are his two settings of **Salvator mundi**. The first was evidently suggested by Blitheman's second *Gloria tibi trinitas* (MB 1/92). As there, plain semibreves in the right hand are accompanied by an unbroken line of quavers in the left and later by a 2-part texture in tripla; moreover, near the end there is a direct quotation (see Ex. 35).

Ex. 35   *a.* Blitheman

It is difficult to read Byrd's purpose in this piece; the style, particularly in the first half, allows very little individuality to come through. This is the only example in his work of a bald variety of bicinium that is found as early as Redford and was to become popular not only with younger Englishmen such as Bull, but with Sweelinck and his followers. Byrd's aversion to it might cast doubt on the authenticity of the piece were it not for the hint, at the beginning of the tripla, of more personal traits which come rapidly to the fore in the second verse. This starts off as a right-hand study in answer to its left-hand companion. However, the figuration later changes position – not phrase by phrase as in Blitheman's *Gloria tibi trinitas* Nos. 3 and 5 (MB 1/93, 95), but in sections as one means of structural differentiation. Although the textures themselves in the various sections can all be matched in earlier composers, the changes in texture coincide with points of cadence which arise from a strong major mode harmonic sense foreign to the tradition behind the piece. The harmonic language shows Byrd at about the stage he had reached in the first 4-part consort settings of *Sermone blando* (see p. 58), but enjoys greater independence here because the bass line has no obligations to imitative counterpoint. The harmony can thus fall naturally into step with, and help to define, the predominantly regular periods.* As a result the music strides out with the same certainty of purpose that must have sounded so novel in the early Fantasia 6/F (see p. 65).

Byrd's two **Miserere** settings occur in an earlier source than any other keyboard music of his, and as it happens they were probably composed earlier too. Their only modern feature, one that they share with all his organ pieces, is a liking for quick note-values. The first is a 2-part setting that immediately recalls, and not only in technical externals, the type of Redford piece so pointedly excluded by Mulliner from his collection. Byrd shows the same feeling for melodic continuity as Redford, the same understanding of the possibilities of melodic sequence, and the same urge to shape the whole piece entirely by melodic gradation. However, his inexperience amusingly lets him down: he runs out of breath before the end and has to mark time through a double repetition so that his last word loses its effect.

The second *Miserere* belongs to a minor species of 3-part setting in which the cantus firmus, in plain semibreves in the treble, is supported by two rather fast-moving parts that sometimes tend, though not in Byrd, towards figuration. Examples range from Redford to Blitheman (MB 1/38, 52) but the nearest parallels to Byrd's are two rather crude anonymous pieces, the very first to be copied by Mulliner into his manuscript (MB 1/5, 6). These two pieces and Byrd's are all built on very similar canonic snatches punctuated at frequent intervals by the same type of cadence. Byrd shows his superiority in a number of ways. His simple counterpoint is smoother, his cadences or near-cadences, falling six times out of seven at the end of the third semibreve, induce not uncharacteristic stability along with much less characteristic monotony, the cadence degrees are well diversified apart from an unfortunate repetition at semibreves 17 and 20, and there is a well-judged canonic coda. All the same it is a rather dull effort.

The three settings of the antiphon **Clarifica me pater** follow the same kind of sequence as the hymns of 'Preston' and Blitheman: an extra contrapuntal strand is added in each so that the first is in two parts† and the

---

*Mostly of four bars (i.e. semibreves) with a cadence resolving on the first beat of the next period; see bars 1–4 . . . 19–24, 25–28, 29–30, and then the four consecutive 4-bar periods before the final chord.

†It is not surprising to find this piece omitted from the set in the later of the two sources (Tregian).

last in four.* There is, of course, no precedent in liturgical practice for a group of settings of an antiphon melody such as this, nor for the upward transposition by a fifth of the plainsong in the middle setting. Although the principle of transposition by an interval other than the octave was not unknown in organ music,† the nearest parallels to the present example are in consort music (see pp. 56, 68). Byrd makes the last note of each setting the root of the final chord, so that the final of the second verse stands in dominant relation to the others, a sharper contrast than the subdominant finals of the very early Consort *Miserere* 1 and *Christe qui lux es* I/2. The first two *Clarifica me* settings may have been influenced by Tallis's *Felix namque* of 1562,‡ for both increase the number of 'crotchets' to the semibreve from four to six and finally to nine, a procedure not met with before Tallis's offertory, and in the second the 9 : 1 proportion begins with almost the same figure as in the Tallis (see Ex. 36). *Clarifica me* 2 has the plainsong in

Ex. 36

a. Tallis   *b.* Byrd

the treble, like Tallis's piece and Byrd's own *Miserere* 2. It starts in much the same way as the *Miserere*, but improves upon it immeasurably as it progresses by smooth transitions through a variety of complex figures. The 2-part setting likewise far surpasses the corresponding *Miserere* in both range and control.

Yet for all their scope and drive nothing in the first two *Clarifica me* settings prepares the listener for the mastery of the third, which might at first suggest itself as a later addition. There are good reasons, however, for rejecting this idea: a 4-part setting restoring the cantus firmus and final to the pitch of the first setting is required to close the set, and the mastery, though impressive, is by no means complete, as Ex. 37 will demonstrate.

---

*J. Caldwell prints the cantus firmi from all three settings in parallel with the chant in 'Keyboard Plainsong Settings in England, 1500–1660', *Musica disciplina*, xix (1965), 142ff.

†See J. Caldwell, 'The Pitch of Early Tudor Organ Music', *Music & Letters*, lv (1970), 156ff.

‡It is worth noting that Byrd left Tallis's hymns respectfully alone. However, though not caring to meet Tallis on his own ground he may be said to have answered him in quite different terms in his last two pairs of consort hymns.

Ex. 37

This shows the melodic peak of the composition, which coincides with the arrival of the plainsong final following the last dominant harmony in the piece. Apparently with the intention of breaking the momentum at the start of his 10-bar plagal coda, Byrd introduces a startling harmonic syncopation. Unfortunately the idea is clumsily executed and the effect decidedly unhappy.

But despite blemishes in the detail the piece is very well constructed (even if the long last section, from bar 28, trails a little), and extremely original; it shows Byrd as one of those rare composers who can run almost before he can walk. There are three sections based on as many points of imitation, somewhat in the style of an In Nomine in halved note-values, though not, of course, the In Nomine style as it appears in organ music by Thorne or Preston. It is more nearly akin to Byrd's own early 4-part In Nomines than to anything in the organ or earlier consort traditions. The main difference lies in the dense texture, which relates to the rather close canonic style of his 3-part pieces, and contrasts strongly with the lean consort works. The structure follows Byrd's In Nomine pattern down to such details as the powerful tonic cadence at bar 11, which exactly corresponds in function to the similar cadence in all his In Nomines at CF 13 or 14 (see p. 36). The whole piece shows such extraordinary powers of melodic expansion and harmonic control that for all its shortcomings it is tempting to place it beside the best of Redford and Tallis among the finest things in English organ music.

In its entirely different way Byrd's **Gloria tibi trinitas** is scarcely less remarkable. Tallis made a little setting of the same chant, typical of its author in its unobtrusive excellence, which Byrd appears to have known. Both pieces employ the old 2-part style with decorated cantus firmus, and the relation between the entries of the stock subject in the extracts shown in Ex. 38 seems too close for coincidence. In general, however, Byrd is here, as in his *Miserere* 1 and *Clarifica me* 1, involved with the letter and spirit of Redford, though he drives the characteristic figures and cross-rhythms harder in order to achieve even greater melodic variety. At the same time, and without undermining the linear tension that gives this vigorous and eventful music its cogency, he further defines the structure with the aid of

Ex. 38

features that also appear in the very different context of his two 4-part In Nomines.

These pieces are probably roughly contemporaneous with the *Gloria tibi trinitas*, since all three share a single irregularity in their common cantus firmus (the reduplication of CF 24) which is not found in Byrd's 5-part In Nomines. The contrasting tonal regions in In Nomine 4/2 and the 8-bar melody at CF 33–41 in 4/1 find parallels respectively in the long passage on the dominant (major and minor) between bars 18 and 31 of the organ piece and the symmetrical periods at its close. These consist of two periods of four bars and one of eight (followed by the final chord) – almost the same pattern as the four consecutive 4-bar periods at the end of the organ *Salvator mundi* 2, but executed in terms of melody instead of figuration.

Ex. 39 shows the last 8 + 1 bars. The first six each contain exactly the

Ex. 39

same melodic pattern at various pitches. This idea derives from one of the commonest techniques in English cantus firmus setting for keyboard, from the earliest known pieces till after Byrd's death: in its simplest form a pattern established upon one note of the plainsong is repeated at whatever level the next note dictates, though sometimes a pattern may span a couple of notes and so require some adjustment. Either way the resulting chain lacks direction, and the technique appealed to Byrd at no period of his life; repetition and sequence only occur in his music as means of building stanza melodies or more ambitious melodic paragraphs, and they always prepare a contrast. Ex. 39 illustrates the process in miniature. The six repetitions are paired in pitch and by harmonic region to form the first three lines of a quatrain which Byrd closes brilliantly by perkily inverting the falling thirds in the last line. This passage, and the two 4-bar phrases that precede it, show the unmistakable influence of secular song and dance melody.

The unprecedented intrusion of secular form and spirit into Byrd's organ music vividly illustrates the deep division between his aims and those of other organ composers of the 1560s and later who became increasingly engrossed in the development of figuration – to the detriment of structure and refinement of expression. For them the plainsong cantus firmus was a convenience; for Byrd it became an encumbrance. Although he soon over-came the stylistic uncertainty that such pieces as *Miserere* 2 and *Salvator mundi* 1 share with many of his earlier consort hymns, and went on to find solutions to the structural problem, such solutions could not hold his interest for long: the success of *Clarifica me* 3 could best be followed up in the 5-part In Nomines, that of *Gloria tibi trinitas* by abandoning cantus firmi altogether – which he swiftly did.

Yet the significance of his brief cultivation of the anachronistic 2-part style can scarcely be overemphasized. It shows, no less clearly than the early consort music but in a different way, that he was preoccupied from the very beginning with the development of self-sufficient abstract forms. It was Redford, as has already been stressed, who provided the example for a melodic style both indigenous to the keyboard and capable of shaping a form. There can, of course, be no certainty that Byrd drew his inspiration direct from Redford, for this style had been used by many composers, including, though probably not in their more recent works, Tallis and Blitheman. But on the available evidence only Redford among Byrd's pre-decessors came near to sharing the acute feeling for linear balance, variation, extension and contrast that characterizes all Byrd's music, and it would be strange indeed if Byrd had learned nothing from his work.

However, there was a limit to the spans that Redford's remarkable powers of linear organization could control on their own, as his longer offertories show. Byrd saw that the licence given by the decorated cantus firmus to the free melodic part could be stretched to allow the introduction of symmetrical melodic periods as a stabilizing factor. But this insight entailed another: if some degree of symmetry was a condition of expansion, so was the freedom to give it appropriate harmonic support. In short, the plainsong cantus firmus could now only hinder the effective articulation of extended instrumental composition, and Byrd turned his back on it for ever.

Nevertheless the vocabulary of organ music continued to make a considerable contribution to Byrd's keyboard style, despite his preference for forms of secular origin. Admittedly, so little secular keyboard music of the mid-century survives that it is hard to tell how far it shared common ground with the organ repertory in matters of style – as opposed to structure. There can naturally have been no hard and fast division between the two traditions: for example Tallis's *Felix namque* settings were undoubtedly regarded as landmarks for keyboard music in general. But the fact remains that in so far as the small change of Byrd's keyboard style, considered in isolation, does not belong to the common international currency of the time, it can usually be traced back to earlier English organ music. Although he used figuration constantly, not as an end in itself but for linear expansion (as Redford had done), he enriched the common stock of figures hardly at all – if they can be considered divorced from their context. Moreover he rarely availed himself of certain forms already present in Redford and Tallis, notably triadic patterns which appear tautological where, as in Byrd, the balance between horizontal and vertical is finer. The little imitative phrases that so often carry his music forward can nearly all be found in Redford and his contemporaries, or in Preston. But Byrd removes all memory of the origins of these ubiquitous ingredients of his keyboard writing by the originality of the conceptions which he calls upon them to serve, and by the distinction of his workmanship.

7
Grounds and Related Keyboard Pieces

Ut re mi fa sol la   BK 58

Short Ground in C major. 20 vars. (+ coda)   BK 43

Short Ground in G major. 38 vars.   BK 86

Short Ground in G minor. 23 vars.   BK 9

Hornpipe   BK 39

The Bells   BK 38

The Hunt's up (Peascod time). 12 vars.   BK 40

Second Ground. 17 vars.   BK 42

Hugh Aston's Ground. 12 vars. BK 20

My Lady Nevell's Ground. 6 vars. BK 57

Chi passa. 3 vars. BK 19

Passing Measures (Passamezzo antico) BK 2

Pavan ○ ○ ○ ○ for each note: 6 vars.

Galliard ○ ♩ ○ ♩ for each note: 6 vars.

Quadran (Passamezzo moderno) BK 70

Notes lengthened as in Passing Measures, with reprises in proportion.

Pavan: 4 vars. 4 reps.

Galliard: 6 vars. 6 reps.

The term 'short' ground refers to the 4-bar basses, not the length of the pieces. The bass of the *Second Ground* was often known as Good Night (see DVB, p. 44), but as the Ground for consort is also based on it the arbitrary title *Second Ground* has been adopted from Nevell (the only source), where it is so called because *My Lady Nevell's Ground* stands first.

Two grounds not listed above but ascribed to Byrd in the sources may be rejected. *Malt's come down* (BK 107) occurs in Tregian (No. 150; also printed in BW 20, p. 116f.). The 8-bar bass belongs to a popular melody (Chappell, 74; Wooldridge, i, 151) which is heard in var. 1 but not alluded to again. There follow a free melodic variation, three variations in crotchets respectively for right hand, left hand and both hands, three more in quavers repeating the same sequence, and a final one on a couple of imitative figures by way of a coda. At a simple level the technique is just about secure enough for the piece to pass muster as a very early work of Byrd. But unless it is seen as a student exercise the lack of any sign of an artistic intention such as even his least mature pieces invariably show must rule his authorship out.

Still less acceptable is a set of variations on the ground to *The Hunt's up* – not the genuine set of twelve, but a very dull set of ten (BK 41) from a late, unauthentic manuscript (Paris, Bibliothèque Nationale, Rés. 1186). Some of the figuration, notably the repeated notes in var. 6, is quite untypical of Byrd, but such evidence is treacherous at best. A surer index lies in the desperate poverty of the harmony, which clings helplessly to the simplest implications of the ground, the lifeless treatment of stock figures, and the appalling pair of variations with which the work peters out. In these the same figure is repeated at a different level in nearly every bar in the worst tradition of English cantus firmus setting. No known work of Byrd sinks to this level. The simplest explanation for the attribution is that the copyist mistook the piece for the well known authentic set.

The term 'ground' is usually associated today with the idea of a ground bass. In Byrd's time it implied a given basis but not necessarily a bass, and so covered a wider variety of pieces. Thus it was applied by Forster and Tomkins to Byrd's purely melodic variations on *The Carman's Whistle*, by Farnaby (or Tregian) to a composition (MB 24/2) based on a constructed cantus firmus which moves from one part to another at various transpositions, and by Tomkins to Byrd's *Browning*. However, the word 'variations', very little used by contemporaries, best describes many of these pieces, so that 'ground' can be reserved for an important series of works, ranging from some of Byrd's earliest to some of his grandest and most mature, which more or less correspond to the modern definition.

A single exception, a ground in the broader sense that can be placed with no other genre, will best be considered straight away, before the main subject of the chapter. As its title **Ut re mi fa sol la** implies, it is based on the hexachord, a standard cantus firmus throughout the renaissance period, in England as on the continent. The scale, which is played in the treble by a second player, ascends and descends again five times in breves, forming a treble ground to five variations. Parsons had adopted the same treble ground in a 4-part consort piece, and had closed the first half with ascending scalar imitations in crotchets similar to the descending ones in Byrd's first variation. Byrd quickens the figuration in var. 2 – the 'second waye' as the only source (in Tomkins's hand) has it – and the last three 'ways' are occupied with popular song tunes, first *The Woods so wild* treated imitatively, and then, from halfway through var. 4, *The Shaking of the sheets*;* the two tunes have

*See Chappell, 84; Wooldridge, i, 228; Simpson, 651; Ward, 73.

certain phrases in common. Details of technique offer no strong reason to place the piece early, but as a whole it scarcely adds up to a proper composition: it opens in F and ends in C, the dull first two variations bear no relation to the other three, and these ramble too much for their charm to hold. In short this demonstration of various ways of setting a cantus firmus was probably written for the benefit of a pupil, who no doubt played the breves. Tomkins, who studied with Byrd, calls it 'a good lesson', but his fellow pupil Morley would certainly not have agreed. In his *Introduction* he expressly condemned some of its salient features.*

Nor is Morley likely to have seen eye to eye with his master on the subject of ground basses. Apart from a contemptuous reference to *Quadran* pavans as barbers' shop music he does not mention them in his book. Having at one time tackled both the stock passamezzo basses himself without much success, he evidently saw no reason to recommend the exercise to his pupils, as Byrd, with a different experience behind him, may well have done. To judge from the scanty remains of mid-century secular keyboard music, most of the more ambitious pieces that Byrd heard in his youth would have relied on some kind of limited and repetitive harmonic pattern. He had been quick to grapple with this legacy, but what he made of it required an intellectual grasp beyond the range of his pupils, even with his example before them.

*This despite his protestation that everything truly spoken in his book proceeded from his master. Grateful pupils, especially gifted ones, commonly entertain mixed feeling towards their teachers, and the sincerity of Morley's 'entire love and unfeigned affection' is not put in doubt by his occasional sniping. In the third part of his *Introduction* he takes on a new pupil who, having previously been taught by 'one Master Bold', serves up some atrocious descants to plainsong. One example contains a quotation from *Sellinger's round* and a weak passage in sesquialtera proportion. Morley's other pupil pours scorn on it, and Morley replies: 'You must not be so ready to condemn him for that, seeing it was the fault of the time [presumably Master Bold's time], not of his sufficiency, which causeth him to sing after that manner, for I myself being a child have heard him highly commended who could upon a plainsong sing hard Proportions, harsh allowances, and country dances, and he who could bring in maniest of them was counted the jolliest fellow.' The marginal comment is 'Proportions are not ridiculously to be taken.' The fictitious Master B**d looks like a creature of Morley's aggression, heavily camouflaged to prevent recognition – perhaps even by its own author. Morley's wholehearted adoption of Italian models, itself a symptom of his inability to absorb Byrd's formal methods, made him view country dances and proportions with distaste. Byrd liked both: he used popular tunes not only in his hexachord exercise but in several of his most important compositions, and tripla crops up everywhere, though never ridiculously. He was not, of course, interested in the old sight-reading games involving hard proportions that Morley goes on to make fun of, but Morley is using exaggeration to disguise his attack and also throws in 'harsh allowances' that Byrd would in no circumstances have countenanced. To excuse Bold as a member of an older generation is a very nice touch: on a twinge of conscience for the covert injustice he immensely and absurdly widens his target – and only makes matters worse.

The earliest English secular pieces of any substance, Hugh Aston's Hornpipe and two anonymous pieces entitled *My Lady Careys Dompe* and *My Lady Wynkfylds Rownde*, occur in a manuscript (Roy.App.58) written not later than the 1540s.* The first two are both based on grounds, though of different kinds. The bass of the dump is shown in Ex. 40. At first sight this simple

Ex. 40

alternation of tonic and dominant hardly looks like a typical ground, but it clearly belongs to the same family as four of the earliest dumps for lute, all of which are based on the same two chords in various patterns of four or eight bars. Later dumps increase their chordal repertory to encompass stock Italian bass patterns.†

The special interest of *My Lady Careys Dompe* lies in the relation of the melody to its plain accompaniment. The melodic line owes nothing whatever to continental dances, and everything to an English tradition of which a sole representative is known: an anonymous piece, in all probability by Preston,‡ called *Upon la mi re* on account of its canonic bass structure (see Ex. 41).

Ex. 41

This ostinato bass provides little more than a drone-like support to the melody, which bears the entire responsibility for shaping the piece, renewing itself and expanding phrase by phrase exactly in the style of the upper line in 2-part plainsong settings by Redford or Preston. It is a remarkably interesting piece, even if the composer misses the sure touch that Redford might have brought to it. In *My Lady Careys Dompe* the cadential implication of the bass exerts some influence on the melody: there are one or two real 4-bar phrases coinciding with the ground, others of two bars incor-

*See especially J. Ward, 'Les sources de la musique pour le clavier en Angleterre', in Jacquot, *Musique instrumentale*, 225ff. The pieces are all printed in *Ten pieces by Hugh Aston and others*, ed. F. Dawes (London, 1951).

†For details see J. Ward, 'Dolfull Dumps', *JAMS*, iv (1951), 111ff.

‡As suggested by D. Stevens in his article on Preston in MGG. These notes are the first three of the popular *Spagna* melody which in one form or another provided a basis for innumerable compositions, from masses to *basses danses*, throughout the renaissance period, and may have influenced the composer. Stevens published the piece in *Altenglische Orgelmusik* (Kassel, 1953). Did Stravinsky come across it before writing the organ interludes in his *Canticum sacrum* of 1955?

porated within larger paragraphs, and some turns on the leading note to emphasize the return to the tonic in the bass. But in most respects the melody pursues its easy course with little concern for the ostinato, finding sufficient means of formal articulation in its own resources.

The ground in the first part of Aston's Hornpipe, which is in F, also consists of only two notes (see Ex. 42), but they are placed roughly speaking

Ex. 42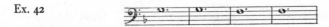

in the tenor instead of the bass so that they act as internal pedals to two harmonic regions: the G permits supertonic and dominant chords, the F subdominant and tonic. Very often two harmonies, in either root position or first inversion, occur in one bar, a rate of harmonic change that the melody can no longer ignore. The melodic line is still paramount, but it develops in more or less well defined 4-bar periods relating to the ground.

Among Byrd's grounds a group of four stand out as his earliest because of their relation to mid-century keyboard music. They consist of three 'short' grounds and a hornpipe. A gap of twenty years or more must separate them from the Aston hornpipe and its companions. In the meantime Italian ground basses had reached England; romanesca and passamezzo basses occur in the earliest extant lute manuscripts dating from the middle of the century. They invoked in English composers, or at least in Byrd, a new sensitivity to harmony as a structural agent that acted powerfully upon the native keyboard tradition. Unfortunately no direct forerunners of Byrd's short grounds survive, but there is a stronger link with Aston's Hornpipe than might at first appear. Byrd adopts almost the same ground for his own Hornpipe, which is in C. (For this and Byrd's other grounds see p. 114f.) Unlike Aston he places it in the bass, except that he occasionally drops a dominant G below the supertonic in bar 2. It will be seen that when this happens the Hornpipe ground becomes very like that of the Short Ground in G. The single difference of the subdominant minim at the end of bar 3 of the latter is more apparent than real: at this point in the Hornpipe there is often subdominant harmony over the tonic pedal, and in both pieces Byrd sometimes substitutes a II^6 chord.

In fact these two grounds consist of nothing else but the cadential formula that terminates every Italian ground: I–V–I–I. It suffers in isolation because the tonic is regained too early, so that Byrd has to keep redressing the balance with a touch on the tiller before the last bar for fear of drifting – an expedient that works very well. On the other hand in the G minor Short Ground the dominant correction at the same point proves altogether too strong; it introduces a second full close only a bar after the first, and this coupled with the odd circumstance that the ground begins on the dominant makes the fourth bar feel like the first. For most of the piece (after bar 20) Byrd accepts the consequences and composes as the ground suggests in phrases from bar 4 round to bar 3. Not much harm is done except that the procedure conflicts with the expectations created by the clear phraseology at the outset.

This difficulty does not arise in the Short Ground in C because the tonic bars come at the beginning instead of the end, as they do in *My Lady Careys Dompe* and most of the first part of Aston's Hornpipe, for after the first 5½ variations Aston treats his ground (Ex. 42) as running from bar 3 round to bar 2. This arrangement was apparently less usual than the reverse one, but had the advantage that each variation was launched by a full cadence. The descending scale in the second half of the bass pattern in the Short Ground in C derives from the English cantus-firmus-like grounds that could migrate to any part. Byrd keeps his ground in the bass almost throughout, but takes the phrase up in other parts as a point of imitation.

The three **Short Grounds** were apparently not widely circulated, for they occur only in Forster, though Tomkins knew the most ambitious, in G major, and called it Byrd's 'old ground' (see MB 5, p. 158). Various uncertainties in formal proportions, in the handling of the ground basses and in technical details confirm their early date. They must be closely contemporaneous because there is no perceptible development between them; the main value to Byrd in composing three such pieces lay in the insight the different grounds afforded into questions of harmonic continuity and scansion.

In vocabulary and shape they have much in common. Each starts with a well characterized section devoted in the C major and G minor pieces mainly to imitative figures, not unlike those found in liturgical organ music, but more lightly handled. The G major starts with dance-like melodies related to the initial phrases of the Aston and Byrd hornpipes. All three then proceed to scalar runs in quavers which serve to re-emphasize the ground by throwing the responsibility for musical continuity almost entirely on the harmonic framework. This stage is best handled in the C major work, where it is followed directly by the coda. In the other two a section in ᵗripla that echoes the plan of the earlier stages of the piece comes next: first a passage of pronounced melodic character – dance-like in the G major, more staid in the G minor – and then scalar runs in quaver sextuplets. In the G major the dance tune contains eight beats and is fitted across the three-beat bars none too skilfully; in consequence the plain harmonic statements supporting the ensuing scales have the merit of restoring equilibrium. All three pieces end well with codas reminiscent of their respective opening paragraphs.

It is easy to underrate Byrd's achievement in these early grounds. They are as yet little touched by the warmth of his maturity, and since his models are lost his advance on them cannot be fully assessed. All the same, it is fairly certain that the easy spans, the deft transitions and the natural grouping of the variations into longer sections would all have been beyond his precursors, as they were beyond the anonymous composer* of *Wakefild on a greene* or Tomkins in his Arthur Phillips ground (MB 5/40). Byrd's material is already too personal to have been picked up ready made, and he was able to carry over much of what he worked out here into his later grounds. The pieces are full of life and youthful drive.

But if the Short Grounds nevertheless contribute little that was not superseded in later works, the same is not true of the **Hornpipe**. Whether or not it is a later composition than its near relative the Short Ground in G major, it is certainly a better one and seems to have been circulated more widely. Its harmonic restriction and its connection either with Aston's Hornpipe or others of the same kind ally it even more closely than the short grounds to the English linear tradition and give it a place of its own in Byrd's output. It begins with a swinging tune that promises to carry the piece quickly forward, an expectation which, to judge from Aston's Hornpipe, would have been reinforced for contemporary listeners by normal practice in such pieces. Instead Byrd plays a cat-and-mouse game. He starts by cheating expectation in two ways: by allowing the impatient tune to get becalmed on the static tonic bass of the second half of the ground, and by developing it in sharply divided 2-bar phrases that prevent forward movement. Not until the ninth variation (which begins at bar 33) does he permit the impetus of a II^6 chord on the third beat of the third bar of the ground to creep in as a fairly regular feature, and only at the end of the twelfth variation (bar 48) does crotchet movement carry over from the last beat of a variation into the next. Even this turns out to be a false breakthrough. The rhythmic flow is immediately checked in var. 13 and disruptive syncopation leads to two variations of pure wait-and-see. Only after that does Byrd allow momentum to gather: at the end of var. 17 (bar 68) a renewed attempt at a crotchet bridgehead succeeds, and the music is free – not to be caught again. The work opens out in a torrent of quaver figuration, which contains no

*Who may in fact have been a precursor. His piece occurs in Weelkes (fol. 56), which contains pieces by Tallis, the elder Ferrabosco, Blitheman and Alwood, as well as later composers.

hint of the monotony that threatens this kind of writing in the short grounds, but keeps breaking into dance rhythms of unquenchable gaiety.

Byrd wrote one other piece on a ground as restricted as that of the Hornpipe – **The Bells**. The resemblance, however, goes no further, for the long melodic lines of the Hornpipe are replaced in *The Bells* by the continual play of imitative figures like peals of bells in two or three parts above the bass. Although an isolated *tour de force* such as this offers few openings for stylistic comparison, the skill with which close 4-part textures are handled and the presence, unusual in 3/2, of lengthy semiquaver runs, suggest a considerably later date of composition; since it is absent from both Nevell and Weelkes it may not have been written before the 1590s. The ground consists essentially of a single bar, containing only tonic and supertonic, which Byrd adheres to very strictly, only occasionally substituting a dominant for the supertonic. But for most of the time he thinks in terms of a 4-bar ground, broken here and there by phrases of two or six bars.

Unfortunately the surviving text is badly garbled, at least between bars 68 and 78,* a passage which as it stands severely damages the larger rhythm of the music. Up to this point an insistent pattern of fourfold repetitions, or more often of twofold antiphonal exchanges, in each 4-bar period is the rule, and the listener finds himself forced into step with it, his expectation of change slowed down until he feels a small intensification in a motive at the beginning of a new 4-bar period positively to require repetition right through the four bars before any further change is appropriate. This slow turn of the wheel builds up a sense of heavy but unshakable impetus that carries (doubtful readings apart) right through to the end of the piece. The contrast here with the light impetuosity of the Hornpipe, and the treatment that

*Tregian divides the piece into nine numbered but musically arbitrary sections, the fifth of which is only three bars long and seems to be a continuation of section 3. It joins on to 3 much better than 4 does (there is even a direct at the end of bar 68 pointing to the left-hand E at the beginning of bar 75), and if bar 77, which is almost identical with bar 76, is removed it completes a 4-bar period on a single subject. This emendation makes a good join between sections 4 and 6, and also between 5 and 4 if an E is supplied in the right hand in bar 69, which bar 71 justifies. (Other doubts remain, e.g. the odd reappearance of the first four bars of section 4 in section 7, as though more than one alternative had got included.) It is not difficult to explain the misplacement of section 5. In a piece as repetitious as this a copyist may easily leave something out (or reduplicate it). If he subsequently notices his mistake and writes the missing bars in the margin, the next copyist may misunderstand where they are meant to go. There is another possible explanation that has the advantage of taking into account the numbering of the sections: that Byrd himself in composing or revising the piece worked it out on different sheets, numbered the fragments (not quite accurately), left the copying to an amanuensis, and failed to check the result. This theory may not accord very well with the little that is known about Byrd, but something of the kind seems to have happened in the revision of *The Hunt's up* (see p. 125).

capriciously holds it in check before finally allowing it its head, underlines Byrd's extraordinary mastery over musical movement. This constant attribute of his music is especially striking in these two pieces because their harmonic limitation forbids the deployment of others.

Byrd's most important grounds are all based on much longer basses than those considered so far, and this naturally leads to a different kind of composition in which each variation has a separate existence as well as a responsibility to the others. Of these large-scale grounds **The Hunt's up** is unquestionably the earliest. Yet despite its immaturity the general formal outline that Byrd worked out in it held good for most of his later examples. The ground is the bass to a tune known either as *The Hunt's up* or as *Peascod time*, and so presumably sung to more than one set of words.* Byrd does not make use of the tune, though Gibbons was later to do so, partly in conjunction with a different version of the ground (see MB 20/30). The ground is a very English affair in more than one respect: the halfway cadence, like those of the Consort Ground and the *Browning*, is on the supertonic, and the second half of each of its constituent 4-bar phrases is static,† three times out of four on the tonic.

Byrd's piece originally consisted of twelve variations, but he later cut out one and changed the order of others.‡ For his first variation he set out to construct a tune on the uncomfortable basis of the ground, employing the stock 2-bar melodic pattern which he also drew on for the openings of his Short Ground in G and Hornpipe. The result is distinctly bumpy: for one thing he adheres too stiffly to 2-bar phraseology throughout, and for another, having arrived at a powerful cadence at the beginning of bars 7 and 15 with two bars on his hands before the end of the 8-bar periods, he fills in with unwanted repetitions of the same 2-bar pattern. 2-bar thinking persists in the next two variations, but here Byrd adopts a mode of writing that was to become a constant resource in his later work, a loosely imitative texture in which for the most part only two voices at a time occupy themselves with the point. Different voices take turns in the lead and more or less successfully paper over the joins between one phrase and the next; indeed, var. 3 is an

*See Chappell, 60, 196; Wooldridge, i, 86, 89; Simpson, 323, 368.

†Compare, besides Byrd's Short Grounds and their forerunners, the piece without title in the Mulliner Book (MB 1/2), which is based on two almost identical 8-bar strains, in both of which bars 3 and 4 are dominant, and bars 7 and 8 tonic.

‡He also changed the detail here and there, but the extent is hard to assess because the only text of the first version (Tregian No. 59) is poor. Hence for practical purposes this version is less well represented by the printed edition of Tregian than by the text of the revised version in BK 40, with the variations taken in the following order: 1–5, 5b, 8–10. 6, 7, 11 (5b is the one omitted in the revision).

excellent piece of work. Vars. 4 and 5 are built out of single-bar patterns, well handled as far as the ground permits. After a variation in quaver scales that he later suppressed, Byrd finds himself only halfway through the round dozen variations that he evidently regarded as normal for a ground bass of this length, and opens a new phase in the composition.

In the next three variations (8–10 in the revised version), whilst still observing the letter of the rather unsatisfactory ground, he breaks away from its stricter rhythmic implications. Taking his cue from the implied hemiolas at bars 5–6 and 13–14 he composes part of var. 7 (= 8 of the revised version) and the whole of 9 (= 10) in what amounts to 4/4 time over the 3/2 of the ground, and he also introduces a passage of 3/4 (or 6/8) in var. 8 (= 9). Unfortunately the result is not, as might be supposed, a remarkably original counterpoint of phrase structure against harmonic change, because the ground, which is the one unifying factor in the composition, loses its grip yet at the same time frustrates Byrd's lively inventions of the harmonic freedom that would serve them best. Nevertheless he is more successful here than in the comparable experiment in the Short Ground in G, and var. 9 (= 10) manages to reconcile the conflicting factors well enough to make an effective interlude. This variation is based on a popular tune that was current during the 1560s, possibly the one known as *The Nine Muses*.* Ex. 43 shows Byrd's melody flanked by an English and a Scottish version up to the points where they diverge.

Byrd evidently now felt that he had gone far enough, if not too far, in obscuring the ground, and turned violently about with two variations in tripla (10 and 11 = 6 and 7 of the revised version) in which the harmonic scheme is so baldly exposed that the melodic figures stiffen and die in its grasp† – a miscalculation that it would be hard to match elsewhere in Byrd. No doubt he threw his weight so far in that direction because he needed not only to restore the balance but to prepare for the well shaped final variation No. 12 (= 11), which again runs counter to the ground. He starts the first 8-bar phrase of this with the last bar of var. 11 (= 7) and then overlaps its last bar with the first of another 8-bar phrase, so that he has room for a 2-bar coda before the additional final chord. This variation eventually caused trouble of a different kind.

Whether to meet a demand or because he himself had a soft spot for it

---

*See H. M. Shire, *Song, Dance and Poetry of the Court of Scotland under King James VI* (Cambridge, 1969), 34ff., 163ff. The tune also appears as cantus firmus to a piece entitled *Salve rex gloriae* in an anonymous Scottish *Art of Music* (Add.4911, fol. 110), and Ravenscroft based a round on it (No. 7 in 'Pammelia', *Now God bee with old Simeon*).

†There is a precedent for the kind of writing used in the central part of var. 11 towards the end of Tallis's second *Felix namque*.

Ex. 43

a. Roy, App. 76, fol. 24

b. Byrd

c. Adeu, O desie of delyt (MB 15/49)

Byrd kept this ambitious but uneven work in circulation and included the revised version in Nevell. The revision is a half-hearted and hasty job on a radically flawed piece, apparently undertaken in the hope of distracting attention from the dull bits and giving more prominence to the variations the composer liked best. Var. 6 is dropped altogether and replaced by the tedious pair 10 and 11, so that the interesting if problematical series 7–9 falls immediately before the last variation. It seems that Byrd did not copy the work out again, but left it to someone else to follow his instructions; at all events he allowed himself to overlook the difficulties. As the last bar of var. 11 carries the start of the melody of var. 12 it had to remain where it was, and consequently var. 7 in the revision (originally var. 11) has one bar too few, and var. 11 (formerly 12) one too many. Later somebody, possibly Byrd, spotted the mistake, for one source contains a new bar at the end of var. 7 to make up the deficiency, and differences at the end of var. 10 (originally 9) that may point to an unsuccessful attempt to put this passage right as well.* This muddle is not the only disadvantage in the revision, for the unsatisfactory original vars. 10 and 11 lose their slender structural justification when moved. All in all the original version is preferable.

*For this important variant, not recorded in BK 40, see *Tisdale's Virginal Book*, ed. A. Brown (London, 1966), No. 8, bars 157–9.

It will be remembered that the first large-scale consort work in which Byrd did himself justice was the Prelude and Ground (see p. 66ff.), a work based on an intricate bass quatrain that defined the musical field with exceptional precision, but at the same time liberated the composer's imagination. Among his keyboard grounds the **Second Ground**, built upon the same bass, occupies a similar place: Byrd no longer struggles against the bass as he had in *The Hunt's up*, but works in step with it and draws inspiration from its special qualities. These have already been described: conjunct motion that carries quite different harmonic implications from Italian bass patterns, song-like features that make it suitable for melodic treatment, and the presence of reprises giving rise to a stanza pattern of $4 + 2 + 4 + 2$ bars. There is little direct correspondence between the two works; the melodies of the first and third variations of the consort piece might be taken at first sight for elaborations of their opposite numbers in the *Second Ground*, but in the general plan the influence seems to go the other way. The consort set contains eleven variations instead of the usual dozen, Byrd having changed his original plan (see p. 68). The keyboard variations consist of eleven with the ground in the bass followed by six for which it supplies the melody (though the reprises remain in the bass).

Here too there are signs of second thoughts. The first ten variations go approximately through the phases that Byrd had established in *The Hunt's up*, with melody dominating at the outset, then imitation, then tripla, and finally a return in the last variation to the simpler texture of the opening. Var. 11, based on quaver runs, serves as a bridge to the last six variations, which rehearse a similar course to the first ten. This second part of the composition is an unusual feature and the suspicion arises that it may have been an afterthought. On this assumption the original set of eleven variations would have been made to the measure of its sister work for consort, and var. 11 would have preceded var. 10, a position that it in fact seems designed for.* Byrd would have changed the order when extending the series to avoid a hiatus caused by the juxtaposition of the coda-like var. 10 with the change of variation technique in var. 12. There is no break in style to suggest an appreciably later date for the melodic variations, but it would not have taken Byrd long to recognize that something more than equivalent length was

---

*The quavers of the second reprise in var. 9 would then prepare for those of var. 11, and the tripla of the first reprise in var. 11 would refer back to var. 9. The tenor crotchets at the beginning of var. 11, which in the final order appear as a diminution after var. 10, would derive equally well, if not better, from var. 9, whilst the effect of augmentation in var. 10 would be enhanced. Had Byrd actually used var. 10 to end the work he would, of course, have provided it with a more decisive close.

needed to match the weightier polyphony and more elaborate organization of the 5-part consort set.

Not that his inspiration flowed any less freely in the relatively slender textures of the keyboard work: his natural bent for line and dialogue, so oddly inhibited in the self-conscious *The Hunt's up*, declares itself from the very beginning. In var. 2 the simple song-like melody from var. 1 (see p. 67n.) takes up a tiny rhythmic characteristic from its own accompaniment as a means of throwing out imitative branches with the aid of which it reaches up to high F – and so prepares an answering descent in var. 3. The same effortless continuity reigns within each variation; Byrd now had no difficulty in taking the 4-bar periods in a single breath,* something that the ground demanded if the punctuating 2-bar phrases were to make their effect.

The tripla variations are especially remarkable in this respect. The tripla sections in Byrd's other grounds and his fantasias vary widely in character, but since they usually take in considerable spans certain techniques are fairly common: a dance-like melody will break up into short, vigorous imitative motives, or merge into quaver runs that bring structural repose beneath a brilliant surface (as in var. 8 of the present work), or do both successively. In some such way Byrd could have covered, and acceptably, the enclosed 4-bar phrases of the *Second Ground* with no trouble at all, but instead he saw the opportunity for inventions too intense to be sustained in a wider context. In vars. 7 and 9 it is the length of phrase and the altogether exceptional lyrical appeal of the imitative dialogue that astonish; in var. 15 textures remotely derived from the syncopations of an older English generation step in and lead, in var. 16, to breathtaking harmonic wealth that stretches the containing structure to its furthest limit.

Throughout the piece Byrd plays on the stanza form of the ground with the same virtuosity as in the consort set. But although, so far as the bad text of the latter work permits a comparison of detail, the keyboard work seems the more mature of the two, he cannot for all his connective skill keep a grip on the larger design quite so firmly, owing to the increased number of variations and the narrower textural range of the keyboard.

No such difficulty arises in the beautifully proportioned work called in Nevell **Hugh Aston's Ground**. The title may mean either that Byrd believed the bass to have been devised by Aston, or simply that he had taken it from a composition by him, presumably in that case the set of twelve

---

*But only in var. 10 do the phrases follow through to include the reprises, as happens in the later variations of the consort set – another special feature that suggests that this variation was originally designed as a conclusion.

variations for 3-part consort entitled *Hugh Aston's Maske.** The second of
these alternatives seems the more likely, because the ground outlines a
strong harmonic progression pointing to a popular origin, like those of most
other grounds, both Italian and English, whereas Aston treats it as bass
cantus firmus and shows no feeling for its tonal implications. His variations
are decidedly unexciting, but he gives as much individuality to each as his
limited stock of melodic shapes will allow.

One of these, involving an accented dissonant passing note, occurs in two
variations (Nos. 3 and 6; see Ex. 44a and b) and evidently lodged in Byrd's

Ex. 44

a. Aston, var. 3.   *b.* Aston, var. 6.

c. Byrd, var. 1.   *d.* Byrd, var. 2.   *e.* Byrd, var. 7.

mind, for it plays an important role in his piece. He based his second
variation on it and worked the dissonance into vars. 1 and 7 as well, emphasizing it each time with an ornament (see Ex. 44c–e). But the influence of
the idea spreads much further than this, for the plangent clash of accented
sevenths and ninths, not necessarily upon the bass, becomes a characteristic
of the vocabulary of the work. It is joined by another: the constant close
proximity or simultaneous use of major third and flat sixth, either on the
dominant or the tonic degree. Whether this factor too was suggested to

---

*Found complete except for the bass in Christ Church Oxford MSS. 982 and 979, with
a wretched additional part in 981 by William Whytbroke, who adjusted Aston's parts
here and there to make it fit (see Edwards, *Sources*, ii, No. 107). The original version
occurs anonymously in the National Library of Scotland Panmure MS. 10, without the
last five variations, but these are unlikely to have been added wholly by Whytbroke
because the part in 981 looks like an addition right to the end of the piece. Panmure 10
contains in addition four anonymous variations (MB 15/84), also for 3-part consort, in
which the ground is laid out in breves, instead of in the equivalent of dotted breves as in
all other settings.

Byrd by earlier settings of the ground is unclear; it is not found in Aston.*
But it makes little difference whether Byrd invented his principles of unifica-
tion or founded them in what earlier composers had turned up at random.
What matters is his extraordinary ability to establish an individual language
and unique musical atmosphere for a particular composition.

The bass pattern of *Hugh Aston's Ground* is exactly the same length as
that of *The Hunt's up*. Although the implied harmonic movement might
seem even slower, its regularity permits a much easier flow. The smooth
stanza form of Byrd's first variation demonstrates this very forcibly, though
its immense superiority to its laboured opposite number in *The Hunt's up*
does not derive simply from the mechanical advantage of a better precompositional basis, but from a shift in Byrd's approach. The change must
have been conscious because, as will be seen, he had the revised version of
The Hunt's up before him while composing *Hugh Aston's Ground*. In vars.
2–5 of the earlier work he had worked an imitative figure very fully in each
variation, choosing successively shorter, more vigorous, and so more
repetitive subjects before breaking into quaver movement in var. 6, which
he later discarded. In the new piece the over-all line of each variation
becomes his first concern; the imitative texture has no function but to
promote it and often steps back where a cadence marks a turning point.

As in the original *The Hunt's up* he gives var. 6 over to quaver movement,
but this time he is determined to do better, not only in the quality of var. 6
itself, but by preparing for it quite differently. There is no shortening of the
imitative figures in var. 5, but instead a marvellous transitional process. It
begins with a sequence of short figures passed down from one part to the
next until they coalesce into a single line carrying its own imitation; the
tailpiece of this phrase becomes the subject for a new imitative passage and
then, while the tenor continues freely, the treble launches into the quavers
from which var. 6 develops. The whole variation demonstrates with special
clarity Byrd's debt to the Redfordian style, but whereas Redford had to rely
on linear development alone, Byrd benefits from the underlying stability of
the ground. Paradoxically it was through harmonic control that he was able

*Weelkes (fol. 97′) contains an anonymous set of fifteen keyboard variations on the
same bass which shares in a much diluted form something of the feeling of Byrd's setting.
The relationship of the two works is hard to determine. The harmony of the first two
anonymous variations, the only ones in the slower note-values of many of Byrd's (cf. Ex.
44), seems rather flat for a composer who knew Byrd's work. On the other hand some of
the faster ones seem to be indebted to him, although each runs its course within the terms
of a single keyboard texture in the manner of Bull rather than Byrd, pointing the way
towards the even more elaborate and vapid set of nine variations on the ground by Cosyn
(R.M.23.l.4, fol. 12′).

to recapture flexibility; when earlier he had failed to come to terms with the ground of *The Hunt's up* his attempts to ignore it had not alleviated the stiffness of the music.

The Hunt's up and its shortcomings continued to haunt him, for the next two variations of the revised version provide the model for vars. 7 and 8 of *Hugh Aston's Ground*, at least to the extent that they are in tripla, and the tripla begins in each work with the same subject in the same bar (the eighth) of the earlier variation. There are, however, no further points of contact between the two works, save perhaps fleetingly in their final variations. Vars. 9–12 of *Hugh Aston's Ground* carry the additional weight needed for the coherence of the whole; they achieve everything in the way of individuality, variety and memorability that the later variations of *The Hunt's up* had striven for so desperately, but without strain and without transgressing, even in the vigorous Nos. 10 and 11, the peculiar, quiet unifying spirit established in the very first bars of the work.

One of the few keyboard pieces by Byrd that can be dated with some certainty is *My Lady Nevell's Ground*, which stands first in the manuscript compiled for her and is likely to have been written specially for her about 1590. It is followed by another piece in a remarkably similar style, also dedicated to her:* the *Qui passe*, or more correctly **Chi passa**. This will best be considered first. The title derives from Filippo Azzaiuolo's *Chi passa per questa strada*, a *villotta alla padoana* which became enormously popular soon after its publication in 1557, and during the next thirty years appeared in innumerable instrumental arrangements all over Europe. Probably only the earlier Italian arrangers knew this vocal version: new features, notably a hemiola in the first half to match the one at the final cadence, soon became standard and are already present in early English versions.† In these pieces such traces of Azzaiuolo's limited little tune as occur may be ascribed to the bass, just as the harmonic progressions of the stock passamezzo patterns give rise to coincidental melodic resemblances between different settings. Some kind of *Chi passa* melody, it is true, must have been current in England because ballads were sung to it,‡ but the harmonic structure was the only constant in instrumental settings.

Byrd accordingly ignored any melody he may have known, as he had in

*The placing of the dedication in Baldwin's manuscript suggests that it may have been an afterthought, which perhaps explains why the piece turns up in Forster whereas neither of the other two pieces dedicated to Lady Nevell is known outside her book.

†e.g. two for cittern in the Mulliner Book (see D. Stevens, *The Mulliner Book; a commentary* (London, 1952), Appendix Nos. 3 and 7) and DVB/30.

‡See J. Ward, 'Music for "A Handefull of Pleasant Delites" ', *JAMS*, x (1957), 166.

The Hunt's up, and composed upon the bass.* He treated it, naturally enough, as an Italian bass, allowing himself frequent passing bass notes and harmonies between those of the fundamental scheme, just as he did with the passamezzo basses. On the other hand he deviates very little from grounds of English origin, which had mostly been employed by composers brought up on cantus firmi rather than popular songs and dances. This does not mean that Byrd thought in terms of national traditions, but merely that he absorbed and built upon the type of treatment associated with each ground rather than upon the bass pattern as an abstraction.

The tradition of *Chi passa* arrangements did not offer Byrd much material for development, and he chose to adopt a course of which a small detail is symptomatic: the absence of a tripla section. In all his other grounds except for the Short Ground in C and the *Quadran* galliard there are passages in tripla, whereas in his ordinary pavans and galliards, with the sole exception of Galliard G2, there are none. This suggests that the 3/2 of the grounds was traditionally slower than that of the galliards. Owing to its Italian origin the *Chi passa*, which had not become acclimatized like the passamezzo basses, was not associated with tripla. Byrd included none in his version, but filled it with the figures and rhythms typical of his galliard style, employing no more imitation than he would normally do in a galliard.

Most of **My Lady Nevell's Ground** is in the same style, even though var. 5 is in tripla and there is an unusual flourish of semiquavers in the coda to var. 6. The connection between the two works is pinpointed by a tiny detail illustrated in Ex. 45, which shows the openings of var. 2 of the *Chi*

Ex. 45

a. Chi passa, var. 2. *b. Lady Nevell, var. 6.*

passa and var. 6 of *My Lady Nevell's Ground*. Byrd used the repeated chords of continental popular music elsewhere only in his descriptive pieces *The Battle* and *The Barley Break*. But Azzaiuolo's original *Chi passa* consisted of little else and the texture persisted strongly in the kind of arrangement that Byrd knew. This explains its brief appearance in his own version, from which the similar example in *My Lady Nevell's Ground* assuredly derives.

The genesis of the latter work may perhaps be reconstructed as follows.

*He deviated from it only once, with C instead of A in bar 5 (and 13) of var. 2.

Byrd wished to compose a sizeable piece for Lady Nevell and turned to his recent set of three variations on the *Chi passa* bass for inspiration. Each half of this ground ends with the same tonic cadence so that the work falls into six sections, alternately of sixteen and twenty-four bars, counting the repeats. He accordingly planned the new piece in six variations, and taking the second section of the *Chi passa* as his measure devised a ground of twenty-four bars incorporating elements from both sections: at the outset a move from dominant to tonic corresponding to the first half, and at the end a progression from flat seventh to tonic corresponding to the second, with a subdominant interpolation separating the two. There is nothing in this scheme, considered simply as a basis, so varied as the 12-bar span of the second section of the *Chi passa*, but the harmonic scheme with its descent through IV to VII and quick scoop up again to I is a very strong one, and the insistent chord changes call forth a richer musical texture. For melodic fecundity, for rhythmic vigour, in fact for sheer uninhibited music-making these two brilliant pieces could scarcely be bettered. Nor is there any hint of superficiality; yet by comparison with the *Second Ground*, *Hugh Aston's Ground* and the two passamezzo settings they lack the sense of a special experience unique to the particular work, or of a progression of feeling within it.

Byrd's most ambitious grounds are two pavan and galliard pairs called the *Passing Measures* and the *Quadran*, and based respectively on the *passamezzo antico* and *passamezzo moderno* basses. Passamezzos on these harmonic patterns became extremely popular throughout Europe during the 1540s and were produced in vast quantity until the early years of the next century. They were often followed by a galliard or saltarello on the same bass, and each dance might consist of a single setting or a series of variations; the number of variations fluctuated, but in early years three was popular, and later on six or twelve. Such pieces carried enough prestige to take pride of place in certain printed collections: the keyboard *Intabulatura nova*, published by Antonio Gardane in Venice in 1551, has three settings of the *moderno* bass at the beginning followed by three settings of the *antico* halfway through, and the show pieces of Marco Facoli's two harpsichord collections of 1586 and 1588 are settings of the *antico* and *moderno* basses respectively.*

*The 1586 book is lost, but is at least partially preserved in the Royal College of Music MS 2088; see Brown [1586]₂. The 1588 book and the *Intabulatura nova* have been printed in *Corpus of Early Keyboard Music*, respectively in No. 2, ed. W. Apel (1963), and No. 8, ed. D. Heartz (1965).

Byrd must have been familiar with Italian bass patterns from his youth, since they occur regularly in mid-century English lute and cittern collections, and to judge from his own settings he had also encountered matching sets of variations on the two passamezzo grounds like the Italian examples already mentioned. His *Passing Measures* Pavan contains six variations and its galliard nine; each variation is of the standard length: four semibreves to each main harmony in the pavan, and two dotted semibreves in the galliard. The *Quadran* is more complicated because the *moderno* bass is followed in many settings, including Byrd's, by a reprise (*ripresa*) which may take various forms but is always half the length of the main section.* Byrd has only four variations in his *Quadran* Pavan, but inserts two settings of the reprise after both the second and fourth, so that the total length equals the six variations of the *Passing Measures* Pavan. Similarly the six variations of the *Quadran* Galliard are made up to the equivalent of nine by the insertion of a double reprise after every second variation. This procedure originated in Italy; Facoli, for instance, uses a variant of it: his *passamezzo antico* contains twelve variations (with a single reprise by way of coda), his *moderno* six variations with a pair of reprises after each.

The dance character of the passamezzo governs the musical style of the great mass of earlier lute settings and the keyboard examples in Gardane and Facoli; somewhat stereotyped melodic runs and patterns are accompanied by reiterated or spread chords which frequently omit the third. But by the time Facoli's pieces were published the basses were being used in association with quite different styles. In Italy Andrea Gabrieli, who died in 1589, combined the *antico* pattern with solider contrapuntal textures,† and independent local traditions had established themselves in Germany and England. The Dublin Virginal Book, copied about 1570, contains a pavan and galliard and a ground on related basses.‡ The melodic patterns here are still quite close to the earlier continental style, and so up to a point are the supporting broken fifths and octaves, though they take the less emphatic form found in English pieces such as *My Lady Careys Dompe* (Ex. 40). National habits of mind, however, come out in the treatment of the underlying scheme, which is felt less as a harmonic progression than as a

---

*For a detailed discussion see R. Hudson, 'The ripresa, the ritornello and the passacaglia', *JAMS*, xxiv (1971), 364ff.

†A. Gabrieli, *Intonationen für Orgel*, ed. P. Pidoux (Kassel, 1959), 36ff.

‡DVB/1, 2 and 9. The ground (No. 9) is on the *Romanesca* bass, which is the same as the *passamezzo antico* except that the first and fifth notes are both mediants. The pavan and galliard (Nos. 1 and 2) are on the complementary variant, in which these notes are both tonic. The latter (which is also found in an anonymous galliard in Weelkes, fol. 84′) permits a major-mode treatment.

bass cantus firmus. There are two consequences: reluctance to admit extraneous chords by breaking the bass leads to harmonic limitation, but in the pavan and galliard opens the way to the free play of keyboard figuration above the bass in both hands simultaneously, a common feature in English liturgical keyboard music.

Whatever stimulus Byrd may have received from the ample layout of the larger continental passamezzos, his interest did not extend to content, for the stylistic traditions he drew on in his settings are demonstrably English – a term which covers, of course, continental elements acclimatized at an earlier date. His first concern in the **Passing Measures** was to establish the character of a pavan, for character was no less important to him than structure, and he classed the work with pavans and galliards in Nevell. He accordingly begins with solemn rising phrases in imitation, one of his favourite types of pavan opening taken over from earlier English examples. But he maintains the imitation only long enough to fix the mood of the piece before thinning the texture down to melody and accompaniment, preparatory to building the work up on similar lines to his earlier grounds. Thus var. 1 plays the usual expository role of mapping out the harmonic field without contrapuntal distraction, with the difference that there is much more ground to be covered. So instead of a stanza melody Byrd develops a long line out of phrases of varying length and speed in his most Redfordian vein, and breaks the accompaniment as in Ex. 40. This figure scarcely appears in his other grounds, even the earliest;* his use of it here is not an indication of date, but provides another illustration of his tendency, when adopting some technical feature such as a bass pattern, to draw on the whole tradition of composition associated with it.

Var. 2, like var. 1, begins by offering allegiance to pavan style for twelve semibreves† and then, from the cadence on D, pursues a freer course, this time in a 3-part imitation on a broader scale than was possible in his other pavans and grounds, and with corresponding weight and momentum. The two halves of var. 3 occupy the position of vars. 5 and 6 in the grounds with twelve variations. The first half contains imitations, not indeed on a shorter subject (the dimensions of the piece forbade it, and in any case *Hugh Aston's Ground* shows that Byrd had tired of a technique that bordered on the repetitious), but with a shorter interval between entries: a minim in place

*Exceptions usually have a particular purpose. For instance in *The Hunt's up*, bars 55–56, it accompanies a little melodic figure that does not lend itself so easily as most to imitation, and many years later Byrd was still using the same rather agreeable dodge; see the *Chi passa*, bars 47–49, and the *Quadran* Galliard, 55–56.

†Or 'bars'. The more accurate term is used here to avoid confusion to users of BK, where the piece is barred in breves.

of the semibreve of var. 2. The second half of var. 3 rounds off the first half
of the piece with the usual quick scalar runs.

The second half of the piece recapitulates the general course of the first
in the more intense terms of faster note-values. Var. 4, like the greater part
of var. 1, is purely melodic, but in the tripla that had become normal at this
point in Byrd's grounds. In var. 5 he was faced with a more difficult problem:
it was one thing to match the contrapuntal texture of var. 2, but quite
another to outdo its dynamic force. His brilliant solution depends on a kind
of trick, almost a joke. After the first four semibreves (on G) he derives from
the melody a not unpleasing little figure that circles round in static imitation
over the F in the bass (Ex. 46). This does well enough for two semibreves

Ex. 46

but becomes a little tiresome when the exchange is repeated note for note,
and almost intolerable when the whole pattern is shifted up a tone as the
harmony returns to G (major) and even seems momentarily to promise
reduplication on this degree too. This is the stuff that a great deal of inferior
keyboard music, especially but not exclusively English, is made of; only
Bull could sometimes brazen it out by the sheer accumulation of shameless
repetition. To come across anything of the kind in Byrd, of all composers
the most averse to it, is a shock. But he is teasing: at the last possible moment
he breaks out of the circle and shoots forward to a close on D to mark the
end of the first half of the variation.

The effect is brilliant, and might be thought justification enough for the
opening gambit. But Byrd takes his debt very seriously, and repays it in a
flood of imitative scale passages that act as a vehicle for continuous development right through to the end of the variation. After this it is up to var. 6
to touch once again on a more pavan-like movement, which it does after
capping the imitation at the minim of var. 3 with one at the crotchet. The
second half corresponds closely to that of var. 3; the usual close in longer
values is held over for the galliard.

Each variation of the galliard is exactly the same length as those of *The
Hunt's up* and *Hugh Aston's Ground*, but it is probably intended to move
faster. Quite apart from references to galliard style, the textures are generally

lighter, influenced by the more linear sections of the pavan; there is also a little less emphasis on the individual character of the variations, and the tripla sections contain hardly any quavers. Other differences arise from the connection with the pavan: var. 1 is not in the usual stanza form because the internal subdivisions are modelled on those of var. 1 of the pavan. In general the galliard is less formal than the other grounds, and the phrases move less closely with the harmonic scheme, though without risk of confusion. The variations run a fairly normal course: vars. 2 and 3 are imitative (though 3 reverts to galliard style later); 4 and 5 have quaver runs in right and left hand respectively; 6 begins a quieter interlude which gives place to tripla during 7; var. 8 is also in tripla, and starts with quotations first of a tune called *Lusty gallant** (Ex. 47) treated in canon, and then of Ex. 46; var. 9 has the customary long note-values of a final variation.

Ex. 47

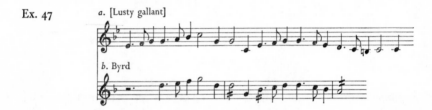

a. [Lusty gallant]

b. Byrd

The *Passing Measures* Pavan and Galliard survive in two versions. The differences between them are mostly small, but in version II† var. 5 of the galliard is missing, and the last bar of var. 4 differs accordingly. The earliest source gives version I, but there is no reason why the three later manuscripts that give II in somewhat varying texts should not go back to an earlier original, as has in fact been argued on the basis of certain points of rhythm and figuration.‡ However, since the work belongs in any case to Byrd's maturity such points are hard to interpret, and the only really revealing one surely points the other way: the substitution in II of contrary for parallel motion in bars 7 and 12 of the galliard.§ This chronology receives support

---

*See J. Ward, 'Music for "A Handefull of Pleasant Delites" '. *JAMS*, x (1957), 169. The tune as given in Ex. 47 comes from Archbishop Marsh's Library MS.Z.3.2.13.p.61. The title is supplied from a duple time version in the Ballet lute book (Trinity College Dublin MS.D.1.21). See also Chappell, 91; Wooldridge, i, 234; Simpson, 476; Ward, 58.

†The designation I and II for the versions is taken from BK. Much of the information about II is provided there, but all three sources of it are bad and it needs editing separately from I.

‡See A. Brown's unpublished dissertation *A Critical Edition of the Keyboard Music of William Byrd* (Cambridge, 1969), i, 110.

§Compare the revision, made before publication in 1611, in bar 97 of Fantasia 6/g2, involving the same technical point in a quite different context.

from another consideration. Var. 5 of I is lacking in II. It seems inherently more likely that a composer as interested in measurement as Byrd should originally have planned nine rather than eight variations for the galliard to the six of the pavan. The left-hand variation of the galliard is not one of the most interesting, and is less easily seen as a later addition than as an impatient cut made after 1591, when the composer had forgotten or lost interest in the question of relative proportions. In the light of this evidence it is not difficult to recognize various minor changes in II as the composer's retouchings to avert possible monotony (pavan: end of var. 1), to provide livelier detail (galliard: bars 61–63) or to avoid anticipating the climax of runs (pavan: beginning of last quarter of var. 6; galliard: bar 50).*

Before turning to the *Quadran* Pavan and Galliard it will be as well to recapitulate briefly the development of Byrd's grounds. As usual it is easier to arrive at an approximate chronological sequence than to suggest dates. The Short Grounds are certainly early; they presumably date from the 1560s. The same may be said of the immature *The Hunt's up*, which nevertheless set the pattern for the next three grounds, all of them among Byrd's finest keyboard works. Of these the *Second Ground* perhaps comes first, occupying a similar place to its consort counterpart; the other two, *Hugh Aston's Ground* and the *Passing Measures*, follow the same line of development to its furthest point, and in that respect stand close to another culminating work in a peculiarly English mode of composition, the *Browning*. It is reasonable to suppose that among Byrd's greatest achievements in instrumental music those that show their roots in native traditions most clearly should have been the earliest, and that they should have belonged to much the same period in his output. There is evidence to suggest that the *Browning* was composed in the later 1570s (see p. 70); this is an equally credible date for the *Passing Measures*. The *Browning* marked a turning point in Byrd's consort music: having nothing to add in the field of the consort variation he turned to other forms. Similarly he could scarcely have improved upon the perfect equilibrium in the great paragraphs of the *Passing Measures* Pavan between the Redfordian modelling by means of varying pace, phrase length and texture, and the stabilizing influence of the simple harmonic foundation. When he turned to grounds a decade later in

---

*A pavan and galliard on the same bass by Peter Philips, credibly dated 1592 by Tregian (Nos. 76, 77), provide a clue of a different kind. Despite many continental traits the fundamental character of this work allies it to other English settings of the time. Echoes of Byrd's setting are incidental but plentiful, and although Philips may have been sent a copy from England the chances are that he knew it before his departure in 1582. The version he knew is likely to have been the earlier, and it probably contained var. 5 of the galliard, because Philips's vars. 5 and 6 are a pair for each hand like Byrd's 4 and 5.

the *Chi passa* and *My Lady Nevell's Ground* it was with a rather different aim.

The only large-scale ground that Byrd did not include in Nevell is the **Quadran** Pavan and Galliard, a circumstance that serves, if nothing else, to underline the isolation of that extraordinary work. Either, as seems likely, he had not written it by 1591, or he thought its complexities too daunting for the recipient. As in the *Passing Measures*, the Italian framework supports a distinctively English structure, but the precise antecedents are much less obvious: there is no trace of the style of the Dublin grounds, and the musical material is generally less closely related to that of mid-century keyboard music or Byrd's other grounds. Among pavans and galliards the style recalls the William Petre pair of about 1590 (see p. 196) rather than any of his earlier pieces. No *Quadran* settings by other composers share Byrd's dense contrapuntal textures and correspondingly fast rate of harmonic change. These components of the work's extremely individual language are the outcome of an entirely original insight on Byrd's part into the structural implications of the ground, from which he drew very far-reaching consequences.

The matter can best be approached by way of a detail in the harmonic scheme of the *passamezzo antico*. In its simplest form this contains no V–I cadence except at the end, but an A was sometimes introduced before the fourth note (D) so that the final cadence was balanced at the end of the first half by a full close on the dominant; Byrd almost invariably adopts this modification in the *Passing Measures* as a means of structural definition. When, as in Byrd's *Quadran* Pavan, the same insertion is made in the *moderno* bass, the effect is rather different, for the bass then falls a fifth at every step except at the approach to the third and seventh notes, implying in any sizeable setting no less than five perfect cadences.

An illustration of the dangers of this scheme is provided by Morley's *Quadran* Pavan, written under the influence of Byrd's *Passing Measures* – not of his *Quadran*, which Morley apparently did not know.* In var. 1,

---

*Morley composed a feeble *Passing Measures* Pavan in two variations (*Keyboard Works*, No. 4), modelled respectively on vars. 1 and 5 of Byrd's setting. The influence of Byrd's var. 5 persists in var. 3 of Morley's rather stronger *Quadran* Pavan (*Keyboard Works*, No. 3), and in rep. 3 of this work there is a quotation from the middle of Byrd's var. 6. (It is impossible to write about the *Quadran* Pavans and Galliards of Byrd, Morley and Bull without causing confusion to users of the current editions. These pieces are all based on an alternation of two variations on the main ground followed by two reprises. In the editions the pairs of variations and reprises are consecutively numbered, and the second variation or reprise is marked 'rep.' in each case. So vars. 1 and 2 are marked 1 and 'rep.' in the editions; reps. 1 and 2 = 2 + 'rep.'; vars. 3 and 4 = 3 + 'rep.'; reps. 3 and 4 = 4 + 'rep.'; and so on.)

where he adopts the traditional accompanying figure of Ex. 40 which Byrd had used so well in the *Passing Measures*, the regular cadences cut the music up into equal slices (an effect exacerbated by Morley's symmetrical phrases). Byrd saw that to avoid shortwindedness each group of four bars (i.e. four semibreves) must be so far expanded by the pressure of its own eventfulness as to require the cadence, and this despite the need for each 4-bar phrase to remain in touch with the single fundamental harmony provided by the ground. He supplied the pressure through dense contrapuntal activity, often but by no means always imitative, and harmonic diversity achieved partly by frequent excursions away from the main bass note, and partly through a wealth of passing harmony, much of it exceptionally dissonant. Dissonance plays an extraordinary double role in the piece: having made its appearance as a by-product of the structure, or more accurately as a structural support, it becomes the source of the highly individual sound of the music. Just as *Hugh Aston's Ground* is characterized by specially favoured sonorities, the language of the *Quadran* Pavan is unified by diatonic dissonance and the conflict of sharp and flat leading notes: F♯ against F, B against B♭, C♯ against C.

The enormous difference between the *Quadran* Pavan and every other ground by Byrd, or any other composer, is felt at the very beginning. In place of the usual relatively simple initial texture the first four bars present a 3-part imitation close enough, and in short enough values, to have completed a small exposition before the cadence marking the first fundamental harmonic change. This sets the scale of the piece. Naturally Byrd sees to it that the remaining seven 4-bar periods in the variation are not all as firmly enclosed as this one, but the sense of a progression through a number of well defined stages stretches the scope of the music beyond the supple linear paragraphs of the *Passing Measures* Pavan, where the harmonic pulse is slower and the spans are longer. In general layout the two pieces have certain features in common: the cumulative imitation in var. 2 of the *Passing Measures* and the semiquaver runs in vars. 3 and 6 are all fairly closely paralleled at the corresponding points in the *Quadran* (respectively var. 2, rep. 2 and rep. 4). Yet any resemblance is obliterated by the denser, tougher textures, the sheer weight of content in the *Quadran*.

In the later variations of his grounds Byrd habitually aimed at diversity of character, and here the *Quadran* Pavan surpasses all others. In the brilliant var. 3 material and treatment are equally original: at first the harmonic scheme of the ground appears to be entirely in control, forcing the rather sprightly subject in dotted notes to go through prescribed motions, but at bar 8 something slips, and although the ground changes on time the music seems to overlook the fact till a bar later, making a 5-bar phrase which is promptly followed up by another. After this the music becomes as fluid as the phraseology: it breaks into semiquavers that might be expected to run on to the end of the variation, in accordance with Byrd's favourite device of reasserting harmonic stability beneath the play of quick notes. Instead he writes a marvellous built-in rallentando, checking the semiquavers with the clangour of thoroughly Italian open fifths and octaves in the left hand, then gliding into a smooth imitation in quavers and finally closing with a few quiet crotchet chords. From here var. 4 makes a meditative start, but no mood persists for long in this work and a peculiarly oppressive imitation builds up until dispersed by a tripla section, and this in its turn progresses from serenity to astonishing exuberance. This gives place in rep. 3 to the most intensely dissonant music of all before the semiquaver coda provided by rep. 4.

One of the greatest strengths of the *Passing Measures* Pavan and Galliard lies in the perfect consistency of tone that runs through the whole work: the two pieces are perfectly attuned to one another as two aspects of one conception. By contrast the *Quadran* settings are designed as contraries. The process of expansion in the pavan is replaced in the galliard by a contraction, and as with the pavan the artistic decision is linked with a technical one. Because the two dotted semibreves allotted to each note of the ground in the galliard allowed no time for an episode between each main harmonic change, Byrd went to the other extreme. Instead of taking his bigger 3/2 grounds as models, as he had done at least in part in the *Passing Measures* Galliard, he looked to the swifter movement of his ordinary galliard style as giving best scope to the propellent force that the harmonic scheme could provide if used in a relatively direct form. This course apparently did not occur to him at once, for var. 2 contains just the type of imitation usually found in his grounds at this point. But that road would have led to the degree of expansion he needed to avoid, so with reps. 1 and 2 he left it abruptly and thereafter substituted for progressive movement a network of almost rondo-like cross-references (vars. 3 and 5; vars. 4 and 6; reps. 3 and 6; the recurrent dominant minor harmony in the reprises). The lack of development is a link with the *Chi passa* and *My Lady Nevell's Ground*, but the style is leaner and more athletic; nothing is admitted, not even a tripla section, that might detract from the contrast with the extravagant pavan. In consequence the identical dimensions of the *Passing Measures* and the *Quadran* Pavans and Galliards are not reflected in performance: the *Quadran* Pavan takes more time to play than its opposite number, the Galliard less.

It is worth attempting to place the *Quadran* Pavan and Galliard rather more exactly in Byrd's output. Plainly they cannot fit into the clear development which culminates in the *Passing Measures*. The stylistic evidence of the bafflingly original pavan supports a relatively late date: independence of any very precise stylistic tradition, a tendency to vary the ubiquitous parallel thirds and sixths of English keyboard style with more frequent contrary motion, and perhaps too the bold coupling of each pair of reprises with long passages of figuration – a device found elsewhere only in the *Chi passa*.* But a number of other features, though ultimately pointing to the same conclusion, offer curious parallels with early works. The characteristic harmonic pulse in crotchets, though most closely matched in the third section of the latish D minor pavan, is more often found in early works, for instance *Ut mi re*, *The Hunt's up* and the A minor fantasia, and also *Clarifica me pater* 3 where it has the same effect of bringing about an unprecedented expansion of the underlying framework. Here and there the ground ceases to control the music, as happens in *The Hunt's up* and nowhere in Byrd's later grounds, but with the difference that he is now in complete command, able to blur the tonal outline with subsidiary harmonies and bring it back into focus again at will. Something of the wilfulness of his very early part-writing returns in the high-handed grammar of the headiest contrapuntal textures, especially in rep. 3.

In fact throughout the work the drive towards extremes and a certain sense of strain that contributes to its character bring to mind Byrd's youthful tendency to overreach himself in his impatience to excel. Restlessness was a part of his nature; he never cared to repeat his successes, and in composing the *Quadran* as a complementary sequel to the *Passing Measures* he accepted the impossibility of surpassing the latter in its own vein as a challenge to break new and difficult territory.

Yet if, as is likely, the *Quadran* postdates the *Passing Measures* by at least a decade, the desire to write a sequel would have lost some of its force if something had not intervened to give it fresh point. In fact it seems clear that an additional stimulus was provided by the *Quadran* settings of some of his younger contemporaries who were making their mark in the 1580s. Four settings are involved. One is an anonymous pavan and galliard in Weelkes (fol. 17'), a rather rudimentary effort on a smaller scale than Byrd's. The rest are made to the same measure as his: there are separate pavans by Morley and Bull (MB 19/127a), and a second, definitive pavan by Bull (MB 19/127b–c) with a galliard (127d–f). The anonymous work bears no relation to the pieces by Morley and Bull. The opening of its galliard is shown in

*Between the second half of var. 2 and its repeat (and in a different way at the corresponding point in the first half).

Ex. 48

Ex. 48. The melody contains both the subjects of Byrd's first galliard variation. In this case it is unclear who was the borrower; if it was Byrd he must have based the opening (bars 1–8) of his pavan on that of the galliard, instead of the other way about.

There is, however, a point of contact between Bull's first pavan and those of Morley and Byrd which establishes the sequence of these three pieces

Ex. 49

a. Morley, bars 32 & 96 (= 61 & 191)   *b.* Morley, bar 87 (= 173)

c. Bull, bar 61.   *d.* Byrd, bar 61.

e. Byrd, bar 125.   *f.* Byrd, bar 173.

with some certainty. Morley introduced an approach to the tonic cadence which he proceeded to elaborate rather well (Ex. 49a and b*). Bull's pavan contains no antecedent for his version (c), so he presumably appropriated it from Morley.† Byrd's three versions (d–f) are much further developed. It will be seen that he twice adds an imitative entry in the tenor; he also reinforces the III⁶–IV–V–I cadential pattern in each case by reduplicating it immediately before the quotations given here, and except in the last example starts his imitations at this earlier point. It is very difficult to see the simpler versions of Morley and Bull as deriving from Byrd. On the other hand Byrd's examples accord very well with his customary radical treatment of his models; moreover, two of his late pavan and galliard pairs, F2 and C3, are partially based respectively on pieces by Morley and Bull (see pp. 206 and 210).

It follows that the extensive semiquaver passage work in his *Quadran* Pavan was partially suggested by Bull (or Morley), though he backed it up with far more harmonic and contrapuntal substance, and that the rather untypical figures in bars 1–4 and 5–9 of his rep. 1 contain reminiscences of Bull's lengthy use of similar patterns in var. 4 of his first pavan.‡ Byrd's pavan (rep. 3, bars 1–4) and galliard (var. 4) recall in a similar manner rep. 1 and var. 5 respectively of Bull's galliard, though there is no reference to Bull's second pavan (which suggests that Bull originally composed his galliard for his first pavan, and later transferred it to his second). The difference between Byrd and Bull was put in a nutshell by Tomkins, who described one of Bull's *Quadran* Pavans as 'excellent for the hand', and Byrd's *Quadran* Pavan and Galliard as 'excellent for matter' (see MB 5, p. 158). It is precisely the Byrd pavan's inexhaustible richness of matter, to which the lighter galliard acts as a foil, that places the *Quadran* among his very greatest instrumental works. In scarcely any other is the texture of the musical language so complex or so densely charged with expressive inflection.

---

*The barring of the Morley edition is not in semibreves, like those of the other two composers. For purposes of comparison the semibreve numbers have been given in brackets in Ex. 49a and b, with allowance for the omission by Morley (or Forster) of three semibreves from var. 3 (one where the editor has supplied a reconstruction, and two more on the tonic at the end).

†The openings of var. 1 of Bull's first pavan and var. 2 of his second resemble respectively those of Morley's vars. 1 and 4.

‡Note that among the features of Bull's pavan which Byrd did not take up even briefly are figures containing repeated notes (var. 2) and broken chords (var. 4). The runs in both hands simultaneously without supporting bass (var. 3) can only be matched in Byrd in early works: the Short Ground in G, Fantasia C4 and *The Hunt's up* (var. 6, which he discarded when revising the piece).

8

Keyboard Variations

All in a garden green. 12 bars. 6 vars.
BK 56
(Chappell, 110; Wooldridge, i, 79; Simpson, 10; Ward, 28)

Callino casturame. 8 bars. 6 vars.
BK 35
(Chappell, 793; Wooldridge, i, 84; Simpson, 79; Ward, 33)

The Carman's Whistle. 12 bars. 9 vars.
BK 36
(Chappell, 137; Wooldridge, i, 253; Simpson, 85; Ward, 34)

Fortune my foe. 24 bars. 4 vars.
BK 6
(Chappell, 162; Wooldridge, i, 76; Simpson, 225; Ward, 41)

Gipsies' Round. 20 bars. 7 vars.
BK 80
(Chappell, 171; Wooldridge, i, 255)

Go from my window. 16 bars. 7 vars.
BK 79
(Chappell, 140; Wooldridge, i, 146; Simpson, 257)

John come kiss me now. 8 bars. 16 vars.
BK 81
(Chappell, 147; Wooldridge, i, 268; Simpson, 396; Ward, 50)

Lord Willoughby's Welcome home. (Rowland.)
24 bars. 3 vars.
BK 7
(Chappell, 115; Wooldridge, i, 152; Simpson, 467; Ward, 57)

The Maiden's Song. 16 bars. 8 vars.
BK 82

O mistress mine I must. 14 bars. 6 vars.
BK 83
(Chappell, 209; Wooldridge, i, 103)

Sellinger's Round. 20 bars. 9 vars. BK 84
(Chappell, 69; Wooldridge, i,
256; Simpson, 643; Ward, 72)

Walsingham. 8 bars. 22 vars. BK 8
(Chappell, 121; Wooldridge, i,
69; Simpson, 741; Ward, 79)

Wilson's Wild (Wolsey's Wild). 20 bars. 2 vars. BK 37
(Chappell, 87; Wooldridge, i,
267; Simpson, 791)

The Woods so wild. 8 bars. 14 vars. BK 85
(Chappell, 66; Wooldridge, i,
119)

The references given above cover information about other sources of the tunes and the words to which these were sung. The assumption by Chappell and Wooldridge that *O mistress mine* was associated with the song in Shakespeare's *Twelfth Night* is invalidated by Tomkins's addition of the words 'I must' to the title (see MB 5, p. 158; also V. Duckles, 'New Light on "O mistresse mine" ', *Renaissance News*, vii (1954), 98ff.). For *John come kiss me now* see also J. Ward, 'Music for "A Handefull of Pleasant Delites" ', *JAMS*, x (1957), 177.

Byrd's setting of *The Ghost* is dealt with in Chapter 9 because the melody is in alman form. The unreliable New York Public Library Drexel MS 5612 attributes a set of variations on *Bonny sweet Robin* to Byrd, but this is by either Bull or Farnaby; see BK 106, MB 19/65, MB 24/35.

The majority of Byrd's instrumental works – the hymns and antiphons, the grounds, the dances, even on occasion the fantasias – make use of the variation principle in some form, but it is convenient to restrict the generic term 'variations' to pieces based on popular dance or song tunes, and appropriate in so far as they show some affinity with variations of later times. The connection lies less in technique than in the role of the theme, which sets its stamp on the whole composition as no plainsong or ground bass can. It has been seen that Byrd sought out additional means of characterizing his grounds over and above the harmonic provisions of the bass; in his variations he found what he needed for developing the extraordinary individuality of each work in the qualities of the chosen melody itself.

The English school of variation composition is often said to have originated from the Spanish, which was already flourishing by the time Philip II visited the English court in 1554–55 and 1557 with a considerable retinue of musicians – including Cabezón on the first occasion. However, English variations show no trace of the distinctive types of piece or modes of thought cultivated by the Spaniards. A very large number of Spanish variation sets are based on either *Conde Claros*, in effect a kind of short ground in the treble, or *Guárdame las vacas*, a triple-pulse *romanesca* pattern. If the English had composed under Spanish influence they would surely have adopted these variation schemes, as they did the Italian basses.*

Again, the only features shared by the variations of Cabezón and Byrd belong to the common international usage of the day: scalar runs sometimes involving imitation, various details of melodic decoration, the rotation of the melody through the parts. Cabezón almost invariably employs a consistent 4-part texture which he decorates on the lines of his intabulations of vocal music, a form of keyboard composition scarcely known in England. The decoration is accordingly quite neutral in character, drawing nothing from the subject of the variations. Even the beautiful (but probably incomplete) set on the *Canto del cavallero* (MME 29/79), though more varied in contrapuntal conception, shows the same habit of mind. Byrd never wrote in this style; he may have heard about Spanish variations, but nothing in his work suggests that he had heard them.

Although no direct antecedents for Byrd's variations survive, the earliest relate plainly enough to indigenous traditions in both technique and sensibility. His fourteen sets differ too widely for any comprehensive chronology to suggest itself – where every case is special the identification of certain sets as early or late will not necessarily help to place others – but two of them stand out as marking the earliest stages in his development of the form. One, *The Maiden's Song*, draws on the techniques of English polyphonic variations; it will be discussed later. The other, *Gipsies' Round*, reflects more directly the taste for popular music found in all spheres of English society at the time.

In the early years of the century songs of a strongly popular cast were welcome at court, and the earliest lute and secular keyboard sources of the mid-century already contain the simple transcriptions of tunes that were to remain a feature of domestic manuscript collections until the end of the seventeenth century, and beyond. One such simple setting of *The Maiden's Song* (a late, anonymous addition to Mulliner) consists of a pair of varied statements and so must count as an early example of English keyboard variations – indeed as the only known example that may antedate Byrd's earlier sets. Although Byrd must assuredly have had more fully developed models than this, it represents the first step on the road from a naïve type of

---

*Two sets of lute variations on *Conde Claros* are the only settings in English sources; see J. Ward, 'Spanish Musicians in Sixteenth-Century England', in *Essays in honour of Dragan Plamenac*, ed. G. Reese and R. Snow (Pittsburg, 1969), 363.

arrangement for untutored listeners to his elaborate compositions. As with other great music that retains the common touch, the road appears at once short and long: Byrd's respect for the melodies that he varies enables him to draw strength from an otherwise remote background.

Despite various signs of inexperience which betray its early date, **Gipsies' Round** is in many ways a thoroughly characteristic work incorporating, sometimes in a rather simple form, most of Byrd's standard techniques of variation. The melody may be accompanied purely harmonically, as in var. 1, or by an independent imitative texture (var. 4), or by imitations to which it contributes itself, usually with the aid of decoration (vars. 2 and 3). It may receive extensive decoration, most typically in the form of runs of quick notes, in which case there often follows a balancing passage in the left hand against which an undecorated segment of the melody can re-establish the norm (var. 6). Very occasionally Byrd departs from the melody altogether for a few bars (var. 5), but this can only happen in works like the present one in which the harmonic scheme is constant enough to bridge the gap, and the effect is always of an extension or development of the prevailing melodic character. When the decoration leads the melody rather far afield he may touch in some notes of the original in the tenor (var. 4, bars 74 and 79).* These techniques rarely hold sway for long singly, but constantly alternate or merge into one another within the individual variations. Byrd already handles them with complete confidence in *Gipsies' Round*, but within limits set by the special mode of keyboard writing that he adopts here. Taking his cue from the dance character of the tripla tune, which is not known to have been set to words, he drums out the brisk rhythms in a much more densely chordal texture than those of comparable pieces such as the early anonymous *My Lady Wynkfylds Rownde*, Aston's or his own Hornpipe, or any of his other variations on tripla melodies, with the one exception of *Sellinger's Round*.

The latter work and *Gipsies' Round* are the only two sets of variations to resemble each other at all closely, and the reason seems to be the usual one when Byrd comes near to repeating himself – that he was dissatisfied with his first attempt. Both melodies consist of a stanza of five 4-bar lines on the pattern AABCC, which on account of the tonic close at the end of C feels like a quatrain with the last line repeated. Line A ends on the subdominant in both tunes, but whereas *Gipsies' Round* gets stuck there throughout line

*Other examples occur in *All in a garden green* (beginning of var. 5), *Fortune* (see p. 159n.), *Go from my window* (last three bars of var. 5), *O mistress mine* (bars 37 and 55), and the *Ut re mi* fantasia (last two notes of statement 15 of the cantus firmus).

B, *Sellinger's Round* moves to the dominant. *Gipsies' Round* also implies rather static harmony in line A, and there are uncomfortable moments when Byrd seems to tire of devising harmonic movement and a suggestion of the curious old tradition of rigid harmonic textures in tripla* creeps in. In *Sellinger's Round* he introduces more frequent and more varied passing harmony for which the tune itself is only partially responsible.

Even so Byrd's early mastery in *Gipsies' Round* can sometimes astonish, as in the double statement of line C that closes var. 3 (Ex. 50). The quietening

Ex. 50

of the music in the last bars by melodic and rhythmic nuance, supported by the earlier return to C♮s, shows how his spontaneous formal sense could already triumph over a structural repetition in a distinctly rigid context. This sense, so characteristic of all his music, has special importance in the variations, for the melodies define the small-scale form so exactly that variety can only be achieved if their simpler implications are very firmly glossed and modified.

The only known text of *Gipsies' Round* appears to be incomplete. The

*As in *The Hunt's up*, original version, vars. 10 and 11 (see p. 124).

sixth of the seven variations begins with two statements of line A which obviously go together, followed by a third statement which belongs with what follows. Apparently Tregian or an earlier copyist skipped the last three lines (BCC) of what may be called var. 6a, the first line (A) of var. 6b, and perhaps one or more intervening variations. Enough of the work survives, however, to show that Byrd had not yet full control of the wider form. The ideas behind the first five variations are clear enough: he keeps var. 1 fairly simple, works quavers into 2, introduces imitations above the melody (partly by inversion) in 3, starts 4 with longer imitative points and then changes to quaver runs in anticipation of freer figuration in 5. But the design is weakened by too narrow a range of vocabulary; the recurrence of similar patterns and motives blurs the individuality of the variations and the sense of progress. Thus a rhythmic pattern of four quavers and a crotchet plays a big part in vars. 2 and 3 and crops up again in 4 and 6b, while 6a and 6b echo the beginning of 3 and the later part of 4 respectively. Var. 7 begins well, and closes with an apt 2-bar coda, but the middle would fit equally well in several of the earlier variations.

Byrd's task in **Sellinger's Round** was thus to clarify and differentiate without breaking the cumulative effect of the vigorous dance character. He starts with a very simple expository variation, admitting the bare minimum of motives in the accompaniment to prevent stagnation. This leaves him with something in hand for var. 2, and he does not need to introduce the four-quavers-and-a-crotchet figure till near the end of 3, where it prepares for the quaver runs of 4. In var. 5 the melody is in the alto, a device which Byrd usually reserves for the final variation but here advances; perhaps he was influenced by the early appearance, in third place, of the comparable variation in *Gipsies' Round*, or anxious to mitigate the danger of melodic monotony threatened by the special style chosen for the piece.

Each of the later variations is similarly based on a particular idea, quaver movement in 6 (different from 4), homophony and 3/2 syncopation against the prevailing 6/4 in 7, suave imitation and melodic variation without recourse to quavers (except at the end) in 8, and a firmly controlled ninth variation announced by an arresting harmonic twist to clinch the series. The general plan here – a sequence of variations (1–4) culminating in fast note values followed by a more diverse group – clearly derives from the standard one in Byrd's larger grounds, and as *Sellinger's Round* is the only set of variations to adopt the second stage of this scheme, it may belong to the same period as the grounds, most probably the 1570s. The increasing speed of the first stage, however, occurs in all his variations where the number of variations in the set and the nature of the melody permit it.

This is not the only feature that connects the variations with the grounds, for the two forms were both partially rooted in cantus firmus technique. The incorporation of popular tunes in the *Western Wind* masses and the *Browning* variations in a singularly direct form, as cantus firmi that could travel through all the parts from treble to bass, has already been discussed (p. 65). In a sense English grounds and melodic variations may both be considered special cases of the same form, the first confining the cantus firmus to the bass, the second to the treble. In practice these limits do not always hold: in Byrd's Consort Ground and in his *Second Ground* for keyboard the bass, which has melodic character, moves into other parts in the later stages, while in only a minority of his sets of keyboard variations is the tune confined entirely to the treble. If a simpler tradition of keyboard setting appears nearer the surface in the early *Gipsies' Round*, another early, but more accomplished work, **The Maiden's Song**, shows Byrd working out the implications of the cantus firmus tradition.

The melody approaches more nearly than most the simplicity of rhythm and contour found in ground basses, and it shares their 3/2 measure. In the first six of the eight variations it is placed in the treble, so that the layout of the music resembles that in the last six variations of the *Second Ground*, where the main sections of the bass line occupy the same position. Each piece momentarily crosses into the territory of the other. In the first two treble variations of the ground (12 and 13) the cantus firmus acquires melodic status through the quiet support of the lower parts, so that var. 13 comes very close to var. 3 of *The Maiden's Song* (see Ex. 51). The *Maiden's Song* variations follow the usual course of increasing activity found in the

Ex. 51

a. Second Ground, var. 13.

b. The Maiden's Song, var. 3.

grounds until, with var. 6, the melody assumes a very cantus-firmus-like air against a single line in tripla (there is no comparison here with the fine tripla variations in the *Second Ground*). Yet elsewhere, even in these two exceptional pieces, the difference of emphasis cannot be missed. In the ground the cantus firmus has a neutral function; it receives no decoration except for cadential purposes, and the musical argument lies overwhelmingly in the rest of the texture. In *The Maiden's Song* the melody dominates; the sparing decoration serves to relate it motivically to the other parts, the function of which, until the later variations, is to support it with varying movement and harmonic colour even where, as in Ex. 51b, they introduce independent imitations.

The Maiden's Song comes nearer to the consistent polyphony of consort variations than any other of Byrd's keyboard sets. Neither the frequent use of extra notes where a chord needs greater sonority, nor the occasional division of the melody between two parts conceals the polyphonic basis of each variation. Var. 1 is in three parts, without treble, 2 and 3 are in four parts, 4 and 5 essentially in three and four parts respectively. Var. 6 is the only one in any of Byrd's sets entirely in two parts; some decoration of the melody and the supervention of a solid tutti with var. 7 help to make it acceptable. In the last two variations, both in four parts, the melody plays its part in an imitative texture, taking the tenor in 7 and the alto in 8.

Although Byrd was never to lose his flair for applying musical procedures in new contexts for new purposes, so thoroughgoing an adaptation of consort variation technique to the keyboard marks out *The Maiden's Song* as the work of a young composer bent on enclosing a wider field of action. Indeed in the bicinium of var. 6 he takes in almost too much: except in his early plainsong settings he left this style to others. Nevertheless, viewed as a whole this composition, in which Byrd responds in the sober accents of an earlier generation to a melody that was soon to lose its popularity, holds its own with all but his very finest variations. He drew on the experience of this set in a number of later ones, but only once, in *Walsingham*, returned to the consort variation for the scheme of a whole work.

In the great majority of the twenty-two variations of **Walsingham** the melody behaves as a cantus firmus, but the treatment is much freer than in *The Maiden's Song*. Segments of the melody change part and octave within single variations, parts appear and drop out again more freely, and the melody is frequently decorated, here and there becoming dissolved in accompanied treble figuration in purely keyboard style. The differences between the two works result from the intentions behind them. In *The Maiden's Song* Byrd evidently set out to adopt as much from consort-variation style as might be useful on the keyboard; in *Walsingham* he shifted the emphasis. His aim here was to compose a counterpart to a particular consort work, the *Browning*.

He accordingly chose a melody of the same length (eight 3/2 bars), and adopted the same initial plan of four groups of five variations each. This scheme was designed as much for his own guidance as for the final product, and he modified it, as he had that of the *Browning*, where musical considerations demanded it – notably by the insertion of two extra variations in the middle of the work. That the groups of five variations derive from those in the *Browning*, rather than the other way about, is certain: as has been shown (p. 69) the latter originated in the rotation of the melody through the five parts of the instrumental ensemble, whereas no such internal origin can have determined those in *Walsingham* because the number of parts in the keyboard texture is variable, and in any case rarely touches five.

Nevertheless, rotation persisted in the first and last groups (vars. 1–5 and 18–22). In the last the texture is fairly consistently in four parts, and the melody, despite occasional straying, rotates through tenor, alto, bass and treble in vars. 18–21 respectively, returning for var. 22 to the alto part, which Byrd particularly favoured for final variations. Similarly, in the first group the melody takes the treble, tenor and bass lines in vars. 3–5, but there is no consistent alto variation because, as in the *Browning*, vars. 1 and 2 are for reduced voices. Vars. 5 and 20 are the only two in which the melody is entirely in the bass; they clearly owe their presence to the rotation idea. In the central sections of the composition, which give fuller scope to keyboard techniques, the melody for the most part divides its time between the treble and tenor parts.

In the *Browning* Byrd had ensured the coherence of the groups of variations by three means: pace, technical affinity and transposition of the melody. The last plays no part in any of his keyboard variations (except of course at the octave), and he did not break this rule in *Walsingham* – it is hard to imagine the beautiful and highly characteristic harmonic outline (G minor – B♭ – G major) required by the melody fitting in at any other level. Nor is such a wide range of device available in keyboard textures as in a 5-part consort: motivic and imitative work is largely confined to the slower-moving variations, and so plays a narrower structural role. On the other hand the polyphonic density of the *Browning* precludes very fast divisions,* so that the fastest contain only three notes to the minim as compared to four and six in *Walsingham*, where pace consequently becomes the dominant formal factor. Thus the first three stages of the work present three crescendos in speed, of

---

*This has nothing to do with the capacity of viol players, as the Consort Prelude and Ground shows.

increasing intensity. After a slow beginning broken quaver movement occurs in vars. 4 and 5; var. 6 drops back and takes stock before quavers reappear in 7 and continue unchecked except at final cadences from 8 till towards the end of 10.

At this point there is an irregularity. The five variations 13–17 continue the sequence begun by 1–5 and 6–10: 13 is predominantly in crotchets, 14 in quavers, 15 introduces tripla which continues, partly in quaver sextuplets, to the end of 17. Vars. 11 and 12 are respectively in crotchets and quavers like 13 and 14, and one pair or the other must have been an afterthought. The reduplication shows Byrd sacrificing his precompositional scheme for musical reasons: by inserting a false start to the third of the three similarly planned groups he averted too great a feeling of symmetry, and at the same time introduced a more effective contrast at the half-way mark (cf. vars. 11 and 12 of the *Browning*) than a single quiet variation could provide. It might be thought that the second object would have been better served by placing the two slow variations (11 and 13) together, but that would have anticipated too strongly the return to imitative motives and slower movement in the last group of five (18–22).

This final section needs to be felt as balancing the opening one, so that the contrast between them can underline the sense of accumulated experience in the crowning sequence. The expository variations (1–5) are relatively simple, closely controlled by the melody: the imitative elements all derive from it, and its down-beat crotchets ($\textstyle\int\!\int\!\int\!\int$) launch each variation and govern its rhythmic character. In the comparable variations 11 and 13, however, the countersubjects, following upon the continuous quavers of vars. 8–10, become more sustained and more independent, while vars. 18–20 take the development a stage further, combining great contrapuntal density and melodic breadth, as though reconverting the energy of the preceding tripla variations into matter. They form a superb climax to the work, after which var. 21 eases the tension a little (cf. var. 6) with a last statement of the melody in the treble before the impressive final variation and brief toccata-like coda.

Walsingham contains more variations than any other set by Byrd, and the over-all structure is correspondingly complex. However, the debt of the finished composition to the *Browning* is small. The *Browning*'s concentration of thought, which no keyboard work could match, involves the formality proper to polyphony: each variation commits itself to a certain path, the music develops powerfully but deliberately, and the sections of the work are carefully balanced against one another. By contrast the music in *Walsingham* is constantly in a state of transition, and this mobility leads to a more linear conception of form. Thus within the broadly similar framework of the two pieces, Byrd works out contrasting modes of expression in accordance with the nature of the instrumental textures.

Walsingham is unlikely to have been written much later than the *Browning*, and may therefore be placed towards the end of the 1570s, considerably later than *The Maiden's Song*. These works offer no basis for dating the only other set of 3/2 variations in Nevell, **All in a garden green,** which is composed on different lines. As a short series of variations on a longish melody of lyrical appeal it has something in common with *The Maiden's Song* in externals; but there the resemblance ends. Whereas in *The Maiden's Song* Byrd combines simplicity of melodic treatment with harmonic variety, in *All in a garden* he adopts a fixed harmonic structure which enables the melody to branch out in profuse decoration. The six variations fall into a familiar pattern: vars. 2 and 3 introduce imitations, fast runs set in towards the end of 3 and dominate, with some dance-like interruptions, till the end of 5, and 6 clinches the series in slower values with the melody shifted for the first and only time from treble to alto.

In the main this is a fine work, but a slight stiffness here and there suggests that it was not one of the more recent of the pieces chosen for Nevell: imitation finds itself rather cramped because both treble and bass are broadly predetermined, and the alternation of runs between left and right hand seems a little rigid. The latter feature is very common in Byrd, of course, but whereas in the wider context of *Walsingham* or the *Passing Measures* Galliard it plays a constructive role, in a slow piece like *All in a garden* every passage must speak for itself. The fact that the tune, like that of *Gipsies' Round*, is unrecorded elsewhere also suggests a relatively early date for the variations, for if it had remained popular until the 1580s or 1590s other arrangements would surely be known in lute or keyboard sources.

The origins of the fixed basses in pieces like *Gipsies' Round* and *All in a garden green* are not easily traced. The bass of the latter is scarcely more freely handled than those of the grounds, and hasty technical analysis might term the work a ground as readily as a set of melodic variations. The music, however, plainly centres upon the melody; what must remain uncertain, since no other setting of the melody survives, is whether Byrd composed the bass or whether it belonged traditionally to the tune like those of *The Hunt's up* and *Malt's come down*. Fortunately all the melodies that he set, except for *Gipsies' Round* and *All in a garden*, occur in other instrumental arrangements, and from these two points emerge: the melodies were by no means standardized, and even when they were commonly associated with a particular harmonic matrix melodic variants sometimes required its modification. When he foresaw the need for harmonic stability in a set of variations Byrd no doubt took the claims of the bass into account in planning the melodic detail. For instance in *Sellinger's Round* he adopted a form of the melody, or adapted it, in accordance with a harmonic structure that would carry the vigorous composition he had in mind, and in all probability he set about *All in a garden green* in much the same way, working out a harmonic framework to contain the lyrical expansion, very moderate pace and copious semiquaver divisions for which he saw the opportunity. But the primacy of the melody as the mainspring of the composition is never in doubt.

To the composer who seeks to derive the character of a complete composition from the melody on which it is based, relatively slow-moving melodies offer considerable advantages. Quick, jig-like tunes in compound triple measure give very limited scope to the contrapuntal treatment or melodic elaboration found in *The Maiden's Song* and *Walsingham* on the one hand and in *All in a garden* on the other. Yet Byrd's concern for character is nowhere better illustrated than in the three sets of variations on tripla melodies in Nevell – *Sellinger's Round*, *The Carman's Whistle* and *The Woods so wild* – each of which is composed on quite different lines.

Carmen apparently contented themselves with whistling a very monotonous stanza of six 2-bar lines on the pattern AABB'BB', in which A is based on the descending upper tetrachord and B on the descending lower tetrachord shadowed at the third above. As though to show what he was up against in **The Carman's Whistle** Byrd points out the connection between A and B in a little 4-bar introduction to var. 1 in which A is followed by its transposition to the lower tetrachord. He avoids the obvious dangers of uniting such a limited melody to a fixed harmonic basis by drawing in about equal measure on what may be called the harmonic and contrapuntal traditions that go back to *Gipsies' Round* and *The Maiden's Song* respectively. He starts out with two variations on a more or less well defined bass, which thereafter reappears quite often in snatches, usually of four bars, but never for a whole variation. He shows less concern than usual to carry through each of these short variations in a single vein, or alternatively to effect any decisive transition within them. Instead each is firmly characterized at the outset and then allowed to run to a close as it will. Thus he starts var. 3 with a new type of harmonization, 4, 5 and 6 with a variety of sequential countersubjects or imitative motives, 7 with another harmonization and 8 as a bicinium;*

---

*Did the last four bars of var. 5 originally form part of var. 8?

in the last variation, as so often, the tune moves down to the alto to make way for a melodic culmination.

By means of this wide variety of techniques Byrd achieves an expressive range that the tune might not seem to encourage: for instance the archaic-sounding 6–5 progressions of vars. 4 and 7 bring an unexpected strain of pathos to the predominantly cheerful music.* Yet he reinterprets the melody with such tact that what he really imposes upon it seems to have been elicited from its own inner resources.† The work may be one of the later ones in Nevell: technical range is a feature of post-Nevell variations, and his conscious exploitation of an old-fashioned technique finds a parallel in **The Woods so wild**, which is dated 1590.‡

The variations on this melody are built entirely on the simple cantus firmus or ground that runs continuously through Aston's Hornpipe, namely F alternating with G. The melody itself must have originated as a descant to this pattern, as its curious tonality shows. Whereas Aston's piece is in F, so that the ground, placed in the tenor, fits into a normal tonal field (see p. 119), Byrd's is in Mixolydian. In consequence the ground, which he uses as a bass more often than in a middle part, implies a raw juxtaposition of F major and G major chords. There can be little question that this reflects a mode of popular improvisation, and one that few composers would have cared to imitate. It is altogether typical of Byrd that he should have done so, and that he set about making it his own not by civilizing its character away, but by accepting all its salient features, confident that in this way he would find more rather than less scope for his capacities. For most of the time he keeps strumming out the cantus firmus in minims (dotted minims in transcription): four on F, four on G, and then the same again apart from a substitute, usually A, for the second G the second time round in order to

---

*Byrd's habit of accompanying a descending melodic phrase with a bass in tenths and 6–5 suspensions in the middle part goes back to his very early consort settings of *Christe qui lux es*, in particular I/3. Var. 7 of *The Carman's Whistle* provides a specially clear example. The influence of the pattern can also be felt not only in var. 4 of the same work, but in var. 3 of *The Maiden's Song* (see Ex. 51b) and var. 6 of *O mistress mine*.

†*The Carman's Whistle* was not only very popular in Byrd's time (it occurs in seven manuscripts, beating *The Woods so wild* by one) but was his first keyboard piece to be revived: Burney printed it in Volume 3 of his history (1789). Since then it has never quite been lost sight of. It appeared in the *Harmonicon* in 1826, Chappell & Co. published an edition in 1814 which was reprinted at least twice in the next twenty years, and Farrenc's edition of 1863 was followed by others in 1870 (W. H. Holmes) and 1879 (E. Pauer) before the appearance of the Fitzwilliam Virginal Book in 1894–99. It was played by Anton Rubinstein in his historical concerts in 1885–86, and published by Yurgenson in Moscow.

‡In Nevell, and also in Tregian – but in a later hand. The writer may simply have copied the date from Nevell.

introduce a II⁶ or dominant harmony for the final cadence to each variation. He usually smoothes the way back to F at the halfway mark with an anticipatory B♭; otherwise almost the only chords on either degree – if it is appropriate to speak of chords at all in textures so light, fast moving and linear as these – are 5/3 and 6/3, with the addition of the chord on the fifth below when the cantus firmus is not in the bass.

The plan of the work, which in 1590 consisted of only twelve variations (1–11 and 14 of the final version), follows none of Byrd's usual procedures, except that it contains two gradual crescendos in speed arriving at continuous quavers respectively in vars. 6–7 and in 10–11. This is because the technique of variation itself is different. The complete melody is heard in only six of the twelve original variations, but always in its simplest form without decoration or any significant change, so that it becomes very firmly fixed in the mind; in vars. 1, 2, 7 and 12 (which later became 14) it is in the treble, and in 3 and 6 in the middle part. In the other six variations the harmonic scheme is embodied in the free play of motives that either derive from the melody or coincide sporadically with its unexpressed line. Here Byrd stands indebted to the tradition of improvisation behind his material for opening up an entirely new field of action to his subtle and in no way improvisatory workmanship. The music has no parallel in his other sets of variations, where the melody is rarely abandoned altogether, and then only briefly, nor in his grounds, where he builds with material of a quite different and more independent kind.

At some time after 1590 he evidently became dissatisfied with the rather hasty preparation at the end of var. 11 for the return of the melody in the final variation – a miscalculation due to his strict adherence to the standard clutch of a dozen variations.* He accordingly inserted two new variations to effect the transition more gradually. The melody re-emerges in the middle part halfway through the new var. 12, comes nearer the surface in 13, and thence regains the treble in the grandly harmonized var. 14 – in contrast to otherwise similar final variations such as that of *The Carman's Whistle* where the melody steps down from the treble for the first time to make way for a closing melodic flourish.

Two smaller sets of variations on tripla melodies are not found in Nevell.

---

*Perhaps most of Byrd's variations were first planned in relation to the number 12, like *The Hunt's up*, *Hugh Aston's Ground* and probably the consort variations on *Te lucis ante terminum*. Disregarding the pair on *Wilson's Wild*, the larger sets (*Walsingham* and *John come kiss me now*) and the incomplete *Gipsies' Round*, the others all contain 12, 9, 6 or 3 variations except *The Maiden's Song* (8), *Go from my window* (7) and *Fortune* (4). Were these altered in the course of composition, like the Consort Ground and *Walsingham* (and perhaps the fantasia on *Ut mi re*), or revised, like *The Hunt's up* and *The Woods so wild*?

One, **Wilson's Wild**, is of little importance. The tune is a five-line stanza of exactly the same length and design as those of *Gipsies' Round* and *Sellinger's Round*, but Byrd does not adopt the same emphatic manner or make a special point of any kind. Perhaps in response to a request he simply made a couple of settings, stylish enough as far as they go, and left it at that.* The simplicity of the six little variations on **Callino casturame** is quite another matter, for here Byrd deliberately restricts technical means in order to concentrate attention in a certain way, very much as he used the limitations of the Hornpipe and *The Bells* to special ends. The melody is short, the bass fixed and extremely simple, and the texture at every stage in the quiet increase in activity up to the penultimate variation correspondingly transparent. As a result the smallest melodic variant, which in another context would claim very little for itself, becomes magnified by isolation. For example, the listener takes in to the full the difference in balance and emphasis between the bars in Ex. 52, which shows the beginning of the second half of vars. 1, 2

Ex. 52

and 6. By scaling down, Byrd finds enough matter to give the piece a place of its own among his variations. Its presence in Weelkes's manuscript puts it in the period covered by Nevell, or not much later.

Nevell contains only one set of variations in duple time, on a tune most commonly known in England as **Lord Willoughby's Welcome home** or *Rowland*. The former title must refer to Lord Willoughby's return either from Flanders in 1589, or less probably from France in 1590; it is the one that occurs in Nevell and most of the other sources of Byrd's forceful and effective composition, which therefore presumably dates from the same period. The work differs markedly in character from the variations on **Fortune my foe**, even though the two tunes match each other exactly in length and stanza structure and Byrd treats them similarly in confining them almost entirely to the treble over a fixed bass. In *Lord Willoughby* he allows nothing to stand in the way of the bold forward movement established right from the outset. In *Fortune* he adopts a pavan-like character appropriate to a

---

*Tregian, the only source, omits four bars from var. 2, but the piece is probably complete in other respects: Forster, who intended to copy it but for some reason neglected to do so, did not leave very much space for it.

tune traditionally sung to doleful words and often associated with a harmonic scheme allied to the *passamezzo antico*. He employs a version of this scheme, and along with it figures and textures very like those of his *Passing Measures* Pavan, both in the slower variations and in the final one in semiquavers. The stylistic similarity is close enough to suggest that *Fortune* was composed at about the time of the pavan, in the 1570s. It is the only set by Byrd to end with a variation in rapid keyboard figuration, like the final verses of some of the Marian organ hymns. There is no preparation in the preceding variations for the more brilliant style, which makes a rather incongruous impression.

In *Fortune my foe* Byrd pays particular attention to decorating the melody, perhaps because the static Ds at the beginning of the second part of the tune invited it. The skilful refashioning of the melody in var. 3 must have impressed Dowland, for he took it over almost unchanged for the second of his pair of lute variations on the same tune.* His interest is symptomatic of a changing approach to some of the tunes that Byrd varied. The grounds that Byrd had handled in the 1570s had become vehicles for extended virtuoso display, and musicians began to look about for less well worn and perhaps simpler harmonic fields for composition, and no doubt for improvisation. They found them in the harmonies popularly associated with certain well known melodies. In var. 1 of his *Fortune* Dowland keeps fairly close to the tune (though he seems reluctant to declare his theme at once†), and the variation that he takes from Byrd is by no means independent of it. But in his variations on *Go from my window*‡ he moves progressively further from the melody after var. 1, just as Byrd had long before omitted the melody of *The Hunt's up* altogether from his setting of its bass. History does not repeat itself exactly: for instance, in five of the eight variations on *Go from my window* by Morley or John Mundy,§ which show the same process at work in keyboard style, the composer frees the typical countersubject

---

Collected Lute Music, No. 62. Byrd's var. 3 is missing from Forster's text, but this is probably an accident (like the absence of var. 2 of *Lord Willoughby* from the same source; see BK 7, commentary), for it hangs closely with the rest in style and in structure. For instance, at the repeat of the first phrase in each variation except the first, Byrd underpins the top line, which can be heard as a version of the phrase itself, with snatches of the original undecorated version in the tenor before moving on to freer treatment in the second half. Var. 3 is therefore unlikely to have been a belated addition in homage to Dowland. Moreover Dowland's version removes the surely integral imitations at the end, and Byrd's interest in his younger contemporaries is not known ever to have expressed itself in the form of such direct quotation.

†A not uncommon feature; cf. William Randall's arrangement of *Lachrymae* (No. 9 in *Tisdale's Virginal Book*, ed. A. Brown (London, 1966)), and lute versions of James Harding's celebrated galliard.

‡*Collected Lute Music*, No. 64.

§Morley, *Keyboard Works*, No. 13; Tregian Nos. 9 and 42.

figures from the melody but fails to invest them with the stamina necessary for a more independent structure over the bass. As a result the music becomes rather shortwinded and loses character. Small wonder that Byrd, except in the rather different case of *The Woods so wild*, never cared to attempt this mixed type of composition.

His retention of the melody and failure to adopt a fixed bass in his own variations on **Go from my window** do not, therefore, indicate that he wrote them before the most obvious harmonic implications of the tune had become standardized into an unadventurous quatrain consisting essentially of I, II, II–V, I. It was second nature to him to avoid such a limited scheme as surely as it was Bull's to embrace it,* and there are reasons for placing this set in the post-Nevell period along with *John come kiss me now* and *O mistress mine I must*. Byrd's later keyboard music is marked by greater flexibility in his treatment of figuration; in particular he likes to pass it freely from one hand to the other in unbroken lines instead of disposing it in alternate left- and right-hand passages.† At the same time he devotes great care to the rhythmic life not only of the figuration but of all his linear material, and this leads to a new intricacy in the part-writing and new melodic wealth. The variations on *Go from my window* show these developments in a relatively simple form. As usual when he employs a melody as a kind of cantus firmus Byrd is very sparing of decoration. In vars. 2–4, where the melody is most subtly harmonized by independent accompanying imitations, he seems to look back to *The Maiden's Song*, but the character of the motives has all the refinement of his late style, var. 3 making use of similar figures to those in the corresponding variation in *O mistress mine*. The semiquaver runs in the accompanying parts in vars. 4 and 5 traverse the whole keyboard texture in the late manner, and near the end of var. 5 the melody has to jump from bass to alto to avoid the impetuous figuration; there are comparable shifts in vars. 10 and 13 of *John come kiss me now*. As for the miraculous final variation, Byrd celebrates the lyrical side of popular melody here as nowhere else outside *O mistress mine*.‡

*See his variations, MB 19/123. A later, anonymous composer, probably Orlando Gibbons, shared Byrd's point of view: he built his ten variations for 6-part consort (ed. S. Wilkinson, London, 1958) entirely round the melody except in var. 8, where he substituted the standard bass as though to show that he was aware of the alternative.

†The prevalence of this feature in late works is emphasized in A. Brown's unpublished dissertation *A Critical Edition of the Keyboard Music of William Byrd* (Cambridge, 1969), i, 220. Isolated examples, however, occur in earlier works, e.g. the A minor fantasia and the *Ut re mi* fantasia.

‡If Byrd composed his *Go from my window* with the examples of Morley/Mundy and Bull before him, as is possible, he showed himself sharply critical of them. But the pieces offer no internal evidence betraying their relative chronology.

What *Go from my window* lacks by comparison with other late works is the exceptional concentration of invention in the bar-to-bar musical texture for which the experience of the *Quadran* Pavan had perhaps laid the foundation. *John come kiss me now* and *O mistress mine*, with their abundance of strongly characterized and closely worked countersubjects and imitative motives, typify the late style more fully. Since the tune of **John come kiss me now** is only eight semibreves long it might seem an odd choice for such elaborate treatment, but the apparent contradiction was no doubt part of the attraction for Byrd. In its long international history this melody frequently appears as a descant to the *passamezzo moderno* bass, though the variant adopted by Byrd required a substitution of VII (or II) for the subdominant in the sixth bar (see p. 115). He also allowed himself many more chord alterations than would be possible in composition on a ground, and restricted decoration of the melody correspondingly.* The originality of the work lies not in the larger plan – the sixteen fast-moving variations are grouped in pairs of related character† and increase fairly constantly in speed up to the penultimate pair – but in the pressure of content. Despite their brevity many variations contain two distinct phases, and to a remarkable degree the countersubjects, figuration and even some of the more extended runs are built from motives derived from the melody. In no other set does Byrd achieve such concision and such wide-ranging vivacity.

The work concludes with a brilliant feat of compression. In the first half of the last variation (quoted complete in Ex. 53a) the melody, in the alto, is accompanied by a dialogue, based on its rhythmic diminution, between bass and treble in ascending sequence, while the passamezzo harmonies are reached in the second half of each bar. An answering descending sequence between treble and tenor begins in bar 5, and the listener immediately anticipates something like Ex. 53b as a foregone conclusion. Probably Byrd did so too in the first place, but found it scarcely possible to fulfil all three expectations in the sixth bar (the tune, the sequential dialogue, and the VII chord), as Ex. 53b makes painfully clear, and rather than juggle with the passage decided to forgo it altogether. Instead he overturns the prevailing

*Var. 6 is a partial exception: after two variations of greater harmonic mobility the stock bass returns in its simplest form to allow rhythmic displacement in lines 2 and 3 of the four-line melodic stanza, and motivic variation reminiscent of *The Woods so wild* in line 1.

†The introduction of tripla in var. 12 might seem to divide it from var. 11, but Byrd often changes to tripla in the middle of a variation when he wants to avoid too sharp a break; see *The Hunt's up*, *Hugh Aston's Ground*, *Passing Measures* Galliard, *Walsingham*, *Quadran* Pavan.

Ex. 53

pattern of harmonic strong beats with a suspension halfway through bar 6,* changes rhythmic step, doubles the sequential pace, and finishes early by the standard of the preceding variations with the air of having put in an extra bar.

With *John come kiss me now* Byrd says his last word on variations in quick tempo; with **O mistress mine I must** he does the same for those on a longer, slower melody. He sets the curious stanza – seven 2-bar lines in 3/2 in the pattern AABCDCD – only six times, so that in its general proportions as well as its mainly lyrical character the work belongs to the family of *The Maiden's Song, All in a garden green* and *Go from my window*. Like the first and last of these it dispenses with a fixed bass and relies to a considerable extent on contrapuntal texture. But the tune, placed in the treble throughout, is not treated with cantus-firmus-like severity; on the contrary, it is occasionally as richly decorated as that of *All in a garden*, despite the absence of a constant harmonic framework.

The reconciliation between the apparently opposing principles underlying *The Maiden's Song* and *All in a garden* comes about as a by-product of

*Whether by design or coincidence Byrd touches on the regular subdominant of the *passamezzo moderno* at this point for the first and only time.

Byrd's ever increasing absorption in his melodic material: in working out-wards from the chosen melody he has recourse to decoration as a means of compensating for his greater caution in admitting independent contrapuntal motives or set harmonic schemes. In *John come kiss me now* the same interest results rather differently in great motivic concentration, because the tune offers neither scope for decorative development nor material for more than a single variation (var. 15) in true imitation. The melody of *O mistress mine* on the other hand contains several workable figures for imitation, and Byrd widens their possibilities in a succession of beautiful elaborations, so that he is able to devote a considerable part of each variation (starting from the first, which in all previous sets he had kept very simple) to imitations directly dependent upon the melody, and to bring any that start independently into the melody's orbit.

He had, of course, used this technique fitfully from *Gipsies' Round* on-wards, but except in the strict polyphony of the last two variations in *The Maiden's Song* he had never tried to take it very far. Its flowering in *O mistress mine* is sudden, profuse, extraordinarily varied, and capable of opening out, especially in vars. 3–5, into contrasting episodes based on other techniques – or at least on quite different applications of the prevailing one, for whether in a count Byrd's range of variation techniques would be found greater here than in, for instance, *The Carman's Whistle*, would depend on the whim of analysis. What is certain is that although one mode of writing cuts across or merges into another with unexampled freedom, the unity of spirit remains secure because everything emanates from Byrd's response to the melody not only in derivational terms, but in a broader sense too. Beyond a certain point the language in which such a response expresses itself, the unrepeatable combination to which all musical elements momen-tarily agree, belongs to intuition. Byrd is one of those composers whose capacity for taking pains and rare intelligence are rewarded in one major work after another with a quality of uniqueness a little beyond their conscious grasp.

9
Almans, Smaller Dances, Arrangements, Descriptive Music

Monsieur's Alman G1. 2 vars.	BK 87
Monsieur's Alman G2. 3 vars.	BK 88 (Simpson, 495; Ward, 58)
Monsieur's Alman C1. 1 var.	BK 44
The Ghost. 2 vars.	BK 78 (Edwards, *Sources*, ii, 205)
The Queen's Alman g1. 3 vars.	BK 10 (Simpson, 590; Ward, 66)
Alman G3. 1 var.	BK 89
Alman g2. 2 vars.	BK 11
Alman C2. 2 vars.	Neighbour 1 (listed in BK, second edition, 117)
Galliard Jig	BK 18
Jig a1	BK 22
Coranto (Jig) C1. 2 vars.	BK 45
Coranto a1	BK 21a
Coranto a2	BK 21b
Coranto a3	BK 21c
Volte G1. 2 vars.	BK 91 (Chappell, 169; Wooldridge, i, 232; Simpson, 237; Ward, 41)
Volte G2. L. Morley. 2 vars.	BK 90

Johnson's *Delight* Pavan and Galliard   BK 5

Dowland's *Lachrymae* Pavan   BK 54

Harding's Galliard   BK 55
                                                     (Edwards, *Sources*, ii, 171)

The March before the Battle (*The Earl of Oxford's March*) BK 93

The Battle   BK 94

The Barley Break   BK 92

Dances are denoted here, as in Chapter 10, by final and mode. The above list excludes several arrangements attributed to Byrd in the sources, one or two of them adequate run-of-the-mill jobs which Byrd could conceivably have produced on request (the *Primero* medley) or for his own interest (Parsons's In Nomine), but the majority obviously spurious. As they are in most cases represented in BK only by incipits, references to other printed editions are given below.

The most important of the doubtful arrangements is not ascribed to Byrd at all. There exists in a late manuscript a thoroughly amateurish version of Dowland's *Piper's Galliard* (BK 103; BW 19/40) impertinently attributed to Byrd. It cannot possibly be by him, but another arrangement of the same work (BK, second edition, 118) lays claim to more serious consideration. It is one of the anonymous pieces in Forster, several of which are by Byrd. Tuttle printed it (p. 80) under the misapprehension that it was a better text of the setting ascribed to Byrd. Forster's title 'If my complaints, or pypers gal' is misleading, because instrumental arrangements (the two referred to here not excepted) invariably derive from Dowland's galliard and not his vocal version of the same music. Most of the quirks in Forster's text are easily amended, though unfortunately not his omission of the varied repeat of the third strain, for which he left a blank page. An ascription to Byrd would have been perfectly credible, for the style is characteristic so far as it goes, and so is the insertion of an additional imitation in the antepenultimate bar. But as the setting is far less elaborate than the authenticated pavan and galliard arrangements the stylistic evidence is too slender for absolute certainty.

The keyboard intabulation of Parsons's famous 5-part In Nomine (BK 51), attributed to Byrd by Forster, is another borderline case. The work is singularly unsuited to the keyboard, but as Byrd's own In Nomine 5/5 shows that he shared the general admiration for it in his early years (see p. 46ff) he may have tried his hand at an arrangement at that time, with predictably clumsy results. Tuttle tentatively attributed a keyboard arrangement (BK 110; BW 20, p. 146) of Byrd's famous *Lullaby* (1588/32) to the composer, and printed it from the inferior source (p. 82ff). It contains more decoration than most of the other intabulations of Byrd songs and motets in Weelkes and Forster; Byrd could have made it, but there is no reason to suppose that he did. Nor does Forster's ascription to him of an arrangement of a short alman or toy in G (BK 109; Tuttle, 126) carry much conviction; it is hard to credit Byrd with pointlessly changing the melody of the second strain so that F♯ is followed by D instead of top G, as common sense and an anonymous lute arrangement of the same tune (Add.15117, fol. 2) require.

Byrd's name is associated with keyboard versions of two medleys. These were suite-like pieces in several sections, and in some cases at least the title carries its old sense of a combat. The most popular one was composed by one of the Johnsons; it was sometimes called the *Old medley* to distinguish it from another called the *New medley*, and was old enough to appear in a garbled form in Adriansen's *Pratum musicum* of 1584 as 'Pavane a l'englesa' (No. 16 in *Monumenta musicae belgicae* 10, ed. G. Spiessens (Antwerp, 1966)). Anonymous arrangements of both are in Forster, who attributes the Johnson work (BK 111; Tuttle, 98ff.; BW 19/24) to Byrd in a rather confused way in the index, which is in any case unreliable (see p. 178): the page reference to the medley is followed on the same line by another to a piece which Forster gives to Byrd in the body of the book, so that his name may be meant to apply only to the second reference. The arranger, whose figuration has the habit of rushing full tilt up to the final chord of a phrase and stopping dead on it, cannot have been Byrd. Another medley (BK 112), called *Primero* in some sources, is attributed to him by Tregian (No. [172], misnumbered [173] in the printed edition; also BW 18, 73ff.). The first section, like that of many battle pieces, starts with a version of a tune known in England as *All in a garden green* (not the one used by Byrd for variations), and the third derives from Janequin's *La guerre*, which also turns up in the majority of continental battles; the fourth is a trumpet piece and the fifth a setting of *The Bells of Osney*. The original was certainly not compiled by Byrd for, as the entirely different keyboard arrangement in Susanne van Soldt's manuscript (No. 33 in *Monumenta musica neerlandica* 3, ed. A. Curtis (Amsterdam, 1961)) and the version for mixed consort (Edwards, *Sources*, ii, No. 645) show, it was an artless affair of no great distinction. The arranger of the Tregian version, whether or not he was Byrd, introduced some lively touches of his own but produced some rather stiff decoration because the simplicity of each section allowed him too little scope – a limitation which restricts both the evidence for authenticity and the importance of any decision about it.

The late sources of *The Battle* contain extra pieces at the end which are certainly spurious (BK 113; My Ladye Nevells Booke, ed. H. Andrews, London, 1926, 38f.; BW 18, 126f.). One manuscript contains a meagre little *Morris* and *Soldiers' dance*. The latter is a setting of a tune usually called *Who list to lead the soldier's life* (Chappell, p. 144; Wooldridge, i, 303; Simpson, 773) which became popular in Byrd's last years at the earliest, and perhaps not till later. Two other late sources contain a setting of *The Bells of Osney* (in one case entitled *The Burying of the dead* and followed by a different, and even less convincing version of the *Soldiers' dance*). In the better source it builds up slowly in the manner of several of the *Battle* pieces and matches them in general dimensions, but it carries simplicity to extremes; it is much more wooden than the short setting of the same tune in the doubtful arrangement of the *Primero* medley, and would come oddly from the composer of *The Bells*, to which its bass relates it. Nor would he have fumbled the change from triple to duple measure at the end.

In recent years Byrd's authorship has been proposed for two short anonymous pieces, *Watkin's Ale* and the *Coranto Lady Riche* (BK, second edition, 119 and

120; Tregian Nos. [179], misnumbered [180] in the printed edition, and [265]), but it is difficult to understand what prompted either claim.

A number of dances to be considered in this chapter are arrangements of popular tunes and so stand closer to Byrd's variations than to his pavans and galliards, which are freely composed. Two of the most ambitious pieces are his G major versions of **Monsieur's Alman**, a dance found mainly in English sources, though apparently named after François Duke of Alençon, who died in 1584. Like many almans it contains two strains, and each complete statement or variation consists of two settings of A followed by two of B. Byrd adopts the same harmonic framework, which is more or less the standard one, for all his settings, and uses the melody for a good part of the time as well. This leaves him little room for development: the melody is not positive enough to give a lead, yet gets in the way of any free construction on the bass.* The first G major version contains two variations, and the second three. The possibilities offered by the theme and Byrd's approach to it last very comfortably for the duration of var. 1 of the first version (G1), but after a promising start var. 2 lapses into remarkably uninteresting quaver runs.

Version G2 is a much more elaborate affair described by Tregian as a 'variatio' of G1, but probably intended to supersede it, since Byrd included only G2 in Nevell. For once he seems to have undertaken to improve on an unsatisfactory piece without having diagnosed the cause of its defects, so that he runs into the same difficulties again. He attempts greater brilliance in var. 1, using semiquavers in the repeats of each strain, and finds himself with nothing much to add except still more semiquavers in var. 2. Even the syncopated imitation in strain II seems perfunctory and there is no sense of contrast or progress. In a desperate effort to save the day he quickens the tempo in var. 3 by changing the time signature, and plays for more direct melodic appeal. But in strain II he flags, refers back to the syncopations of var. 2 and finally introduces empty arpeggio decorations, a device he normally eschews.

Despite frequent touches that proclaim their composer, these two pieces, of which the second at least presumably belongs to his maturity, fall short of his usual standard. Nor is the third version, a single setting in C, a particularly notable work, but it is a much later one containing detail of some distinction and several of the headlong dashes from one end of the keyboard

---

*Compare what Byrd was able to do with the admittedly less unwieldy bipartite ground of the *Chi passa* when unhampered by the melody.

to the other of his post-Nevell style. Perhaps it embodies an admission that one lightweight setting was all that he should have attempted.

The nearest relative to the G major versions of *Monsieur's Alman* in Byrd's keyboard music is **The Ghost**. The tune, which is also known as the *Voice of the earth*, is nowhere referred to as an alman but is constructed in the same way. It has two repeated strains of 8 and 16 semibreves, as compared with 16 to each in *Monsieur's Alman*, over which it has the slight advantage that the second strain begins in the supertonic instead of dully in the tonic. Byrd accepts a current version of the bass* and turns his main attention to the leisurely melody, varying it with his usual grace. The piece pretends to less than the second version of *Monsieur's Alman*, but in a quiet way offers more.

Although the alman was danced at the English court as early as 1554† a settled musical tradition seems to have been slow to establish itself. The almans in the Dublin Virginal Book, copied about 1570,‡ are notated like the pavans, though their simpler character presumably implies a faster pulse. Byrd accepts this notation in all his settings of *Monsieur's Alman*, and the semiquaver divisions in vars. 1 and 2 of the second version enforce a pavan-like tempo. However, the quicker speed of var. 3 shows him conscious of having stretched its natural measure. In later almans he halves the note-values; the fastest divisions are still semiquavers, but they are equivalent to the quaver divisions in the earlier notation so that the real speed implied, as well as the notation used, is faster. This is also the situation in almans by Morley, Marchant and Tisdale. Bull and younger composers, such as Gibbons, use the same notation but no semiquavers, implying a still faster pace.

Byrd's choice of the newer notation for his setting of the **Queen's Alman** places it later than the first version, at least, of *Monsieur's Alman*. The tune, of continental origin, had become internationally popular in the 1560s; Byrd adopted both the melodic outline and a standard harmonization.§ Although its dimensions, despite appearances, exactly match those of *The Ghost*, the fact that cadential suspensions and resolutions still require, as previously, the space of a minim before the final chord shows that the faster notation really does imply a quicker pulse. The melody consequently retains its natural movement, and this enables the composer to employ some of his more usual techniques in shaping the three attractive variations.

*Corresponding with the lute version in Trinity College Dublin MS.D.1.21, p. 113.
†See J. Ward, 'Music for "A Handefull of Pleasant Delites" ', *JAMS*, x (1957), 176f.
‡See DVB, Introduction.
§But not the simplest; see J. Wendland, ' "Madre non mi far monaca": the biography of a Renaissance folksong', *Acta musicologica*, xlviii (1976), 185ff.

Thus semiquaver decoration becomes more general in the second and then recedes again in the third, where the melody moves down to the alto.

The three remaining almans, G3, g2 and C2, are all apparently original compositions. **Alman G3**, unlike the other two, employs the older convention of notation, indicating an earlier date. On this occasion Byrd did not attempt the pavan-like elaboration of his settings of *Monsieur's Alman* but emphasized the dance element, marking out the rhythm in plain left-hand chords until, in the last strain, the vigorous melody breaks bounds and sets up a fragmentary dialogue with the bass. The sheer vitality of this excellent little piece places it closer to *The Barley Break* than to the other almans.

Among the anonymous pieces in Forster there is a crudely composed alman in G minor (fol. 232′) both strains of which progress from B♭ to G, the second corresponding closely to the second half of the *romanesca* or *passamezzo antico* bass. It is certainly not by Byrd, but it may be connected in some way with his own wholly characteristic **Alman g2**, in which the bass of the first strain differs from the *romanesca*-like pattern of the Forster piece only in the postponement of the dominant by a minim. To start on a degree other than the tonic was an exceptional step for him, but in the context of a two-strain dance it would have had the attraction of avoiding tonal monotony. Since opening strains almost invariably run from tonic to tonic, a two-strain dance normally gave little opportunity for tonal digression, and it is significant that Almans G3 and C2 belong to the rarer three-strain variety.

Alman C2 is one of two anonymous almans in that key in Forster. Thanks to Tregian, Morley is known to have composed the other (*Keyboard Works*, No. 10); it is one of his best efforts, for its short strains do not overtax his uncertain formal sense in keyboard music. The two pieces resemble one another in general character, and there is some correspondence between their simple harmonic schemes up to the beginning of strain II. But wherever a direct comparison is possible, and indeed everywhere else, Morley finds himself outclassed. The other composer was undoubtedly Byrd. The piece abounds in figuration typical of his later work, and if few of the figures taken in isolation are entirely confined to his music, in context and in quantity they make a strong impression of authenticity. So do the typically late-period diversity and exactitude of detail, especially in varied repeats of already well characterized sections. Although the strains are too short to provide very much structural evidence, the acceleration in harmonic pace in the penultimate bars in strains 2 and 3 is typical of Byrd's acute feeling for gradations of this kind, particularly in strain 3 where the music tumbles downhill and almost gets out of control before it is neatly scooped up and set down safely by the cadence. His perennial concern for the top line as a formal agent makes itself felt in var. 2, where he strengthens the second statement of strain II by denying the first statement its second top G, and ends the first statement of strain III on the dominant below the usual tonic in order to give that note greater emphasis at the final cadence. This alman is more refined in workmanship than any other in the whole repertory of virginal music.

The odd title **Galliard Jig** belongs to an odd piece, probably a survivor, though not necessarily a typical one, of a vanished species. It has the 3/2 time of a galliard and a mosaic-like structure succinctly described in the commentary to BK 18 thus: 'each 8-bar section consists of 4 bars and varied repeat; section 4 is a varied repeat of section 2, and sections 5 to 8 a varied repeat of 1 to 4'. Its only near relative, and a poor one at that, is an anonymous piece without title in Mulliner based on two alternating 8-bar strains.* The long lines of Byrd's piece, surely one of the earliest selected for Nevell, recall parts of his Hornpipe, but miss its energy.

Byrd's other jigs belong to an entirely different group of works consisting of simple arrangements of popular dance tunes, and including the corantos and voltes. The partial correspondence of **Jig a1** with a little piece by Tisdale† shows its popular origin. **Coranto C1** is also called a jig in the less authoritative of the two sources. This seems the more appropriate name because the tune looks English;‡ perhaps Byrd wrote it himself. **Corantos a1–3** are settings of French tunes, as are also, presumably, **Voltes G1 and 2**. The corantos belong in sequence, for an independent lute arrangement contains their constituent eight strains in the same order.§ Byrd does little more than tidy up the tunes and harmonies of the current versions and add varied repeats. The voltes are more substantial because in addition to internal repeats he adds a complete varied statement to each dance. It is unclear whether G2 is dedicated to Lord or Lady Morley.

*It is one of the late additions to the manuscript (MB 1/2). There is one other piece, Inglott's *Galliard Ground* (Tregian No. [250]), based on a similar alternation of 8-bar strains, but it is less linear in style; much of the texture is imitative.

†No. 4 in *Tisdale's Virginal Book*, ed. A. Brown (London, 1966).

‡The editorial repeats in BK 45 are surely mistaken: the tune is an ABCC quatrain.

§In British Library, Hirsch M. 1353 (North No. 12). Coranto a1 is connected with the pavan 'Belle qui tiens ma vie' in Arbeau's *Orchésographie*, and the tune 'La dama le demanda', on which Cabezón wrote variations (MME 29/80, 81). There are arrangements of Coranto a2 in Tregian (No. [205]) and the Thysius lute book (see J. P. N. Land, 'Het Luitboek van Thysius beschreven en toegelicht', *Tijdschrift der Vereeniging voor Neder-landsche Muziekgeschiedenis*, i–iii (1884–88)).

The arrangements of other composers' pavans and galliards offered Byrd more scope than these trifles, even though he departed very rarely from their melodic outlines and never from the harmony. The certainly authentic settings contain more decoration than his own dances, because the first statement of each strain varies something already known to the contemporary listener, and the varied repeat goes a stage further. This is true even of the **Johnson's Delight Pavan and Galliard,*** the soberest of the group and, although a mature production, certainly the earliest. Various passages in this work, for instance the dance rhythms and harmonic sequences of the related third strains of both dances, are quite foreign to Byrd's style, and at one point in the pavan he seems to have lost patience with his model. In the last eight of the twenty bars of the second strain the harmony suddenly becomes sluggish, supporting a dull sequential melody that peters out altogether four bars before the end.† Byrd skilfully refashions the melodic line of the whole passage, but not without a touch of savagery in the varied repeat where he highlights his new conclusion by unnecessary impoverishment of the preceding bars (63–66).

The arrangements of **Dowland's Lachrymae Pavan** and **Harding's Galliard** belong together. The Dowland is set in D minor, a fourth higher than the original, to bring it in line with the Harding, and the two are paired in Tregian (as are other versions of the same pieces in both lute and keyboard sources). The features that distinguish the figuration in the latest works – great variety of pattern and its diffusion throughout the keyboard texture – are developed very fully here, and in Harding's Galliard the semiquaver divisions slacken the hold of the original dance measure, as scarcely happens in Byrd's own galliards. He manages this with such tact as never to do violence to the original,‡ but although the setting contains no critical element, as nearly all his musical commentaries on other men's work do, his attitude remains neutral. To *Lachrymae*, however, he responds with the

---

*Tregian names Edward Johnson as the composer at the end of his transcription of Byrd's setting. If this had Byrd's authority it is likely to be correct. There are lute arrangements ascribed to R. (Robert) and John Johnson, and a cittern part ascribed to Richard Johnson; it is unclear whether composer or arranger is meant.

†Bars 45–52. Compare the versions printed in *Early Scottish Keyboard Music*, ed. K. Elliott (London, 1967), 2f., and *An Anthology of English Lute Music*, ed. D. Lumsden (London, 1954), 21ff.; also the version for mixed consort, Edwards, *Sources*, ii, No. 717.

‡Strictly speaking the original is unknown, but the close correspondence of the 5-part consort setting in Add. 17786–91 (printed by Fellowes as No. 1 of *Eight short Elizabethan Dances* (London, 1924)) with Byrd's version shows that its melody and bass, at least, represent Harding reasonably faithfully; the only doubtful passage is at the end of the first strain where Byrd's tenor appears in the treble. These two versions establish a norm from which various others, for consort or lute, can be seen to deviate.

unmistakable sympathy that he usually reserves for popular music. The spacious pavan framework allows him room not merely for the most imaginative flights of figuration, but for far-reaching elaboration of the melody and contrapuntal reflection upon it in the manner of *O mistress mine*. His excursions away from his model do not aim at correction, like those in Johnson's *Delight*, but pay it the compliment of treating it as a source of inspiration. By comparison with such a work Farnaby's setting seems mechanical and Sweelinck's undistinguished.

Byrd's contribution to martial music, **The Battle**, must have enjoyed exceptional popularity, since it occurs in no fewer than four very late sources which can muster only two or three other genuine Byrd pieces between them – and a similar number of spurious ones. Nothing illustrates more vividly the huge losses in keyboard manuscripts, for despite its wide dissemination it is found in only one earlier source, Nevell. Byrd does not adopt the plan, standard in the innumerable continental battle pieces and medleys of the sixteenth and seventeenth centuries, of a continuous sequence of contrasted sections. The work consists of a suite of short, self-contained descriptive pieces. All are in C, but in Nevell, where it occupies fourth place, it is flanked by a *March before the Battle* and a *Galliard for the Victory* which are both in G; these are significantly numbered separately as 3 and 5. The galliard is in only one of the late sources of *The Battle*, and the march in none, though it occurs on its own in Tregian as the *Earl of Oxford's March*. It seems likely, therefore, that Byrd decided to associate the march with the *Battle* only when he was assembling material for Nevell, and then wrote the admirable galliard to balance it in the same easy, confident vein as the two grounds composed to head the collection. The *Battle* itself, which includes an *Irish march*, must allude to one of the Irish rebellions of the 1570s or early 1580s.

   The music of *The Battle* stands as a tribute to Byrd's versatility, but unlike any other sizeable work of his it has dated irrevocably. Even though he clearly did not intend it very seriously he relied, as any composer until the eighteenth century or later could, on the associations of trumpet and drum to numb his audience's normal responses for a while. In the *Trumpets* movement, for instance, the mounting excitement is most skilfully handled through 48 semibreves of C major fanfares, but it requires a considerable effort today to enter the world of toy soldiers and catch the echo that would have stirred a contemporary – and without that the music falls lifeless.

   The work opens with *The Soldiers' summons*, an agreeable little piece which lulls soldiers and listeners alike into acceptance. But the heavy C major tramp of *The March of the footmen* gives warning of the rigours to come: it contains almost four times as much tonic as dominant and almost nothing else. Byrd shows ingenuity in devising schemes for the ensuing pieces within comparable limits. *The March of the horsemen* consists of imitations on a tune also used in a piece called *A Battle and no battle*, probably by Bull, and in Dowland's *King of Denmark's Galliard*;* the bass is largely confined to tonic and dominant. After *The Trumpets* come an *Irish march* in tripla in the form of a I–IV–I–V ground,† and *The Bagpipe and the drone*, based on a tiny cantus firmus heard at the outset four times over in the treble (towards the end the pattern changes to admit a V–I cadence). The realistic style of *The flute and the drum* was widely known;‡ Byrd's contribution lay in shaping it in six lengthy 'changes'. In *The March to the fight* he attempts on a smaller scale and with limited success the kind of slow build up that he achieves in *The Bells*; the change to the dominant when 'the battels be joyned' and the ensuing helter-skelter are most welcome after sixty bars of tonic. *The Retreat* recapitulates this sequence of events very briefly, starting with dignity and ending in a rout. The battle proper ends here in Nevell, and there is no agreement beyond this point in later sources. The additional pieces found there are discussed at the head of this chapter.

The addition of the G major march and galliard in Nevell was not a happy idea. True, the first section of **The March before the Battle** is harmonically rather similar to *The March of the footmen*, but the resemblance only serves to emphasize their stylistic incompatibility. Far from scaling the popular march melody§ down to toy realism Byrd arranges it as a real-life keyboard piece in which the figuration, especially in the second of the two variations, loses nothing in military verve by acknowledging a convention, even if it cannot entirely compensate for the all-too-simple harmonic basis. In the excellent *Galliard for the Victory*, which despite its title has no

*For the Bull see MB 19/108; for the Dowland, also known as his *Battle Galliard*, see *Lachrymae*, ed. P. Warlock (London, 1927), 24, and *Collected Lute Music*, No. 40.

†Fellowes argued with some justice that four minim beats may have been lost from the later stages of this piece; see BW 18, p. xxii.

‡Following a battle piece and its saltarello in one of the sixteenth-century manuscripts of Italian keyboard music at Castell' Arquato there is a short piece in F on the same bass in the same drum rhythm as Byrd's, supporting a melody that shows the same tendency to emphasize the subdominant degree at the upper limit. Arbeau illustrates the same melodic style in the 'tabulation du fifre (ou arigot) du troisième ton', and quotes the same drum rhythm, in his *Orchésographie*. For Byrd's 'changes', not so marked in Nevell, see BW 18, 116ff.

§Simpler forms occur in Morley's *First Book of Consort Lessons* (ed. S. Beck (New York, 1959), No. 14) and the Thysius lute book.

special pictorial aim, Byrd's normal harmonic, melodic and motivic freedom returns (see p. 202); it certainly brings succour to the wounded, but in the form of forbidden fruit.

The Barley Break, which follows immediately upon the *Galliard for the Victory* in Nevell, has a closer affinity with the battle sequence than might at first appear. Its subject has been described as follows:* 'In the country game of barley-break the two couples at either end of the field attempt to change partners without being caught by the couple in the middle (called hell). The couple in the middle must hold hands while chasing the others, and if they catch any one member of an opposing couple before they meet as partners, that pair must take their place in hell.' Byrd's music takes the form of a suite of thirteen short dance-like sections, each followed by a varied repeat, but since the game could never in its nature have been formalized into a dance his aim must have been purely descriptive.

In fact a simple programme can be discerned. He starts by marshalling his six players before the fray, like the footmen, horsemen and so on in *The Battle*. They are represented by six movements, linked in pairs by the use of dance styles, the only characters available to abstract music of the time. First come two galliard movements, and since each has its own distinctive rhythmic pattern and closes in self-contained fashion in the tonic, they are clearly not holding hands. The middle pair, however, which are jigs, are closely joined, as the game requires – by a dominant cadence at the end of the first, and by greater similarity of character. The third pair, in alman style, also resemble one another; taken together they stand in the supertonic of the work, that is to say the first begins in A minor and the second ends there, but they keep their distance because the first is an arrangement of the *Browning* tune, and so closes in G, the main tonic. In the seventh section battle is joined, as plainly as though the direction were written in, with a flourish of mock trumpets. The next section is based on a melody found in many battle pieces,† with an admirable continuation of Byrd's devising. Further skirmishes follow in four very short alman-like sections cadencing in the tonic, supertonic, dominant and supertonic respectively.

Finally the players may be imagined to leave the field in the long concluding section in pavan style, pivoting on the very English tonic-supertonic axis that dominates the whole work. The fundamental structure is extra-

---

*In *The Poems of Sir Philip Sidney*, ed. W. A. Ringler (Oxford, 1962), 495. See also Chappell, 135; Wooldridge, i, 270.

†For instance, Banchieri (*Organo suonarino*, 1611), Mercure d'Orléans 1615 (*Oeuvres des Mercures*, ed. M. Rollin and J. M. Vaccaro (Paris, 1977), 54), Vallet 1616 (*Oeuvres*, ed. A. Souris (Paris, 1970), 245).

ordinarily simple, a series of six 4-bar phrases in the pattern AABABA, in which A consists of I–V–I–(I) and B of II–VI–II–(II). The A scheme is essentially that of the Hornpipe and Short Ground in G (see p. 119), though in practice the harmony in both A and B moves on after the central progression to effect a transition to the next phrase, and only remains static through the fourth bar at the final cadence. In a wonderful stroke of imagination Byrd brings the turmoil of the game to rest through the gentle rise and fall of these insistently repeated cadences. No music in the surviving repertory approaches the swiftly changing high spirits and sheer physical vitality of this delightful work, the most important, apart from the late Dowland and Harding settings and Alman C2, to be discussed in this chapter.

10
Keyboard Pavans and Galliards

a1 Pavan		Galliard	BK 14
a2 Pavan: the Earl of Salisbury		Galliard 1	BK 15
		Galliard 2	
a3 Pavan		Galliard	BK 16
a4 Pavan			BK 17
Bb1 Pavan		Galliard	BK 23
C1 Pavan		Galliard	BK 30
C2 Pavan: Kinborough Good		Galliard	BK 32
C3 Pavan		Galliard	BK 33
C4 Galliard: Mary Brownlow			BK 34
c1 Pavan		Galliard	BK 29
c2 Pavan		Galliard	BK 31
d1 Pavan		Galliard	BK 52
d2 Galliard			BK 53

F1 Pavan: Bray [music] Galliard [music] BK 59

F2 Pavan: Ph. Tr. [music] Galliard [music] BK 60

G1 Quadran Pavan and Galliard (see p. 115) BK 70

G2 Pavan [music] Galliard [music] BK 71

G3 Pavan [music] Galliard [music] BK 72

G4 Pavan [music] Galliard [music] BK 73

G5 Pavan: Echo [music] Galliard [music] BK 114

G6 Pavan: Canon [music] BK 74

G7 Pavan: Lady Monteagle [music] BK 75

G8 Pavan [music] BK 76

G9 Galliard [music] BK 77

G10 Galliard for the Victory [music] BK 95

g1 Passing Measures Pavan and Galliard (see p. 115) BK 2

g2 Pavan: Sir William Petre [music] Galliard [music] BK 3

g3 Pavan [music] Galliard [music] BK 4

In this list the pieces have been grouped according to their finals, as far as possible in conformity with BK; major modes are indicated by capital letters, minor by lower case. Each group starts with pavan and galliard pairs followed by separate pavans and separate galliards, and each sequence is arranged by source in the following order of preference: Nevell, Parthenia, Weelkes, Tregian, Forster, others. An exception has been made for the two works on passamezzo basses, which head their respective groups; they are discussed in Chapter 7 but are listed here because Byrd included the *Passing Measures* among the other pavans and galliards in Nevell. The *Galliard for the Victory*, from Nevell, is placed after the G major galliard from Forster because no source transmits it as a fully independent work. Byrd's arrangements of pavans and galliards by Johnson, Dowland and Harding are dealt with in Chapter 9.

Perhaps as a result of writing Byrd's name so often against his many pavans and galliards, copyists presented him with several more that he would certainly not have welcomed as his own. These are omitted from the foregoing list; as they are represented only by incipits in BK, references to printed editions are given in the following brief account of them. Pavan and Galliard in C (BK 100; Tuttle, 55ff.; BW 19/23), the only presumably false ascription to Byrd in Weelkes: in the pavan each strain makes for the cadence before anything has been achieved, and the galliard recapitulates it in unequal strains of 5, 4 and 6 bars respectively; it is difficult to believe that Byrd could have produced this poverty-stricken work at any period, unless in a satirical spirit, but oddly enough it seems to have some connection with the two pavan and galliard pairs that immediately follow it in the manuscript – G4 (a weak but apparently authentic work) and C1 (given anonymously).

Pavan and Galliard in A minor (BK 99; Tregian [173, 174], misnumbered [174, 175] in the printed edition): the pavan is a poor arrangement of No. 35 from Holborne's *Pavans, Galliards, Almains . . . in five parts*, 1599, and is wrongly associated with the galliard, a variant text of which is found anonymously with a different pavan (not printed) in Paris, Bibliothèque Nationale, Rés. 1186; the simple, often chordal style of this pavan is remote from Byrd, like the broken-backed structure of strains I and III of the galliard and its frequent passages in parallel tenths between melody and bass. Pavan in C (BK 101; Tregian [256]): ragged in style, uncontrolled in form and incompetent in harmony (e.g. the move from a 6–4 on II to another on VI in strain II). Sir John Gray's Galliard (BK 104; Tregian [191]), ascribed to 'W.B.': the initials fit the name of William Byrd, among others, but the strumming left hand, the parallel tenths and seventeenths, and the treble pedal in strain III do not.

Galliard in G (BK 105; Tuttle, 96f.; BW 19/33), attributed to Byrd at a rather confused point in the index to Forster, although its companion pavan was left anonymous: if anything this pair is even emptier than the C major pieces in Weelkes (BK 100). It is followed by the spurious arrangement of Johnson's Medley (see p. 166), which Fellowes printed as a pavan and galliard (BW 19/24).

Pavan and Galliard in A minor (BK 98; Tuttle, 40ff.; BW 19/20) in New York Public Library, Drexel 5612: there is no reason why Byrd should not have adopted figuration used by younger contemporaries or written for a keyboard of wider compass in a late work, but he would have remained incapable of the feeble construction of strain I of the pavan, the flimsy 3-part writing of strain II, or the repetitious character of strain III of the galliard; the composer of these pieces thought primarily in very simple harmonic terms, using few suspensions, and he had a trick of filling out a rhythmic pattern by moving to another chord and then straight back to the first (pavan III, galliard I and II) which is very rare in Byrd (see beginning of Galliard c1/III). Pavan in F (BK 102; Morley, *Keyboard Works*, No. 1) in Drexel 5612: the ascriptions of this piece, which is by Morley, and of

Byrd's Pavan and Galliard F2 have simply been transposed in the manuscript. The so-called galliard in F in Christ Church 1175 (BK 108; Tuttle, 79; BW 19/36), really a very crude alman, is attributed in Rés. 1186 to Mr Lever.

A pavan and a pair of galliards preserved only in lute sources are highly unlikely to go back to originals by Byrd, the pavan (North No. 9) because, apart from anything else, the three strains contain 10, 11 and 10 bars respectively, and the galliards (North Nos. 10, 11), which are in any case only attributed to 'W.B.', because they rely heavily on bar-by-bar rhythmic repetition and the second has an untypical cantus-firmus-like melody in strain III. Byrd is given as composer and Cutting as arranger of a lute version of Morley's A minor pavan (*Keyboard Works* No. 5) in Cambridge University Library, Dd.9.33 (North No. 8); the ascription appears to belong to the preceding piece, an arrangement by Cutting of Byrd's Pavan F1 which bears Cutting's name only (North No. 2b).

Tomkins possessed a pavan and galliard in F by Byrd dedicated to Sir Charles Somerset (see MB 5, p. 158). This may be lost, but was possibly the F2 pair, a late work that would fit in with the other pavans and galliards in Tomkins's list, which are all relatively late: G1, G5 and g2. Tregian labelled F2 'Ph. Tr.', which has been interpreted as Philippa Tregian (see E. Cole, 'Seven Problems of the Fitz-william Virginal Book', *Proceedings of the Royal Musical Association*, 79 (1952–53), 56); if correct this may not have been Byrd's original title, for Tregian rechristened *Hugh Aston's Ground* 'Tregian's Ground'.

The following conventions are adopted in this chapter. A 'bar' means a semibreve in pavans (regardless of whether the BK text is barred in semibreves or breves), and a dotted semibreve in galliards. A '16-bar pavan' is one that contains sixteen semibreves in each strain; similarly an '8-bar galliard' contains eight dotted semi-breves in each strain. The three strains of each dance are numbered I, II and III, the two halves of each strain are lettered a and b, and the repeats are denoted by a superscript stroke. Thus the decorated repeat of the second half of the second strain in the William Petre Galliard is referred to as Galliard g2/IIb'.

The Pavans and Galliards in Nevell

No feature of My Lady Nevell's Book shows Byrd's guiding hand more clearly than the selection and arrangement of the first nine pavans and galliards (the tenth pair stands apart, having been added as an afterthought near the end of the manuscript). The sequence is laid out with the regard for symmetry and variety that he habitually brought to the planning of a set of variations. The first six pavans are each followed by a galliard. Nos. 1, 3 and 5 are solemn works in minor modes (c1, a1 and c2) with sixteen bars to the strain. Of Nos. 2, 4 and 6, all in the major, 2 and 4 (G2 and C1) are lighter pieces in 8-bar strains; No. 6 (C2) matches the minor mode pavans in dimensions and weight, and closes the first group. Nos. 7 and 8 (G6 and a4), though also 16-bar pavans, differ in having no galliards. The great *Passing Measures* pair (g1) crowns the series.

The equal distribution of mode in Nos. 1–8 goes beyond the simple alternation of major and minor. In his keyboard pavans and galliards Byrd adopts the Dorian form of C, D and G minor, never allowing the chord of the sixth degree in any prominent position, whereas in Aeolian (except in the Earl of Salisbury pieces) he constantly uses F major as the starting point for a new strain or a new phase within a strain – a feature which contributes more to the individual flavour of the mode in these pieces than the choice of secondary cadence degrees. In the G major works, F major characterizes the Mixolydian mode (except in Lady Monteagle's Pavan and, of course, the *Quadran*) in precisely the same way; by contrast the chord of the flat seventh degree occurs only incidentally, if at all, in the B♭, C and F major pieces, all of which are Ionian. Byrd selected two pavans in each mode to make up the first eight in Nevell: Nos. 1 and 5 are Dorian (c_1, c_2), 2 and 7 Mixolydian (G_2, G_6), 3 and 8 Aeolian (a_1, a_4), and 4 and 6 Ionian (C_1, C_2).*

According to Tregian Byrd's Pavan c_1 was 'the first that ever he made', and among his more important pavans it undoubtedly stands out as the earliest in style. It was not mere coincidence that led Byrd to place it first in Nevell, for the next three 16-bar pavans seem to follow on in something like chronological order. This is not to say that chronology would have appealed to Byrd as a deliberate principle of arrangement, but having developed his ideas by stages he would naturally have tended to think of the works that embodied them in sequence. Although he broke the sequence by inserting the two 8-bar examples (Nos. 2 and 4) for the sake of diversity and by leaving the two that lacked galliards (Nos. 7 and 8) till later, an unmistakable progression leads from No. 1 to Nos. 5 and 6 by way of 3. Discussion of the galliards associated with these four pavans will best be postponed.

*In certain, mostly later works these distinctions become harder to draw. In g_3, an out-and-out Dorian work, the persistent sharp sixths rule out any opening or cadence on the third degree, whereas g_2 makes great play with it, as do d_1 and d_2 (in which strain II' even opens on the Aeolian sixth). Consequently these works, which all have Aeolian key signatures, sound Aeolian by comparison with g_3, even though the flat sixth loses its characteristic prominence in transposition. Elsewhere in Byrd, however, less equivocal transpositions occur: the D minor keyboard fantasia is Aeolian, and the pavan and galliard for 6-part consort are in Mixolydian C. An additional feature in Byrd's use of the modes may also be noted. The natural tendency of the note B to flatten intermittently colours the modes on A, G (with major third) and C, though not their transpositions. In C it leads to a decorative Mixolydian element. In the A and G modes, apart from playing a necessary role in relation to F♮, it makes more striking contributions: in the first it introduces Phrygian seconds in the cadential flourishes (Pavan and Galliard a_1, *Hugh Aston's Ground*), and in the second the flat mediant (Pavan G6/III) or flat sixth to the dominant (reprises in the *Quadran* Galliard).

An additional circumstance, apart from its evident early date, makes Pavan c1 the natural starting point for a study of Byrd's keyboard pavans: its survival in an earlier version for 5-part consort. One or two other pavans such as a4 and B♭1 (with its galliard) probably originated as consort pieces; but no such versions have survived, so that an important stage in Byrd's development of the genre is represented by c1 alone. Of all instrumental forms dance music had, for practical reasons, always migrated most freely from one medium to another.* No doubt a band of instruments provided the best accompaniment for dancing, but in its absence a keyboard player or lutenist could make up to some extent for his instrument's smaller tone and lack of sustaining power with broken harmonic figures and melodic decoration. There is little evidence that an independent keyboard style for dance music had grown up in England before Byrd's time. Newman's pavan in the Mulliner Book (MB 1/116) looks like an intabulation of a consort dance, and so do some of the pavans in the Dublin Virginal Book – indeed, the consort original of one of these (DVB/21) is preserved in the Thomas Wood part-books (MB 15/78). Although Byrd clearly conceived his keyboard pavans and galliards primarily as abstract compositions rather than dance music, various formal elements fundamental to his long development of these forms derive from the types of consort dance current during his earlier years.

The largest collection of dances of the period in an English source is contained in Roy. App. 74. All are anonymous, but the titles of some suggest a continental origin. The pavans vary considerably in style and quality. Some embody canons of various kinds, and although none remotely resembles Byrd's canonic example (G6) they show that the principle was already familiar. Of the others, two claim attention for their greater intrinsic interest and their relevance to Byrd; they have been published by Nathalie Dolmetsch.† The first is a 4-part piece to which an unwanted quintus partus has been added by a later scribe. Like the 4-part pavan from the Wood part-books, with which they may be conveniently associated, both pieces make considerable use of imitation. This circumstance does not brand them as English, but it makes Italian provenance rather unlikely because Italian dance music generally favoured simple textures. There is, for instance, no imitation beyond the occasional echoing of passing-note figures in four 5-part pavans by Italian immigrants to England that survive in one of

---

*See for instance the parallel texts of a pavan in versions for consort, keyboard and lute from Attaignant's collections in D. Heartz, 'Les styles instrumentaux dans la musique de la renaissance' (Jacquot, *Musique instrumentale*, 67f.).

†*Two 16th-century Pavans for five viols* (Cambridge, 1970). Unfortunately the edition is none too accurate.

Tregian's score books (Egerton 3665).* In other respects these pieces – two by Augustin Bassano and one each by the elder Ferrabosco and Joseph Lupo – have a good deal in common with the three anonymous pavans singled out above. All, except perhaps the second published by Dolmetsch and the Ferrabosco, were either originally composed in four parts or devised by composers who thought more naturally in four parts than in five, and all are built in 16-bar strains subject to the same types of structural treatment.

It is in structural matters that these pavans bear on Byrd most closely. There are three main types of strain, differentiated by the treatment of the first eight bars. The first may have developed through the extension of 8-bar strains to 16, for it is characterized by an intermediate cadence at bar 7, the point where the final cadence would fall in an 8-bar strain. Whether or not the harmony remains static throughout bars 7 and 8, the cadence rhymes with the final one at bar 15 and creates a kind of couplet. (In a pavan the final harmony of each strain is almost always reached at the beginning of the penultimate bar,† no matter how many bars the strain may contain.) It will be convenient to call this the 'twin cadence' pattern, the identity referring, of course, to the position of the cadences, not their nature. The second type of strain in its most typical form opens with two matching 4-bar phrases governed by melody rather than harmony, though cadences often fall at the beginning of each new phrase (at bars 5 and 9) and serve to articulate the melody. In the third type there is no clear caesura in the middle, though usually some element from the other types – an unemphatic or interrupted cadence beneath the surface at bar 7 or an initial 4-bar phrase – helps the music to keep its bearings.‡

To Byrd, whose early cantus firmus compositions already show his interest in stanza-like patterns as a structural element in textless composition, this tradition had much to offer. The first two metrical schemes outlined above provided a framework firm enough to carry far greater contrapuntal elaboration and cadential variety than his predecessors had attempted, and the third category showed that the conventions of the first two were well enough known for new schemes involving their partial suppression or contradiction to be readily understood. The pavan, with its attendant galliard,

---

*The early 1570s have been suggested as a likely date for these pieces, because all three composers were in London then (see Edwards, *Sources*, i, 16). This was, of course, also the time of Byrd's return to London.

†There are only two exceptions in Byrd: Pavans G7/III and B♭/II.

‡Examples of the first type: Dolmetsch 1/II, Dolmetsch 2/II and III, Bassano 1/I and III, Ferrabosco /II; of the second: Dolmetsch 2/I, Bassano 1/II, Bassano 2/III, Ferrabosco /III; of the third: Wood /I (with weak cadence at bar 7), Bassano 2/II and Lupo /III (beginning with 4-bar phrase).

came to occupy the sort of place in Byrd's output that the sonnet might hold for a poet; during a period of some forty years he returned to it more often than to any other form without risk of exhausting its possibilities.

The consort version of **Pavan c1** bears the characteristic marks of his more ambitious early work: the adoption of elements from more than one quarter, clear declarations of intent, and some uncertainty in execution. The music, which is conceived from the outset in five parts, resembles the Wood and Dolmetsch anonymous consort pavans in making considerable use of imitation. The motives – one to each strain – are mostly shorter; their brevity enables them to move freely through the five parts, intensifying the character of the music without attempting to govern the whole contrapuntal texture, and prevents them from falling into sequential patterns geared to the larger metrical structure.*

In tonal organization, on the other hand, the piece stands much nearer the Italian pavans. The three-strain pavan having presumably developed from the two-strain variety, strain II in some earlier examples still ends in the tonic.† In three of the four Italian pavans this weakness is remedied: strain II neither begins nor ends in the tonic. Byrd goes one better in c1/II, admitting no tonic harmony at all in the whole strain. The tonic has, of course, been well established in strain I, which opens and closes there – the procedure in the great majority of Byrd's pavans and galliards.‡ His treatment of tonality in the second strain is not always so extreme as here, for he occasionally begins in the tonic; but he never closes there§ and the tonic returns at the beginning of III in only about a third of his dances. In short, there is always a tonal excursion, but the placing and duration vary.

In Pavan c1/I Byrd seems to have aimed at the twin cadence type of structure with corresponding cadences at bars 7 and 15, but he made a miscalculation which betrays his inexperience: on a characteristic impulse to give melody the leading role he devised a symmetrical bipartite melody which throws the harmonic scheme out by requiring a half close too soon,

---

*Compare, for instance, Dolmetsch 2/I and III.

†Dolmetsch 2 and Bassano 1 are examples: Dolmetsch 1 has no third strain.

‡The only exceptions: at the opening, Pavans a3, a4, C1, G6 (the first two showing Phrygian leanings); at the close, Galliards a1, d2, g3 (and the second a2, influenced by its two two-strain companions, in which the tonal balance is naturally different).

§Openings in the tonic: Pavans C1, G6 (both compensating for a first strain that opens irregularly on a degree other than the tonic), G2, G3, g2, g3, and Galliards d2 (but not the repeat), F1. The nearest approaches to tonic closes are the tonic chords in Galliards a1 and d1 occasioned by half closes in the subdominant, and a half close in the tonic in Galliard c2 (as distinct from the plagal approach to the dominant at this point in Pavans a3 and a4).

at bar 6. The motive with which both halves of the melody begin is un-obtrusively worked twice into each part in the consort version, but owing to the melodic domination imitation only comes to the fore in II. Here the new subject, foreshadowed in the bass at the end of I, becomes a kind of bass ostinato, as well as providing a sequence in the melody. Its descending intervals, inhabiting the new tonal region of B♭, bring the kind of shift in feeling that gives such assurance to Byrd's formal articulation in the pavans, and indeed in all his music. Here, however, in his concern to establish character through close imitation he perhaps places too much faith in the power of the interrupted cadence at bar 7 and the symmetrical bass line to hold the 16-bar period in shape. Strain III shows similar strengths and limitations. After recalling the opening of I Byrd develops a jagged crotchet phrase as the basis of a concluding phase which, though admirably judged in character, simply fills in its allotted span without following up the first 4-bar period with any effective structural consequent.

In its structural clarity and relatively spare textures **Pavan a1**, the next 16-bar pavan in Nevell (No. 3), exactly counterbalances Pavan c1. Whether it likewise originated as a consort piece may be doubted: the imitative figures in II and III, though of similar stamp to those in Pavan c1, never appear in the bass, as they might be expected to do in consort writing, while the keyboard is suggested more positively by the rather different imitative procedures in I. This strain unfolds in primarily harmonic and melodic terms, the harmony marking out an unequivocal scheme of 4×4 bars supporting a beautiful and by no means foursquare melodic line that first climbs slowly to the subdominant by way of a striking shift from flat to sharp mediant, and later falls back from high dominant to tonic. Within this framework imitation emerges from incidental decoration (treble bar 2, tenor bar 3) and gradually expands in leisurely dialogue to embrace all four parts in the second half of the strain.

Strain II rectifies the weakness of c1/I, cadencing in bar 7 instead of 6, and emphasizes the symmetrical structure with an identical opening to each half, moving from the chord of the Aeolian sixth to the tonic in the first half and in the second to a striking full close in what is essentially the dominant minor. The melodic climax reached here is immediately capped in the second bar of III by the only top A in the piece, and the rest of the strain is occupied by a long, marvellously controlled melodic descent; below this the bass of bars 1–6, with the middle parts that it supports, are transposed a fourth down with very little change in bars 9–14 – a device Byrd never used again.*

---

*But Bassano transposed the first half of the bass in his Pavan 1/III up a fifth in the second half beneath a less symmetrical melody.

At some date that is hard to determine this pavan underwent revision.*
Both versions are for keyboard, but some of the changes resemble those
made in Pavan c1 when it was transferred to the keyboard. The imitative
motives in the first two strains of the consort version of this work employ
only minims and semibreves. In order to preserve their contrapuntal identity
in the chordal textures that they inevitably induce in the keyboard version,
Byrd introduced dotted notes in many of the entries in I and shortened
upbeats in II. In the decorated repeats, which had no counterparts in the
consort original, he went further, turning the upbeats to the motives in
both strains into scalar flourishes. (In III, where the difficulty did not arise,
the close polyphony in any case left little room for decoration.) Strain III of
Pavan a1 shows how close he still was to the consort tradition when he wrote
the piece. The imitative subject is of the same type as that in Pavan c1/II,
and although he sometimes shortened the upbeat in the first version he did
not avoid rhythmic stagnation. He overcame this in the revision by shortening the upbeat more consistently and by bringing forward a number of
features from the decorated repeat – a procedure from which the rather bare
textures of II also benefited.

The repeats of I and II typify two approaches to decoration that Byrd was
to use constantly. In I much of the polyphonic texture is swept away in
favour of quick runs and figuration, so that only the fundamental harmonic
progression and at most the outline of the treble melody remain. The
procedure in II is the exact contrary: the imitation is not only preserved but
its effect intensified by consistent elaboration of the subject.

Whatever the shortcomings of the earlier version of Pavan a1, Byrd
achieved in it a structural assurance that laid the foundation for all the finest
16-bar pavans of his earlier maturity. His next task was to regain a richness
of content comparable to that of c1, but better suited to the keyboard. He
achieved this by replacing density of imitative polyphony with diversity of
material. Thus whereas each strain of Pavan c1 (and also of a1, with the
partial exception of I) had relied on a single motive, every half strain in c2
and C2 (Nos. 5 and 6 in Nevell) except C2/III employs a fresh one. Unlike
the imitative work in c1 this more varied treatment is never cultivated as an
end in itself, but remains subservient to the over-all design; despite occasional
appearances to the contrary it is mainly harmonic and melodic factors that

*The two versions are printed in parallel in BK. Nevell contains the earlier, but the
revision is already in Weelkes and very likely predates the compilation of Nevell. Perhaps
Byrd had no copy of the revision available to send to Baldwin – he certainly provided him
with a poor copy of Pavan and Galliard G2 (see BK commentary).

guide the course of the music. In Pavans c2 and C2, as in a1, the highest melodic point comes in the last strain,* in both cases in bar 2 of the second half prior to a descent to a final cadence that fully reestablishes the tonic for the first time since the end of I.

All three strains of **Pavan c2** use the twin cadence plan to support a melodic antecedent and consequent. The three antecedents, which are all interrelated, reach E♭, E♭ and F respectively; the consequents, which are more varied, reach F, F, and G. It is a subordinate question for the structure, dependent on the needs of the moment, whether the melodic character shall be reflected in the lower parts by means of regular imitation, as in Ib, IIIb and, less pervasively, in Ia, or merely in echoes of the salient motive from the melody, as in IIa and b, or not at all, as in IIIa. Only in IIIb is imitation allowed much scope: it starts independently after the first cadence at bar 7 and momentarily breaks the predominance of the top line. In some of the repeats the picture changes: echoes are worked into IIIa′ to compensate for the loss of some in IIa′ through an invasion of semiquaver runs. These dominate the strain up to the mid-point and so throw into relief the soberly decorated exchanges of the second half. The two types of decoration found here had appeared separately in a1/I′ and II′ respectively. Their combination in the two halves of a twin cadence strain became a favourite device of Byrd's, and a highly effective one; he used it in both earlier and later works than c2.†

In Pavan c2 then, Byrd planned all three strains on similar lines but varied the texture. In **Pavan C2** he adopted the opposite course, constructing each strain differently but using imitation throughout. The pattern of I is the same as in each strain of c2: a twin cadence structure carries a melodic antecedent and consequent reaching F and G respectively. The antecedent becomes the first entry in a 4-part imitative exposition; the consequent, which follows at the upbeat to bar 9, takes third place in a new exposition.

The design of II is entirely different; the melody makes a long descent, from top G in bar 3 (compare Pavan a1/III), for which the twin cadence pattern would not serve because a caesura would engender an inappropriate sense of renewal. Byrd devises a slacker yet controlled structure of the greatest ingenuity. He defines the first half of the strain by means of pairs of imitative entries at bars 1, 3 and 5 which set up a 2-bar rhythmic ostinato. The series continues with a pair at bar 7, but a similar pair of entries having intervened at bar 6, the rhythmic pattern is overlaid, and further obscured by a final

---

*The melodic peaks are anticipated or even overreached in the repeats of earlier strains, but Byrd evidently did not regard decoration as structural in this context.

†Cf. G3/I′, a4/II′, B♭/I′ (and II′), F1/II′.

single entry at bar 8. The prolongation of the harmony of this bar through the first half of bar 9 finally extinguishes the sense of movement imparted by the ostinato. At this point a new figure, derived from the old but more restricted in rhythm and compass, takes up the thread and draws it to the close through seven bars of level dialogue over a scarcely moving bass.

After this III has a good deal of ground to make up to overtop the previous strains, and not much time to do it in. The action tightens in very clear 4-bar phrases, and the melody rises quickly to D in bar 2, then F in bar 7 (not 6) and finally A in bar 10, the sense of urgency enhanced by an imitative entry in every bar till after the melodic peak. The repeats, unlike those of c2, accept the imitative structure as they find it, and elaborate the subjects in the three strains respectively with semiquavers, quavers, and slower figures.

Pavans Nos. 7 and 8 in Nevell (G6 and a4) belong to the same line of development as those already considered, but they embody special technical features which make their place in it more difficult to determine. **Pavan a4** contains passages of consistent 5-part texture that must derive from a consort original, though a later one than that of c1. Strain II, with its twin cadences and imitations based successively on the melodic antecedent and consequent, recalls c2 and C2, but the piece as it stands is less elaborately organized. The recurrent use of phrases culminating in the same sequence of notes CDEFE (in Ia, IIa, IIIa and b) inhibits variety of treatment, and the full harmonic textures that give the piece its special distinction allow limited scope to the varied repeats. The calculated effect of harmonic stagnation at the centre of III is less well judged than the comparable moment in C2/II and reinforces the impression of an earlier date.

Pavan G6 is constructed entirely upon a canon between treble and alto at the fifth below and at the distance of two semibreves. Here again there are 5-part textures, especially in III, which might suggest a consort original, particularly as the lower canonic part often passes uncomfortably from one hand to the other. But even those among the pavans under discussion which were not originally conceived as consort pieces inherit their polyphonic style from consort writing, so that the inclusion of a canonic part of a kind which, however integral to the texture, was traditionally regarded as additional would inevitably lead to rather full part-writing. Various features in the present work point to the surviving text as the original: it is difficult to believe that the inspired repeats formed no part of the original conception, and the confident use of idiosyncratic and somewhat dissonant counterpoint, especially in Ib and IIIb, recalls the keyboard style of the *Quadran* Pavan rather than consort writing. Any affinity with the *Quadran* would seem to place the piece among the later compositions in Nevell, certainly no earlier than the 1580s. Such a date is supported by other evidence. The work draws to some extent on one of Byrd's earlier pavans (G3; see p. 199), a procedure paralleled only in the rather later Pavans g2 and F1, and it is more complex in structure than any other of the first eight in Nevell.

Strain I employs a modification of the twin cadence pattern. The earlier cadence falls in bar 8, splitting the difference between the normal position (bar 7) and bar 9, to which the canonic interval of two bars might be expected to postpone it. Byrd accordingly keeps the antecedent rather short to allow its canonic dependent to end at bar 8; the lengthy consequent begins correspondingly early and rises fairly quickly to a top G, though on a weak beat. The pivotal feature of the antecedent, a fourth rising to a suspension in bars 4–5, is echoed a tone higher at precisely the same point in the antecedent in II, a correspondence which serves to emphasize a turn to the supertonic region, I having been largely taken up with establishing the tonic after an unusual opening on the dominant minor. But Byrd does not intend the more intense beginning of II to prepare a challenge to the high G in the previous strain; that must wait till III. He makes the consequent to the exact measure of the antecedent, incorporating the pivotal feature at the corresponding point and at the same pitch and brings the music to rest smoothly on the dominant.

The melody of III scarcely gives the usual impression of dividing into antecedent and consequent, because the break occurs even earlier than in I. The first phrase in the upper canonic part ends at bar 5, underpinned by a subdominant cadence, after which the second swiftly reaches top G in bar 8. The arrival of this melodic peak strikes with extraordinary force. In the first place the subdominant cadence has led the listener to expect a second 4-bar period followed by some kind of caesura (perhaps in the form of a matching cadence at bar 9), so that the enjambement creates a sharp sense of dislocation. At the same time the harmony, having started from the Mixolydian seventh (the lowest point it has touched) and climbed as steeply as the melody through subdominant and tonic minor to the dominant in bar 7, further enhances the effect of the top G with a powerful vi chord.

This harmonization, like the phraseology at this point, derives its peculiar emphasis from the subdominant cadence at bar 5, which creates with the ensuing tonic minor a transient episode in Mixolydian C. One of Byrd's unmistakable fingerprints is his use, especially in later works, of iii chords with F♯ in Mixolydian as an astringent corrective to the mode's natural subdominant leanings; there is an example, coupled with a suspension, in bar 13 of the strain under discussion. The vi chord in bar 8 acquires the same quality through its corrective B♮, but in even greater measure precisely because its function as a local iii chord is so unexpected. After this climax normal scansion reasserts itself by means of a guiding rhythm ♩ ♩ ♯♩|♯♩ ♩| that takes hold of the music almost imperceptibly on its appearance in the melody in bars 9–10 and descends through the canonic alto to the tenor, supported by harmonic progressions of the utmost subtlety.

Before turning to the two 8-bar pavans in Nevell it will be useful to consider the galliards belonging to Pavans c1, a1, c2 and C2. The traditional way of composing a galliard to follow a pavan was to boil the same material down into half the number of 3/2 bars. The rule was not applied universally. The Dublin Virginal Book, for instance, contains two possible exceptions (Nos. 21, 22 and 26, 27), although the association here of these more or less unrelated pairs of dances may be fortuitous; the other pairs in the manuscript are closely linked. Apart from DVB/21 only two of the pavans singled out above (p. 181 f) for comparison with Byrd's early examples are followed by galliards. These are the two by Bassano; the second is irregular in having eleven instead of eight bars to each strain, but both are exactly modelled on their pavans and can have cost their author very little effort.* Out of his experience of these traditions Byrd adopted two principles to which he adhered in all his galliards without exception. As in the pavans he accepted a foursquare number of bars as his structural basis; the 8-bar strain treated as a couplet or as a short quatrain could withstand the stress of the most varied shifts of emphasis, as well as all manner of rhythmic displacements – especially the interplay of 3/1 (hemiola) and 6/4 with the basic 3/2. On the other hand, although as time went on he showed increasing concern for the congruence of his galliards with their pavans, every one is a new piece with its own melodic and tonal scheme.

In the earlier galliards he is out to emphasize this independence. **Galliard c1** probably goes back to a consort original like the pavan, with which it shares certain characteristics. Although the weight of imitation in the pavan could not be matched in the context of galliard style, there are frequent echoes of the melody in the lower parts of I and III (sometimes partially obscured by the keyboard texture),† and in II some imitations on a counter-

---

*An anonymous composer of about the same time can be seen deriving a galliard from a pavan as a matter of routine in Roy. App. 76 (Edwards, *Sources*, ii, Nos. 487, 567). Having written out his 4-part pavan (fol. 44) he reduces the melody and bass to triple metre (fol. 43′) and then rewrites them (fol. 48′), filling in the two purely harmonic middle parts.

†And further obscured, of course, in the lute and cittern arrangements, where traces of an earlier version may perhaps survive. The three different lute arrangements (North

subject (asymmetrically placed in bars 2 and 5). The only direct references between the two dances, however, are supplied by the beginning of strain III of the pavan, which contributes the first phrase of the galliard and the idea of repeated chords at the beginning of its third strain. Here Byrd shows his anxiety to avoid too close a correspondence: strain II of both pieces having ended on the dominant he begins III a tone lower in the galliard than in the pavan.

The relation of **Galliard a1** to its pavan is also largely confined to general matters. It reflects the lean textures and structural clarity of the pavan; imitation is entirely excluded and the design centres on three top Gs – one on the strong beat of bar 5 in each strain – harmonized respectively by the three possible triads of C major, G major and E minor.*

In the c2 and C2 pairs technical affinity as a means of linking the two dances comes to the fore; melodic ties, especially in the first strains, are also closer, but of secondary importance. Accordingly the exploration of formal symmetry found in Pavan c2 is pursued in the galliard, where the principle is carried to extremes, and Galliard C2 inherits the contrapuntal pre-occupations of its pavan. Each strain of **Galliard c2** is built up through repetition of a strongly characterized rhythmic cell. The 2-bar cells of the outer strains make up quatrains that differ from the similarly constructed c1/I and a1/III only in their emphasis on regularity, but the use of a single-bar cell in the middle strain has no precedent in the earlier pieces.

At first sight it may seem contradictory that Byrd should have employed two subjects to the strain instead of one in Pavan c2, and yet narrowed the range of melodic elements in the galliard. His aim, however, was the same in both: to increase eventfulness. Eight bars in galliard style as he then conceived it could not accommodate the antithesis between antecedent and consequent possible in a 16-bar pavan strain, and the sense of cumulation attainable in a simple melodic statement was obviously limited. The key to

No. 5a, b and c) and the two for cittern (in Holborne's *Cittharn Schoole* of 1597 and Cambridge University Library MS. Dd.4.23) agree to differ from Byrd's keyboard version in three small matters (for Holborne's version see *The Complete Works of Anthony Holborne*, Vol. 2, ed. M. Kanazawa (Cambridge, Mass., 1973), No. 41). In bar 2 of III all insert a passing D between the first two bass notes, making a rhythmic sequence with the second half of the bar; in bar 7 of III all except North No. 5b pass straight from the tonic harmony to the dominant without an intervening fourth degree in the bass; and in bar 1 of II all except Dd.4.23 have E♭ instead of C as the second melodic note. Moreover, a consort version by Byrd would have lacked decorated repeats, like the cittern arrangements; the lute arrangements have them, but they are unrelated to those in Byrd's keyboard version. However, since none of the sources antedate the 1590s they may simply record changes arising from the aural transmission of a popular piece.

*The chord of the Aeolian sixth at the beginning of II in both dances serves as a link, but the same feature occurs in Galliard a3 and Pavan a4.

expansion of content therefore lay in a more developmental style of writing, on the basis of relatively short, sharply characterized motives or rhythmic patterns. Generally speaking structure becomes tauter as subdivision increases, in the following ascending sequence: unbroken melodic span, couplet of dissimilar 4-bar lines (c1/II and III, a1/II), couplet of similar lines (a1/I), quatrain of 2-bar lines (see above), strain developed from single-bar cell (with more potential for the future than appears in c2/II). It will emerge in the course of this chapter that although Byrd used the quatrain all his life he never went beyond it in the scale outlined here in his earlier galliards, and never below it in his later ones.

A comparison of c1 with a1 shows how quickly his feeling for these gradations developed: in the latter the most relaxed strain occurs in the middle and the tautest at the end. Nor did his treatment of the quatrain remain unchanged. Ex. 54a and c* show the very similar melodies of the

Ex. 54

a. Galliard c1/I

b. Galliard c1/III

c. Galliard C2/I

d. Galliard C2/III

first strains of Galliard c1 and **Galliard C2**. The earlier is the more self-contained and consorts well with c1/III (Ex. 54b), another enclosed melody constructed with so little repetition of any kind that its second half is free virtually to recapitulate that of I. By contrast the melody of C2/I is planned with a view to development: in combination with the contrapuntal support for which the crotchet passing notes and the rests give the opportunity, it builds up a greater sense of energy. Moreover, after II has provided a homophonic interlude containing development of another kind (by rhythmic diminution), III (Ex. 54d) picks up where I left off and carries the same line of thought further still. Naturally the contrapuntal aspect of C2 makes it a

*Ex. 54a–d have been slightly simplified.

special case, but representative cases scarcely exist in Byrd's mature work.

Pavans Nos. 2 and 4 in Nevell (G2 and C1) differ from the others in having only eight bars to each strain. An 8-bar pavan was normally followed by a 4-bar galliard, a rule that held good, for instance, in the Dublin Virginal Book. Such a short strain offered the composer very small scope, and Byrd wrote 8-bar galliards for all his 8-bar pavans. The pavans themselves, however, still presented a problem, for if no special role could be found for them they risked playing poor relation to their 16-bar cousins.

This is what happened with the pavan in **Pavan and Galliard C1**. Strain I is taken, with some modifications, from the first half of Pavan a4/II; the borrowing results in a very unusual opening on a degree other than the tonic. Perhaps there was some personal reason for the quotation, for no musical one suggests itself. The antecedent simply appears shorn of its consequent, to which an unexpected allusion is made in the last strain of the galliard. The work also appears to have some connection with its near neighbour in Weelkes, the surely spurious Pavan and Galliard in C, BK 100 (see p. 178). Every strain in this pair begins on the tonic chord with middle C as bass, and no note lower than C an octave below is used. Byrd begins strain II of his pavan and I of his galliard at the same high pitch* with some slight similarity to the corresponding points in the other work; the rhythmic pattern in the second case becomes a kind of motto for his galliard. After the problematical opening of the pavan he continues with rather lighter textures, adding a second strain of some distinction and an unusually sequential final one. The melodies of the first two galliard strains are very simple, almost without caesuras; two 4-bar strains (with inexact repeats) take the place of a third 8-bar strain, as a gesture to tradition. After writing Byrd's name at the end of this piece Baldwin added the comment 'homo memorabilis'. It is odd that he should have chosen the one work in the group that is something of a makeweight.

The **Pavan and Galliard G2** are clearly much later pieces. In the pavan the example of consort texture, never far away in the works so far discussed, recedes, and the lighter, more mobile style hinted at in Pavan C1 comes into its own. The workmanship is no less exact than in the consort-influenced works, but the music wears a less formal air and the quicker note-values natural to the keyboard help to fill out the short strains. In strain I, which is the most elaborate, Byrd explores another means of compensating for the

---

*He allows himself the A below the lower tonic, but not the low dominant. The only other sizeable work of his to share equal limitation is the Galliard Jig, but it is less striking here because A is the final.

restricted space: instead of decorating the close imitation in the repeat he replaces it with new imitations over the same bass. He does not carry this idea through to II and III, however, because he has a scheme in mind that requires the avoidance of any intensification in the last strain.

The plan of the piece somewhat resembles that of Pavan C2: the top note from I (in this case a modest D given extra emphasis in the repeat) is heard again early in II, after which a descent to the cadence is followed by a rise in III. But here there is a change, for the melody refrains from out-topping the earlier strains, and merely regains the same D. The strategy behind this unusual procedure becomes clear with the first bar of the galliard, which brings a top G, the first of many in this brilliant piece. Byrd has used the shorter form of pavan as a means of reversing the traditional balance between the dances and promoting the galliard to the dominant position. The subject matter of each galliard strain goes well beyond the normal galliard vocabulary: the leaping lines of I are matched only in the *Quadran* Galliard (var. 6) and the tripla of II only in the *Passing Measures* Galliard (vars. 7–8), while III, without using tripla, tends towards the style of tripla dances and variations. In all three strains short figures of a bar or less form the basis of exceptionally lively and eventful development.*

The **Pavan and Galliard g2** is the only pair in Nevell in which the galliard equals the density of activity of G2. It does not overtop its associated pavan, which is a complex work in 16-bar strains, but it certainly measures up to it. These magnificent dances stand apart from the others in the manuscript, not only literally, having been entered much later in the manuscript as the tenth pair, but by virtue of their far wider range of style and technique. The dimensions are no different, but the content so far expands the frame from within that Byrd does not attempt an over-all hierarchy of melodic peaks, nor a single all-embracing tonal progression. Melodic climax has enough to do controlling more limited spans, whilst tonal organization operates quite differently between broadly corresponding areas of harmonic influence.

The pavan begins quietly with a twin cadence strain. There is no consequent, but a single subject of a standard kind, rather like the first melody of the *Passing Measures* Pavan† – though the immediate model for the first

---

*Tregian headed his text of the pavan 'Pavan fant.' The interpretation 'fantasia' might apply to the unusual treatment of I'; 'fantastic' (cf. Bull's Fantastic Pavan, MB 19/86) might fit if the galliard were included. Another small irregularity is perhaps worth noting: many pavans and galliards have an extra cadential bar at the end of III', but G2 has a flourish of three bars at the end of the pavan and two after the galliard. These are equalled only in the first version of Pavan g2 and in Galliard C1 respectively.

†Compare also the Wood pavan (see p. 181) and Johnson's *Delight*.

half strain is Pavan a3 (see p. 201). The subject is a long one, more melody than motive, and the imitation an easy dialogue, more closely worked than the *Passing Measures* opening, which has further to go, but with greater tolerance of purely harmonic filling than is usual in the consort-influenced pavans in Nevell. The repeat dissolves the melody into almost unremitting semiquavers in which only a few salient features remain clear, taking the process first observed in Pavan a1/I' a step further. It will be remembered that in the grounds Byrd often uses rapid figuration as a means of bringing the fundamental harmonic scheme back into prominence after a spell of more elaborate treatment. Similarly his replacement of polyphony by figuration in the repeats of all three strains of Pavan g2 draws attention to the underlying harmony, which plays an important structural role.

Two degrees other than the tonic receive special emphasis in I: there is a bar and a half of B♭ sonority at the peak of the opening phrase (momentarily reinforced by a first inversion at the peak of the tenor imitation in bar 5), and a bar and a half of F major at the beginning of the second half.* These quite ordinary features provide the basis for extraordinary developments. Strain II, instead of striking out for new territory, moves in the same tonal orbit, within which two distinct fields begin to assert their influence by association with rather different musical procedures: one centres on the tonic, the other on the third and seventh degrees, with the dominant acting as a mediator between the two regions. The first and last quarters of the strain both begin on the tonic, and the melody is accompanied in imitative dialogue, as in I. The middle is the province of B♭ and F, and the imitation is of a different kind: it follows half a minim or crotchet beat behind the melody and so lacks melodic value of its own, merely contributing to the keyboard texture (see Ex. 55a and b).† No opposition is felt between the two textures because both serve the unbroken melodic paragraph that spans the whole strain, but in III they split apart.

This strain starts like the previous ones with leisurely imitation in the

Ex. 55

a. Pavan g2/II, bar 6.   *b*. Pavan g2/II, bar 11.

*Johnson's *Delight* has F major at this point, but only for the length of a dotted minim.
†Exx. 55 and 56 follow Nevell.

Ex. 55 (Contd.)

c. Pavan g2/III', bar 15.

d. Galliard g2/II', bar 5.

neighbourhood of the tonic; three entries at 2-bar intervals establish strong rhythmic symmetry, so that when a half close in the tonic brings a dominant chord in bar 7, the listener who knows pavans expects nothing new in bar 8, unless perhaps an upbeat or contrapuntal preparation to a consequent that will begin at bar 9. Instead Byrd cuts through every expectation by plunging on to B♭ at bar 8* with an intensification of the type of imitation previously associated with it – a 3-part canon at the octave and fifteenth below at the distance of a crotchet (see Ex. 78a). The shock of this abrupt juxtaposition is absorbed in a gradual return to the tonic by way of a melodic quotation from II (cf. bars 39–42, 75–78).

Byrd originally concluded III' with figuration in the tonic major suggestive of the patterns associated with B♭ and F (Ex. 55c), thereby reconciling the contrasting characters finally established so dramatically at bar 8 of this strain. This idea, brilliant in itself, was misplaced, because the galliard exploits the contrast, and the intervening reconciliation cuts the ground from under it. When he revised the work for *Parthenia* he found the courage to drop the passage. The galliard answers the strenuous syncopations of the repeats in the pavan with a more close-knit vigour. Strains I and III belong to the tonic region, and accordingly to more usual kinds of motivic and imitative work. The motives are shorter than in any galliard in Nevell except G2, and more closely worked than the imitations in Pavan g2; nor are the imitations dropped in the repeats, but intensified in the manner of, for instance, Pavans C2 or G6. Strain II provides contrast by reference to the second character developed in the pavan. The first half is in B♭ and

*The preparation for this bar is the one passage in the pavan where the rhythmic structure is not dissolved in figuration in the repeat.

Ex. 56

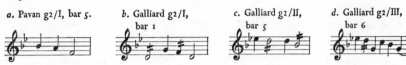

a. Pavan g2/I, bar 5.   *b.* Galliard g2/I,   *c.* Galliard g2/II,   *d.* Galliard g2/III,
                         bar 1   bar 5   bar 6

approaches homophony; the second cadences in F and performs two functions, one in the first statement and one in the repeat. Ex. 56c shows the motive in the first statement; it is linked with the openings of I and III (Ex. 56b and d), and all three derive from a fragment of the melody in strain I of the pavan which Byrd singles out and isolates in its repeat (Ex. 56a).* When repeated, strain IIb′ of the galliard supports the reference to the second musical character, already made by the return to B♭ and F, by introducing the texture linked with them (Ex. 55d).

By good fortune this remarkable work can be dated with some certainty about 1590 or 1591. When Byrd chose the pavans and galliards for Baldwin to copy in Nevell it was evidently not available for inclusion. Since it is entered only two places from the end of the manuscript, after the fantasias, grounds and variations, it must have been a late arrival, and the conclusion that it had only just been written is inescapable. Moreover the dedicatee, William Petre, who was only fifteen in 1590, would scarcely have mastered such difficult pieces earlier, and their style and structure, as has been seen, show many developments not found in the other pavans and galliards in Nevell.

The latter circumstance suggests that the pieces that Byrd selected as his best only a little earlier may not have been very recent (except perhaps G2 and G6). The first of the fine series of 16-bar pavans, though probably written for London rather than Lincoln, is undoubtedly relatively early, and there is no need to suppose that he would have needed another fifteen òr twenty years before progressing to the masterly Kinborough Good† Pavan and Galliard C2. The later 1570s or earlier 1580s would seem a reasonable date for such a work. It brings to perfection the pavan and galliard genres as he originally conceived them, that is as extensions of the consort tradition, and it would not have been surprising if he had abandoned them for that very reason, just as he was to abandon the ground and the fantasia within the next few years. The C1 pair, however, shows that fairly early on he had attempted a lighter style which did not prosper initially, but eventually

*This three-note phrase may be felt to epitomize the opening melodic phrases of strains II (bars 1–4) and III (bars 1–3) in the pavan.

†The dedicatee had changed her name through marriage by 1589; see BK 32a, commentary.

found its full justification in the G2 pair. The more idiomatic keyboard writing of this work opened up new possibilities for the genre; the Petre pair drew on both styles. The pavans and galliards not included in Nevell fill in details of the development traced here, and carry the story on beyond 1591.

Earlier Pavans and Galliards not in Nevell

Among dances found in other sources are the 8-bar Pavans g3 and G4. **Pavan and Galliard g3** make up a rather good pair in the consort-influenced style, but the pavan is naturally more limited than its 16-bar fellows. The openings of I and III recall the corresponding bars in Pavan a1, but its nearest relative is perhaps the 8-bar Pavan C1, not only because it shares the same peak notes in the three strains (F, F, G), but because its galliard, like Galliard C1, substitutes two 4-bar strains for the usual third 8-bar strain.

Pavan and Galliard G4 occur at a confused point in Weelkes. They are preceded by the C major pair BK 100 with an improbable ascription to Byrd, and followed by an anonymous text of the genuine C1 pair. Since they are rather slight in content and occasionally clumsy in detail* doubt arises as to their authenticity. The question can best be tackled by comparing the pavan with three others, the C major BK 100, G7 (Lady Monteagle) and G8. The opening of Pavan G4/III is an almost direct quotation of BK

Ex. 57

a. Pavan MB 100/III   *b.* Pavan G4/III   *c.* Pavan G7/II

d. Pavan G7/III   *e.* Pavan G8/III   *f.* Galliard G3/III

*Pavan II, bars 4–6: the imitation in minims between alto and tenor makes a break in rhythmic continuity that ornamentation cannot disguise (cf. the early version of a1). Pavan IIIb′: the imitations are rather awkward. Galliard III: the melody runs out of steam so that a feebly repetitive extra push is necessary in bar 6 to get it to the end.

100/III (see Ex. 57b and a), but whereas the latter strain virtually collapses after the first two bars, G4 carries on in sequence and then evolves a point from the melody – a sharp enough contrast to suggest a different composer (it will be remembered that the C1 pair also has connections with MB 100).

This same strain contains twelve bars instead of eight. The only other pavan attributable to Byrd to use the 12-bar scheme* – in this case in every strain – is **Pavan G7**, another rather flimsy and colourless piece that does not at first sight suggest his authorship at all strongly. Neither work shows the composer asking himself what special opportunities this type of strain might offer, and the music drifts.† Strains II and III of G7 both open with an alman-like 2-bar phrase (Ex. 57c and d), the first very like those in G4 and BK 100 (Ex. 57b and a), the second like the beginning of G8/III (Ex. 57e). The latter resemblance goes further than the opening, for in each case the first idea leads into the same descending triadic motive. It is difficult to believe that these three G major pieces are not by the same composer, and there are good reasons for accepting the ascriptions to Byrd. There are no other works by named or anonymous composers that resemble them, and although Weelkes, Tregian and Forster are all fallible it would be too great a coincidence for them to have misattributed G4, G7 and G8 respectively. Pavan G8 is in any case a thoroughly characteristic piece; the affinity of its third strain with passages in the other two pavans, far from casting doubt on its own status in the Byrd canon, helps to confirm theirs.

Pavan and Galliard G3 also belong with these works: strain III of the galliard (Ex. 57f) is related to the alman-like pavan strains – especially to G4/III (Ex. 57b) where the resemblance continues for four bars – and the pavan is akin to G8 in structure and expression. Both are 16-bar pavans, both use the twin cadence plan in I but not again (not an uncommon feature), and both attempt a long descent to the cadence of strain II of the kind later managed so perfectly in Pavan C2. Pavan G3/I makes a good beginning in a similar style to a1/I, and, in contrast to G4 and G7, sets a tone no less personal to the composer. This quality persists in the later strains and partially compensates for structural miscalculations. Byrd seems to have aimed at the effect he later achieved in the G2 pair: he prepares for the top Gs and vigorous dance rhythms of the galliard by holding the pavan to a low melodic ceiling and progressively slowing down the harmonic activity with pedal notes in the bass or middle parts. Strain II begins with a quasi-canonic dialogue over four 2-bar pedals (Ex. 81c) and continues with

---

*BK 98a is a 12-bar pavan, but its ascription to Byrd is unacceptable (see p. 178).

†It is symptomatic that the final tonic harmony of G7/III is reached most irregularly at bar 12 instead of 11 without it making any appreciable difference.

monotonously alternating minim chords over a 4-bar pedal, so that the music has difficulty in dragging home to the cadence. By the time Byrd has started III with another 4-bar pedal and refused to allow the harmonic pulse to pick up until bars 7–8, it is clear that he has overplayed his hand.

Pavan G8 is potentially the finer work, but the only source (Forster) gives it in an unfinished state without fully worked-out repeats: the additional decoration in I' is stiff and perfunctory (as in G7/I'), there is hardly any change in III', and no repeat at all for II. In II imitations on a single subject run out into chords alternating round internal pedals, but unlike those in G3/II they are firmly contained within an over-all cadential progression; moreover the crotchet pulse serves to anticipate III, where the alman character takes over and finally justifies itself. The canonic texture exploited in the later strains of G3 appears at the very beginning of G8 in the form of a strict canon between alto and treble – the nearest approach to its disposition in the canonic Pavan G6. However, G3 was to contribute more to that great work: the initial impetus for each strain and the structure of the caesura in bars 8–9 of II.

Pavans G3 and G8 make little use of antecedent and consequent or of any other type of contrast within the strain, a circumstance that places them nearer to c1 and a1 than to the later pavans in Nevell – as do the various marks of inexperience noted above. But in certain other respects they differ from any Nevell pavans: they are less indebted to consort tradition, and although they do not make greater use of idiomatic keyboard writing they show signs of the freer compositional approach that the keyboard allows. One element that Byrd excluded from the more carefully wrought compositions chosen for Nevell was the alman character in the pavans. A comparable feature is found in the galliards. Side by side with strains based on a single melodic span (G3/II, G4/I and III) and fairly regular quatrains (g3/I, G4/II*), these early examples contain others of a strongly dance-like character dependent on 6/4 syncopations within the 3/2 measure (g3/II, G3/I and III†). Such syncopations occur incidentally in nearly all Byrd's galliards, but only here as the central point of interest.

No galliard follows Pavan G8 in Forster, but the unattached **Galliard G9** occurs later in the manuscript, and may possibly belong to it. This suggestion‡ seems improbable from one point of view, for G9 is Byrd's only 4-bar galliard, and if he was unwilling to follow custom in writing this type of

---

*This anticipates the symmetries of Galliard c2. Did Byrd remember it when he composed the corresponding strain in the galliard section of Fantasia 6/g1?

†The syncopations are thrown into relief in this galliard by hemiolas in II – and less happily by the feeble conclusion to III.

‡First made by Tuttle, p. xxi.

galliard for his 8-bar pavans he would presumably have been still less prepared to do so for the 16-bar G8. Yet each strain in this pleasing little piece is related to the corresponding one in the pavan – a simple and obvious means of connecting the pieces which Byrd might have tried out in an early pair.

Only one other pair, the curious and highly interesting **Pavan and Galliard a3**, belongs to this early period, in which it is unmistakably placed by the unbroken melodic treatment of the first galliard strain, the dissimilar lines of the couplet making up the second, and a certain general untidiness resulting from the conception of the work. Here, for the first time in these pieces, Byrd puts the variety of texture and freedom of movement offered by the keyboard to positive use, developing the character of the work directly out of them. The very first bars announce their independence of the contrapuntal formality of the consort tradition, as comparison with the 5-part opening of Pavan a4, with its rather similar quasi-Phrygian harmony, shows very clearly. Everything in this first strain is held in place by the twin cadence structure, but the loose imitation in the first half, the sudden promise of stretto at the caesura and its rapid dissolution in continuous semiquavers* all make an improvisatory effect. In IIa, where the melody is built sequentially on a motive outlining a rising and falling third, there is no imitation; in IIb a short inverted form of this motive splits off in a quick imitative exchange of no fewer than eleven entries.

In III the texture changes yet again, with ingenious rhythmic play accompanying an initially slow-moving treble. There is probably a reference here to the curious cantus firmus treatment sometimes met with in the last strain of pavans and galliards, as there undoubtedly is in Pavan F2/IIIa, the only comparable passage in Byrd (see p. 207). The present example merges into a succession of short segments that echo one another and recall the texture of IIb. (With so much invention and assurance in these two strains it is surprising to find Byrd reaching the dominant too soon in III, in bars 11–12, and fumbling to get into position for the final cadence.) Since strain III of the galliard is modelled on that of the pavan, segmental treatment appears here for the third time and consequently operates as a kind of thematic texture in the work. It lends striking individuality to the music, but its distribution (Pavan II and III, Galliard III) is lopsided and suggests that Byrd did not plan the idea beforehand, but stumbled on it while com-

---

*It is not uncommon for the cadential flourish in an undecorated pavan strain to occupy the last four bars, but there is no other in Byrd where the figuration begins a bar earlier and becomes a feature in its own right.

Ex. 58

a. Pavan a3/I

b. Pavan g2/I

posing. Years later he saw unrealized possibilities in the use of characteristic textures, and worked them into Pavan and Galliard g2, reinforcing them with contrasted tonal areas (see p. 193f). Ex. 58, which shows the openings of the two pavans, confirms the connection.

The fine **Pavan and Galliard B♭1** is the one pair outside Nevell written in the consort tradition, and its nearest relatives are the mature examples c2 and C2. As in them each half strain of the pavan receives a new motive, and as in c2 the peak notes in each strain are respectively E♭ and F, E♭ and F, F and G (see p. 186).* Unlike the two Nevell works, however, it seems to have its origin in a lost consort version which is detectable in various details of the keyboard arrangement. Suspensions, which occur more often in consort polyphony than in keyboard style, need some form of decoration to make their best effect on the keyboard. The frequency of these decorated resolutions is noticeable in the keyboard version of Pavan c1/II and III, and also in B♭/I and II.† The dense imitation in Ib and IIb of the pavan suggests consort style, and the motive and treatment in IIb recall the corresponding strain in Pavan c1.‡

*This ignores the top G in bar 8 of III, which looks like a mistake in the earlier source, on which the later is apparently dependent: it is not in the repeat, nor in the admittedly sketchy arrangement for lute and bass viol in the Weld lute book (North No. 3) – and it makes no musical sense. (Byrd seems to have felt with some justice that the G in bar 10 was not forceful enough, and so added a second, extremely telling one at bar 15 in the repeat.)

†The Weld arrangement, for what it is worth, gives plainer resolutions in most cases, and so may go back to an earlier version, presumably for consort. It has no repeats, but lute arrangements often omit them.

‡The last bass entry causes an interruption in the final cadence so that the chord of resolution is delayed until bar 16; perhaps that is the reason for its extraordinarily heavy instrumentation.

Strain III is the only one in Byrd to run to eighteen bars instead of sixteen. It quite often happens that the first half of a strain requires an intermediate cadential chord at bar 9, but except in the present case he avoids this pattern in the second half. However, in the last strain of a consort pavan there would have been less objection to such a plan, for in the absence of a differentiated repeat the extra bars needed to accommodate the final harmony would occupy a similar place to the additional flourish of a bar or so that often rounds off the repeat of a final strain in keyboard dances; thus strain III of the Consort Pavan 6/C extends to seventeen bars. In the B♭ galliard the rhythmically displaced imitative entry in the treble at the end of I suggests consort writing, as do various features in III. This is based on the opening of the last strain in the pavan (which, exceptionally for this type of pavan, adopts a variant of the alman-like style illustrated in Ex. 57). The melody of the first two bars is echoed an octave lower as though by lower instruments, and the repetition in bars 6 and 7 of the alto part looks like an antiphonal exchange between two instruments at the same pitch.*

The unattached **Galliard d2** is difficult to place in relation to Byrd's development of the genre. The exceptionally clear articulation of the caesuras, the sense of spaciousness that these create in I and II, and the purity of melodic line all show considerable maturity, though to judge from the simplicity of texture and the couplet construction of each strain, within his earlier years. It must surely have been composed well before the **Galliard for the Victory (G10)**, which belongs unquestionably to the latest stratum in Nevell. The nearest stylistic relative of the latter work is Galliard C2, but, with all allowance made for a certain deliberate formality in the Kinborough Good pieces, the even more developmental nature of G10/III, the assurance of the irregularly planned imitations in II and the general richness of detail place it nearer the William Petre pair (g2).

Later Pavans and Galliards

Apart from the late pieces in *Parthenia* there remain for discussion five pavans, all of the 16-bar type, and their galliards. All are highly individual compositions in which, as in the g2 pair, faster note-values and harmonic pulses lead to a vast expansion of content. The increased eventfulness, in both structure and decorative detail, could not be contained within the kind of framework that Byrd had perfected for such pairs as c2, C2 and B♭1, and although he drew at will on structural elements used in these or less mature works he did so only in the service of much more specialized developments

*Is it chance that the bass in these bars echoes the motive of I?

dictated by particular conceptions. Of the five pairs two, F1 and d1, have a certain amount in common with g2 and the *Quadran*, and would appear to date from the same period; the other three are probably later.

Pavan F1, rather too vaguely entitled 'Bray' by Tregian, was in circulation by 1596, for an orpharion arrangement by Cutting appeared in William Barley's *New booke of tabliture* in that year. To describe its most original first strain as a twin cadence structure with a different imitation in each half would be accurate but would give a misleading impression. The imitation is mostly tenuous, and the intermediate cadence provides very little fresh impetus, merely introducing a 4-bar dominant pedal – and tonic or dominant pedals take up a large part of the strain. The inactive accompaniment throws into relief a quiet top line which would otherwise scarcely have asserted itself but, with this encouragement, ventures ornamentation of great refinement at the cadential approaches. In the repeat it increases its hold and refuses its more persistent imitative shadow (in the second half) any part in its dominance. The whole strain is an essay in line drawing, and line is the theme, in the wider sense, of the whole work.

For the material of the other two strains Byrd goes back to his early Pavan G8. He bases II entirely on a very similar point to that of G8/II, and at one moment almost borrows the treatment too (see Ex. 59). But the

Ex. 59

a. Pavan G8/II, bar 5   b. Pavan F1/II, bar 9

experience of the intervening years is not lost: there are now two fairly regular imitative expositions separated by an emphatic twin cadence pattern. All this might appear to have little to do with the concept of line, but Byrd has not lost sight of it. In the first place he adopts a procedure that he had learnt to avoid: he admits a lot of note-against-note movement so that the part-writing tends to coalesce and give prominence to the treble. Then, in the repeat, by decorating one part at a time he produces an entirely new line of almost unbroken quavers and semiquavers that passes through the whole texture – and in the process rediscovers for himself, and puts to a special purpose, a technique very generally used on the continent in intabulations of vocal music.

In III he takes up the old alman character from G8 (see Ex. 57e – both move to the major harmony of the local second degree in bar 4 and the local subdominant in bar 5), and spices it with little imitations that do not detract from its essentially melodic nature. The repeat adds a dialogue in semi-quavers between right and left hand and can be compared to no decorated pavan strain before g2 and the *Quadran*.* The contribution of Pavan G8 to this work (unlike that of a3 to g2) is secondary. Its outstandingly melodious quality, to which Byrd pays tribute in F1/II and III, can have suggested the linear idea behind the work only in a very general way, if at all. The real source for the whole conception, including the repeats, is the melodic material of I, the only strain to find no parallel in G8. The galliard, like Galliard d1, fails to live up to its pavan; they will best be discussed to-gether.

In Pavans g2 and F1 Byrd makes reference to early works; in **Pavan d1** he turns to the mature consort-influenced pieces in Nevell. Strain I contains two very full imitative expositions on related subjects, one in each half, entirely in the spirit of these pieces, and in the repeat the whole imitative texture is retained and intensified by decoration. If anything the imitations assume greater importance in the later work because they are no longer subservient to a melodic antecedent and consequent; the more active motives of the new style occasion greater variety of incident than a melodic line can encompass, as the little episode for lower voices in bars 9–10 demonstrates. Events move fast in II as well: in bars 1–4 (very similar to F1/I bars 11–14) and 5–8 Byrd achieves a powerful tonal shift by the same process of partial repetition that he had used in a1/II (see p. 184) but within half a strain, so that room remains for a new imitation on one of his relatively rare circles of fifths in the second half.

Strain III is more eventful still. It starts rather like F1/III, but for the moment with less emphasis on the characteristic rhythm ♩ ♪♩ ♩ . Byrd hastens instead to establish a sense of recapitulation by returning in bar 3 to the tonic, which has been absent during II, and by quoting the closing phrase from Ia (bar 8) in the treble and tenor (bars 4–5), in the second case with its original dominant harmony. A reminiscence of the mid-point of I so early in the strain carries the implication that some new development is imminent. The listener expects it after a cadence at bar 7, towards which the incipient cadential flourish of semiquavers at bar 5 and the twin cadence tradition both point. But instead of a 4–3 suspension in the second bar of dominant harmony (bar 6) followed by the tonic, or a half close on E, Byrd

---

*The semiquavers in the second half of vars. 3 and 6 of the *Passing Measures* Pavan are treated more simply, like enormously expanded cadential flourishes.

simply repeats in bar 7 the heavy dominant chord from the beginning of bar 6, and the listener realizes that a new turn of events has brushed re-capitulation aside without cadential ceremony and is already on him. It takes the form of a sequence on the rhythm of the first bar of the strain reinforced in sturdy homophony, which quickly replaces harmonic stagnation with as many as four real harmonies to the bar (bar 8). Treble and alto in quasi-canon detach themselves momentarily from this texture for top G and top A respectively and are then reabsorbed in a strongly harmonic approach to the final cadence. The cadential flourish in bar 15 refers back to the same point in strain I.

The transition from the elegiac imitation of strain I to the almost aggressive homophony of strain III is immediately confirmed in strain I of **Galliard d1** (Ex. 60d), which reinforces its echo of the dotted rhythm from strain III

Ex. 60

a. Galliard F1/I   *b.* Galliard F1/II   *c.* Galliard F1/III, bar 3

d. Galliard d1/I   *e.* Galliard d1/II   *f.* Galliard d1/III

of the pavan with the same texture.* Strain II stages a battle between the two textures: bar 1 tries to reintroduce independent movement in the parts, but it is brutally contradicted by homophony and syncopation in bar 2, and the process is exactly repeated in each pair of bars to the end of the strain. Homophony likewise disrupts IIIa, dislocating the rhythm by a crotchet in bar 3. However, order is deftly restored in bar 4 and polyphony with a touch of imitation (carefully preserved in the repeat) wins the day.

Each strain of this galliard is based on a version of the same motive, and the same is true of **Galliard F1** (see Ex. 60a–f).† The two motives are almost identical, as d1/III shows by filling in a passing note in bar 1 before quoting from I in bars 2–3, and the d1 motive also links, though less schematically, the strains of g2 (see Ex. 56). This shared preference for single-bar cellular structure forms a bond between the three pieces which counterbalances any impression that Galliards F1 and d1 might be earlier than g2 on account of their greater stylistic simplicity. Moreover their

*Compare the milder treatment of a similar melody in Galliard c2/I.

†If Pavan G8 and Galliard G9 belong together the motive in Galliard F1 will have been suggested by the similar opening of the latter, since Pavan F1 borrows from the former.

impressive pavans yield nothing to Pavan g2, and there is no reason why they should not post-date it. Unfortunately Byrd seems to have lost interest when he came to write the galliards, and applied the motivic idea that he used so imaginatively in Galliard g2 in a more mechanical way, as a means of getting going.

His difficulty is understandable in the case of F1, because the linear idea had already been fully worked out in the pavan. Up to a point there is nothing wrong with the galliard: it is an attractive piece of some individuality that perfectly reflects the linear style of the pavan. In its relationship to its more complex companion it may be compared to the *Quadran* Galliard, but unlike that work it fails to set up its own standard and remains a lightweight pendant. Galliard d1 is a greater disappointment because it has a more important part to play. The homophonic idea, having emerged late in the pavan, needs to be taken up in the galliard; strain I does so rather baldly, which is effective as a means of making the development explicit, but sets a difficult precedent for the rest of the galliard. Byrd does not really face the problem: he uses the later strains to sketch in the final stages of his conception, but without much thought for musical refinements.

No such imbalance spoils the F2, C3 and G5 pairs. Here pavan and galliard complement each other as perfectly as in the g2 pair, but the three works further display the special richness of melodic detail and the diversity of figuration which mark Byrd's latest phase (see p. 160), and which neither the brilliant semiquaver passage-work of the *Quadran* and g2 pavans, nor the refined linear ornamentation of Pavan F1 quite attain. Byrd also seems to have written preludes for each (see p. 224). It has been seen that he took ideas of varying importance from earlier pavans and galliards in some of his later ones: from G3, a3 and G8 in G6, g2 and F1 respectively. He now turned in F2 and C3 to examples by his younger contemporaries Morley and Bull.

In his **Pavan and Galliard F2** Byrd parodied Morley's F major pair, a poorly constructed work presumably written before the composer found his salvation in Italianate formulae. Yet the pavan at least must have been popular, for Farnaby made a more elaborate keyboard setting from the 5-part consort version which may have been Morley's original, and Rosseter included an arrangement in his *Lessons for consort* of 1609.* Strain I, tuneful

---

*The 5-part version survives in the Kassel manuscript mentioned on p. 61. For Morley's keyboard arrangement, with its galliard, see *Keyboard Works*, Nos. 1, 2 (also Tregian Nos. [169, 170]); for the Farnaby, MB 24/17 (No. [285] in Tregian, who does not mention Morley); entitled Southernes Pavin in Rosseter.

in an untidy way, probably earned it its vogue; II has little character and III, following a curious convention found in final strains, employs a treble cantus firmus in semibreves.* This third strain provides proof that it was Byrd who imitated Morley, and not the other way about. Morley's cantus firmus cannot derive from Pavan F2/III, for by the time Byrd has doubled its speed and turned it into a subject for imitation it becomes almost unrecognizable. On the other hand Byrd clearly refers to Morley's countersubject, refashioning it in an entirely original texture† and inverting the one element that he does not use at first to form the equally unusual subject of the second half of the strain (see Ex. 61a–c).

Ex. 61

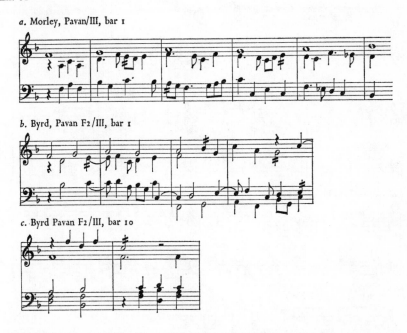

a. Morley, Pavan/III, bar 1

b. Byrd, Pavan F2/III, bar 1

c. Byrd Pavan F2/III, bar 10

Although the third strain of Morley's galliard is independent of the pavan, for the first two he simply converts the corresponding pavan strains into triple measure. Byrd, who never does this, neatly avoids it in his parody of strain I and corrects a weakness in his model in the process. Morley's

---

*For other examples, all highly detrimental to the compositions, see Bull, MB 19/73 and 87a; Philips, Tregian No. 85; Gibbons, MB 20/17. Thurston Dart suggested that the solmization syllables represented the names of dedicatees.

†But cf. Pavan a3/III, discussed on p. 200.

strain I in both dances contains three salient phrases of which the second
and third resemble each other too closely for comfort; Ex. 62a–c show the
galliard versions. Byrd, who could scarcely have wished for a better vindica-
tion of his own preference for bipartite strains, adopts only the first and
third ideas for the first strain of his galliard (Ex. 62d, e), and the first and
second for that of his pavan. In order to avoid duplication of any kind he
inverts the first motive in the pavan;* he also lengthens the second phrase by
combining it with another from strain III of Morley's galliard (see Ex. 62b,
f, g).† In the other strains he takes no more than a hint from Morley's

Ex. 62

a. Morley, Galliard/I, bar 1

b. Morley, Galliard/I, bar 5

c. Morley, Galliard/I, bar 10

d. Byrd, Galliard F2/I, bar 1

e. Byrd, Galliard F2/I, bar 5

f. Byrd, Pavan F2/I, bar 9

g. Morley, Galliard/III, bar 7

*Cf. Pavans G2/I and d1/IIb.
†Note the quavers filling in the interval of a fourth in Ex. 62b. They are present at the
corresponding point in the keyboard pavan, but they are not in the consort version, and
were presumably absent from the consort version of the galliard – if it ever existed.
Byrd's adoption of the figure in Ex. 62f removes any doubt that he was parodying the
keyboard version.

opening melodic notes – the interval of a fourth in pavan II, a hexachord in galliard II, and a 3-note figure in galliard III – and on the basis of the resulting motives replaces Morley's uncoordinated strains with object lessons in economy and cogent development.

The outer strains of the pavan are concerned with the lesson of clarity and balance, to which the complexity of the middle one provides a foil. The former both employ bipartite forms, though of slightly different kinds: having adopted the simple twin cadence pattern in I Byrd postpones the caesura in III till the end of bar 9, thereby giving special prominence to the terminal notes of the cantus firmus – presumably in compensation for its earlier dilution in imitation.* In II the dense imitative development of his 4-note decoration of Morley's rising fourth† and its derivatives allows no central caesura. After an initial 4-bar phrase a very weak cadence at bar 8 is the only signpost on the outward journey; from here the route continues through bass augmentation and a reduced-voice episode, and the listener must concentrate if he is to pick up the first homeward pointer in a similarly weak cadence at bar 13.

Byrd made no attempt to reflect this kind of writing in the galliard, although, having rejected Morley's routine repetitions as a means of linking the two dances, he needed to establish some other bond between them. His solution to this problem, as so often a highly original one, was to base each strain of the galliard on a harmonic progression analogous to that at the opening of the pavan. This begins with two bars each on the harmonies I–IV–II–V, a less common opening than might be supposed.‡ The idea of harmonic symmetry built on a pair of interlocking fourths or fifths is taken up in the galliard as follows: strain I begins with one bar each of I–V–ii–VI; strain II contains a quatrain of 2-bar lines, pivoting respectively on VI–II, V–I (+ II–V), II–V, III–VI; the first four bars of strain III bring I–V–VII♭–IV, IV–I–v–II (–V). Monotony is avoided by the intervening harmonies in II (especially the important dominant cadence halfway through), the differing harmonic paces of I and III and the freer continuations in these two strains. In IIIa Byrd pares away all other activity except for a simple melodic line, and so closes the work by concentrating the listener's attention on the unifying harmonic principle – a brilliant structural stroke.§

*But bars 8–10 also seem to echo bars 2–3 of strain III of Morley's galliard.

†A common figure, but it is perhaps worth noting that Morley himself uses it at precisely this point in his A minor pavan (*Keyboard Works* No. 5; Tregian No. [153]).

‡Dance strains in English virginal music provide only two other examples, both by Byrd: Galliards G2/I and G3/I.

§In Tregian the bass notes are not struck again on the last crotchet beat of bars 1–3 – an odd reading but, since it further emphasizes the harmonic symmetry, possibly correct.

In Forster an anonymous text of the galliard is preceded by an anonymous prelude in F which is clearly Byrd's work. It follows the harmonic scheme of strain I of the pavan very closely – in particular the all-important initial harmonies, which it announces with a minimum of decorative distraction – and so serves to counterbalance the absence of any follow-up of the harmonic idea in strains II and III of the pavan.*

Although Byrd incorporated his criticisms of a particular Morley work in his highly personal F2 pieces, Morley's keyboard style held no wider interest for him. When, however, he turned to Bull in his **Pavan and Galliard C3** his object was to put to the test the principles underlying Bull's keyboard style in general. He did not select any of Bull's works for parody, but he quoted from one of them, presumably in acknowledgement of the source of his critical exercise. Ex. 63a and b show the openings of Bull's

Ex. 63

a. Bull, Lord Lumley's Pavan/I

b. Byrd, Pavan C3/III

c. Bull, Galliard, Parthenia 13/I'

Lord Lumley's Pavan (MB 19/129a) and of strain III of Byrd's pavan. Bull's piece is certainly the earlier: it is in no way involved with Byrd, as

*Interlocking fourths make incidental melodic appearances in both; Byrd cannot have intended them as audible references to the bass of I (or the prelude), but there may have been a connection in his mind.

Byrd's is with Bull, and if Bull had been the imitator he would surely not have swept away Byrd's initial series of 6–5 and 4–3 progressions in favour of his own rather haphazard consonances and suspensions. But the matter is complicated by Bull's use of the same idea at the beginning of both pavan and galliard of the pair printed as Nos. 12 and 13 in *Parthenia* (MB 19/131a, b). The decorated repeat in the galliard (Ex. 63c) is especially close to the Lumley version, raising the question of priority again.

Lord Lumley's Pavan is a fine work, showing Bull's use of virtuoso keyboard style at its most imaginative; the material has a warmth of expression that he rarely achieves, and at first sight the piece might seem later than the less interesting *Parthenia* pair. However, it cannot have been composed later than 1609, the year of the dedicatee's death, whereas the *Parthenia* pieces are not known to have circulated in manuscript and may have been specially written for the 1612/13 publication in an easier style less likely to scare away prospective buyers.* Internal evidence supports this chronology. Strain I of the *Parthenia* galliard is, of course, barred in triple time, but it remains obstinately duple, and the music must have been conceived as such.† It can only have originated in Lord Lumley's Pavan, for its relation to Byrd's C3 is not quite so close, while many of its most characteristic features are altogether lacking in the watered down version that opens the companion pavan in *Parthenia*. This 16-bar pavan employs twin cadence structure in all three strains, and as this device scarcely occurs elsewhere in Bull‡ the inference is that he was consciously adopting one of Byrd's favourite formal schemes. So the following sequence of events suggests itself: certain features of Bull's music prompted Byrd to compose his C3 pair, drawing attention to his interest by quoting from Lord Lumley; by way of returning the compliment Bull used the same quotation as the starting point for a pavan and galliard in which he made an unconvincing attempt to reciprocate Byrd's interest.

The whole of strain I of Pavan C3 consists of imitation on a long subject incorporating a group of seven quavers; this results in a texture of almost unbroken quaver movement such as Byrd had used very occasionally in

---

*This may be true of two of his other *Parthenia* pieces: No. 14 (MB 19/70), an outstanding work among his mainly disappointing contributions to the collection, and No. 10 (MB 19/126a), the *St Thomas Wake* Pavan. Thurston Dart pointed out (MB commentary) that this pavan was probably written later than its galliard; the triple metre version of the tune is evidently the original, and the galliard is found alone in manuscript sources.

†It consists of a 4-bar phrase with an unwanted extra half bar for the sake of appearances (see the dotted bar lines in Ex. 63c), and an 8-bar phrase from which the final minim beat has been dropped because there is no room for it.

‡See his pavans MB 19/66, 67, 86–88, in which only 87/I and 88/II have a cadence at bar 7, neither as emphatic as any in the *Parthenia* piece.

repeats (Pavans G3/IIIa′, B♭1/Ib′), but never before in primary material. There is no overt reference to Bull except in the last bar, where figurative activity continues up to the last beat and ends with his favourite termination of accented mediant falling to unaccented tonic. This is rare in Byrd, but he closes several sections of the present piece with it.* The repeat of I, largely in semiquavers, contains nothing unprecedented in Byrd except the partially inverted antiphonal figuration at the beginning, which again recalls a passage in Bull (Pavan MB 19/66a, bars 72–73). Strain II returns to quavers, but with a shorter imitative point than that of I so that the weave becomes closer and superficially more like Bull's frequent patches of rich quaver texture. Bull usually has two strands of quavers going at once; imitation, if present, is incidental, and the intention, apart from fuller keyboard sonority, is to give a semblance of harmonic activity where the basic pulse is slow and perhaps not very purposeful. For Byrd, who in this piece also keeps the harmonic pace slow, it is the melodic progress within imitation, with its expressive nuances and power of structural control, that counts.

The same difference of approach is illustrated in his use in no fewer than three different figures of the rhythmic pattern ♩♫♫♩ which is common in Bull, but as a repeated pattern virtually absent from his own music outside the present work. Whereas Bull tends merely to work it for a bit and then turn to something else (Pavans MB 19/66a, bars 10–14; 87a, bars 58–60), Byrd gives it a functional role. It first emerges in a subordinate capacity in strain IIb, and when it reappears in IIa′ it is still only as a decoration in a pre-established contrapuntal texture. But this time it takes charge, and by doubling the incidence of the pair of semiquavers manages by purely rhythmic means to bring about a caesura at the end of bar 8* (in the first statement of the strain the first half had been allowed to run on for another bar). The pattern comes into even greater prominence in IIIb with a number of consecutive repetitions almost in Bull's manner. But when Byrd halts development in one dimension it invariably means that something important is happening in another, and in this case it is the return to the tonic. The rhythmic pattern provides the vehicle for this progression, but also makes a more positive contribution by breaking its intervallic sequence

---

*Bull, however, would not have combined this termination with figures reminiscent of Redford (I, bar 16), or of Byrd's own early A minor fantasia (III, bars 15–16). Byrd also worked it into IIIa′ and adopted it here and there in his late *Parthenia* pieces.

†This passage introduces another example of Byrd's developmental treatment of figuration. Descending scales of four semiquavers turn into continuous runs, and then back again into their original form with different accentuation (there is no parallel to this last stage in his earlier use of the idea in Pavan a1/I′). Compare Bull's effective but essentially decorative treatment in the Pavan MB 19/88a, bars 17–32.

to emphasize the mediant E in the crucial unestablished tonic chord in bar 13. In the repeat of this passage, which recalls Ia', Byrd uses a semiquaver figure including a repeated note – yet another importation from Bull's vocabulary.

Paradoxically the near-quotation from Lord Lumley in III brings Byrd closer to his normal territory. Bull's continuation, which passes on to block chords in crotchets and demisemiquaver runs before closing the strain in only eleven bars, is by no means ineffective, but Byrd devises one that does better justice to the main idea. The harmonic adjustments mentioned earlier make possible a sequential prolongation ending in a half close at bar 7, so that the pavan closes with the stability of a most un-Bull-like twin cadence structure.

In the galliard Byrd makes no further reference to Bull. The first two strains are composed in the normal manner for his later galliards – in so far as he may be said to have one – largely with single-bar units. Each is attuned in some way to the style of the pavan, I by pedal basses, II by a repeat that refers back to the subject of strain I of the pavan (down to the position of the ornament on the third quaver of each group); the tendency of the figuration to run through to the last beat of each strain also links the two pieces.

In strain III, as at the same point in Galliard F2, Byrd lays bare the underlying principle behind the whole composition. But in this case the implications are the most extraordinary because at the same time he looks beyond the work itself, and beyond Bull, to a general problem of composition that raises itself in a particularly acute form in Bull's music. The first two bars consist of nothing but a little 2-part canon on the notes of the dominant chord, which is then repeated in bars 3 and 4 on the tonic (the rest of the strain is concerned with turning this excessively plain start to good account with a double canon reminiscent of bars 4–7 of strain II of the pavan). There is no other passage in Byrd's keyboard music that can match the pointed emptiness of these first four bars, yet there is none in which his astonishing analytical intelligence speaks more clearly.

A glance back at the work which this passage summarizes will help to make its significance plain. It has been seen that Byrd's treatment of various figures in the pavan differs from Bull's, but the nature of their common material imposes certain concomitant restrictions on both composers. Just as elaborate ornamentation is seen to best advantage on a flat surface, Bull's highly inventive figuration thrives best in his plainsong settings, in which he sometimes seems to abdicate structural responsibility. In several of his pavans he tries to recreate similar conditions, adopting a somewhat static harmonic plan and using the 16-bar strain as an arbitrary legacy from tradition rather than as a real structural component. When, as in such pieces as the Melancholy and Chromatic Pavans (MB 19/67a and 87a), he seeks contrast in striking harmonic progressions, these cause stylistic inconsistency, not only in themselves but because they resist decoration except on their own terms. At his best Bull managed to overcome such difficulties, notably in his Fantastic Pavan (MB 19/86a), an altogether outstanding piece containing an arresting variety of vigorous textures with excellent decoration in the repeats. Even so, he could not avoid occasional slackness in the structure, particularly in strain II.

Whether or not Bull ever consciously grasped the nature of the technical problem, Byrd undoubtedly did so, as strain I of his pavan shows. His object was not to avoid problems which in any case did not normally arise in his music, but to solve them. He realized that the straight melodic course imposed by a steady stream of passing notes must inevitably rule out many of the most characteristic features of his musical language – the flexible harmonic pulse, the wide range of chordal degree and the extensive use, through chromatic inflexion, of secondary tonal areas – because these depended on variety of rhythm and interval in the melodic sphere. Following this train of thought to its conclusion, he employs a slow succession of harmonies that rarely goes beyond I, V and IV and lacks the muscle for a caesura or any other harmonic event apart from the long-foreseen close. Nor does he ask anything of it that it cannot provide, but instead lightly sketches in a quatrain framework with the aid of subtle rhythmic touches within the linear flow.*

Strain II begins with a vi chord, which is not quite new to the piece, and then slips straight back to the tonic again. From about the middle of this strain Byrd begins to allow himself the greater freedom necessary if the work is to develop properly, for he is always artist before theorist.† But, as has been seen, he finds many ways to preserve continuity with the early part of the work during the quotation from Bull and the dance rhythms of the galliard, and with strain III of the galliard returns to the concept of decorative pattern in its purest form – in fact in a more extreme form than at the outset, for pattern and its static harmonic background now coalesce. The effect resembles the return of a theme in something like its original form at the end of a set of variations; the 'theme' here is a technical concept,

---

*See the correspondence of the bass entries at bars 1 and 5, and the slight check at bar 8 (emphasized by a 6–5 appoggiatura) before the slow treble notes of bars 9–11 echo those of the opening.

†Compare his study of Italian 3-part writing in his Fantasia 3/C3 (p. 96ff).

but it similarly reaffirms the bounds within which the work has run its course, and Byrd perhaps implies in addition that these particular bounds are exacting. Comparison with, for instance, another great C major pair, Kinborough Good, shows that the enormously richer texture has been achieved at a certain cost, while the structural duties laid on the figuration do not allow it the carefree zest of similar decorated passages in Pavan F2, which are carried by the harmony (and sound positively mischievous in relation to Morley's piece).

The **Echo Pavan and Galliard G5**, like a number of other late works (see p. 23), are anonymous in Forster, which is the sole source. However, Tomkins once owned a copy of a work of this title 'in gamut' by Byrd (see MB 5, p. 158), and there is every reason to identify the untitled Forster work with it. That the keyboard repertory contains no other echo pavan or galliard, ascribed or anonymous, is not surprising, because the technique of echoes at the unison employed in the present work originated in antiphony between pairs of voices or instruments, an effect which a single-manual keyboard instrument obviously cannot capture. But Byrd had always been interested in reworking the techniques of consort music in terms of the keyboard, and the echo idea, which plays a considerable part in his two later 6-part fantasias and his 6-part pavan and galliard, offered him a unifying basis for a keyboard pavan and galliard comparable to those in other late pairs. As with some of these, notably C3, the work's originality of conception sets it apart from his other compositions; but it betrays its author in every dimension, from the precision and vitality of detail that characterize his late style to the masterly clarity and assurance with which the design is carried through.

In Byrd's 6-part consort pavan each echo follows its leader at an interval of two bars, which is decreased to one bar in the galliard because the strains are only eight bars long instead of sixteen. In the keyboard work, where longer phrases designed to offset the lack of instrumental contrast might have been expected, Byrd takes the opposite course and makes the single bar the standard unit in both movements. In this way a more adventurous harmonic scheme becomes possible, because the short repetitions allow greater freedom of movement. Thus in each strain of the pavan, after an initial phrase and echo on a static harmony, the bass starts moving away fairly fast, so that the harmonization of each subsequent phrase differs from that of its echo.

To avoid too many exact repetitions is, of course, no more than an elementary necessity of good composition, but if the composer who can do so as skilfully and naturally as Byrd is not altogether common, the one who can draw consequences for the development of a piece from so simple a premise is considerably rarer. That is what Byrd does, carrying the idea into the wider structural field so that melodic stability becomes the counterbalance to a prolonged tonal excursion. Single-bar echoes, all closely related, dominate the first half of each strain: those in IIa derive from Ia by inversion, and are in turn varied in IIIa, though the first phrase here inverts the 2-bar echo from Ib,* which itself may be felt to refer back to the first phrase by inversion. The motivic network embraces the later parts of the other strains as well, where, as in Ib, the echo process is applied differently: in IIb in a more relaxed fashion between detached 2-bar blocks without exact melodic correspondence,† and in IIIb more tautly in short phrases that chase each other at the half bar.

So closely woven a fabric could be relied on to withstand tension, and after strain I Byrd forsakes the tonic until the very end. Strain IIa is entirely in the subdominant; IIb circles round the supertonic and ends with a half close on E. As a result the F major that opens IIIa sounds like an Aeolian sixth rather than a Mixolydian seventh, an impression that seems to be confirmed when A is eventually established at the beginning of IIIb. It is not the progressions here that go beyond Byrd's normal practice in pavans, but the duration of their influence, and he celebrates the long-delayed return of the tonic with a delightful flight of fancy such as only he could imagine.‡

The extremely forceful galliard, which is built from the same motivic material, is the only one by Byrd in which the opening harmonies of all three strains correspond to those of the pavan. However, the continuations differ: II keeps nearer to the dominant and III reintroduces the tonic earlier, though in a very special way. The tonic chord occurs at or near the beginning of every bar of the latter strain from 4 to 8, but it is approached on each occasion from a different angle, and the dominant steps in to confirm it only at the last opportunity. Although the galliard does not permit such a lengthy absence from the tonic as the pavan, this elaborate return emphasizes the importance of the work's wide harmonic field, just as the last galliard strains in the F2 and C3 pairs draw attention to special technical features. There is also a very subtle final twist in the echo structure. The earlier statement in the last exchange enters, not in bar 5 in agreement with the pattern estab-

---

*A reminiscence of Galliard F2; see Ex. 62e.

†Compare the virtual truce to antiphony at this point in Pavan 6/C (see p. 88).

‡For something comparable in substance, if not in spirit, see the end of var. 8 of *John come kiss me now.*

lished in the previous strains, but on the second beat of bar 4. This allows it to expand into an eloquent 2-bar phrase, and makes room for a beautiful alto entry to intervene in bar 5, before the true echo.

Byrd's contribution to *Parthenia*, which was published in the winter of 1612–13, consisted entirely of pavans and galliards, with appropriate preludes. He included only one 16-bar pavan, William Petre's, which after more than twenty years he evidently still thought the most suitable for the purpose, whether on account of its very substantial galliard, or because it avoided any too specialized reference or technique, or simply to honour the dedicatee. The other dances, however, were recent. Mary Brownlow was born about 1591 (see BK 34, commentary) and would have been hard put to it to play the magnificent Galliard C4 that bears her name till some years after the turn of the century; since she did not marry till 1613 it need not have been composed till shortly before its publication. It is followed by the Earl of Salisbury Pavan a2 and two galliards which demonstrably belong with it, although the engraver mistakenly repeated Mary Brownlow's name at the head of the second one. Gibbons also contributed a pavan for Lord Salisbury and a related galliard to the volume, and since the pieces of both composers are sombre in mood and, apart from Gibbons's galliard, lack decorated repeats, it is reasonable to suppose that they were specially written as a tribute to the memory of Robert Cecil, who had died a few months earlier on 24 May 1612. These are the only pavans and galliards in the keyboard repertory for which a commemorative purpose can be adduced with any degree of certainty.

By the time *Parthenia* appeared the galliard had changed considerably in the hands of younger composers. The desire for greater brilliance led them to introduce semiquaver runs which slowed the beat down and dissipated the characteristic rhythmic buoyancy of the dance; there are examples by both Bull and Gibbons in *Parthenia* itself. Byrd subjected Harding's popular galliard to this treatment in his late keyboard setting, but showed no enthusiasm for it in his own compositions. Apart from the cadential flourishes at the end of Galliards g2 and G5, semiquaver figures occur only in the highly ornate **Galliard C4** for Mary Brownlow, and even here only incidentally, in the context of a slow tempo determined by quite different factors. Pattern is Byrd's subject in this work; not, as in the C3 pair, linear pattern placed in the leading role, with its attendant lowering of harmonic activity, but the interpenetration of melodic and harmonic pattern. One result of this is an unusually fast rate of harmonic change, another the frequent fragmentation of melody into smaller developing elements. A third arises from Byrd's habitual dislike of literal sequence, to which pattern naturally leads, and to avoid which he twists this way and that, forestalling the obvious with every kind of variant, transformation and interruption. Even he rarely achieved a musical texture of such density and interest.

All this inevitably puts considerable strain on the galliard structure, which Byrd accordingly provides with an unusually clear foundation. In strain I he looks back to the old tradition of 4-bar strains* and arranges a partial correspondence between the two halves of the strain, with the same bass opening in bars 1 and 5 and a tonic cadence in bar 4 as well as bar 8. The rest of the piece too seems to have been thought out differently from most pavans and galliards, in which the three main strains invariably contain the complete formal conception, however essential the repeats may be to the final effect of the work. Here the opening of I′ provides material for II and later introduces for the first time a recurrent feature of the piece: a heavy open fifth in the bass on the second quaver of the minim beat. Similarly III′ takes up a figure from II.

Beside this most complex piece Byrd placed the simplest of all his pavans and galliards, if a work of such perfection can be called simple, the **Pavan and Galliards a2.** The Earl of Salisbury is the only 8-bar pavan of Byrd's maturity, his only pavan in two strains instead of three, and the only one in which the repeats are undecorated.† The two galliards, which employ the usual 8-bar strain, are likewise the only ones with undecorated repeats, and the first the only one with only two strains. The sober tone of the pavan superficially recalls Byrd's minor mode pavans of the 1570s and 1580s. The mood of such pieces must have appealed strongly to younger composers, for they intensified it a few years later in the passionate pavans of the melancholic vogue.

Byrd's development led another way. From the g2 pair onwards the proliferating invention of his later keyboard style carried too many complex cross-shafts of feeling to allow him to cultivate a single affect at a time, as comparison of his wonderful arrangement of *Lachrymae* with the original shows. Such complexity could find no place in the Earl of Salisbury Pavan, but there was no real return to an earlier style, still less any suggestion of overt lamentation. On the contrary, one of its most striking features, its extreme motivic economy,‡ allies it to the more elaborate late works, whilst

---

*See Galliard G9, the last strains of g3 and C1, and beyond them the Galliard Jig and its forbears.

†It should be obvious that Byrd did not want decoration here; to supply it is an impertinence.

‡For a detailed study of the motivic organization see A. Souris, 'Problèmes d'analyse', in Jacquot, *Musique instrumentale*, 354ff.

the special restraint and poise, in expression as in structure, belong only to itself.

As usual only the pavan bears the dedication, so it is not altogether clear whether the galliards form part of the epitaph. The first matches the pavan so perfectly in proportions and purity of line that its right to the title seems equally good. The second, which was probably an afterthought, follows on with perfect musical propriety, but takes in a larger horizon and is less obviously commemorative in spirit: it forsakes the frequent 3-part writing of the other pieces and introduces cross-rhythms and a more decorative style. The beginning of the first galliard grows straight out of the close of the pavan and also refers to its opening, as Ex. 64a–c show* (there are also various precedents for the dotted note). The second galliard starts with a variant of the same motive, strain II in each galliard with an inverted version

Ex. 64

a. Pavan a2/I, bar 1   b. Pavan a2/II, bar 6

c. Galliard a2(1)/I, bar 1

of it, and strain III in the second with a rather different kind of derivative of strain II of the first; all this resembles the motivic procedure in the pavans and galliards 6/C and G5. There is another technical feature that serves to unify the three pieces, even though it is found in other late works: a bass line of which the essential notes descend by step accompanying a melody at the tenth (or seventeenth) above.† It appears in strain Ib of the pavan, in IIb (starting from the half-bar upbeat) of the first galliard, and in Ib (with varied bass)‡ and IIIa of the second galliard. Despite its close bonds with the first galliard, the second establishes its own identity not only through its

---

*The close imitation at the beginning is paralleled in another late galliard, F2; see Ex. 62d.

†Cf. Mary Brownlow, strains Ib (an octave descent), IIb and IIIb, and strain III of Alman C2.

‡Cf. the penultimate bar of *Oh mistress mine*.

fuller keyboard texture* but by a subtle structural parallel between each strain as it begins to move towards the cadence: bars 6–7 in I are echoed at the same point in both the later strains, in II by an upward transposition and in III by the rhythm of the top line.

Every one of Byrd's more mature pavans and galliards derives individuality and consistency from a particular technique: melodic symmetry (c2), polyphonic formality (C2), keyboard virtuosity (G2), canon (G6), textural contrast (g2 and d1), line (F1), a special type of harmonic progression (F2), figuration (C3), the echo principle (G5). To this list the Mary Brownlow and Earl of Salisbury pieces add not so much fresh technical principles as extremes respectively of exuberance and restraint that Byrd had never touched before. Placed side by side after the William Petre pair in *Parthenia* they demonstrate vividly within the restricted space allowed by the publication the astonishing range of his art.

*In this respect too there are parallels with Mary Brownlow: compare III, and the heavy left-hand chords in bar 6 of both I and II, respectively with I′, and bar 6 of I or bars 2 and 3 of III′, in the latter work.

Keyboard Fantasias and Preludes

Prelude, A minor		BK 12
Prelude, C major		BK 24
Prelude, F major		Neighbour 2 (listed in BK, second edition, 115)
Prelude, G major		Neighbour 3 (listed in BK, second edition, 116)
Prelude, G minor		BK 1
Ut re mi fa sol la		BK 64
Ut mi re		BK 65
Fantasia a1		BK 13
Fantasia C1		BK 26
Fantasia C2		BK 25
Fantasia C3		BK 27
Fantasia C4		BK 28
Fantasia d1		BK 46
Fantasia G1		BK 61
Fantasia G2		BK 62
Fantasia G3		BK 63

No distinction is drawn in the above list between fantasias and voluntaries because, although the three works entitled voluntary in Nevell (C1, C3 and G1) contain noticeably less florid writing than the fantasias, they do not differ structurally from the fantasias and copyists used the terms interchangeably. Tomkins called C4 a 'verse', a term which he applied with no special significance to several of his own free compositions; one of Bull's pieces in similar 2-part style (MB 14/10) is called a fantasia in two of the sources. Within each mode the fantasias are arranged by source in the same order of preference as the pavans and galliards (see p. 177). The canonic fantasia C1 is an unsatisfactory arrangement of the Consort Fantasia 5/C; it is discussed in Chapter 4. The worthless keyboard scores of Fantasias 6/g1 and 2 (printed as Nos. 11 and 12 in *Cantantibus organis* 16, ed. E. Kraus (Regensburg, 1968)) were probably intended only as accompaniments; Byrd can have had no part in them. Two misattributions to Byrd fall within the scope of the present chapter. The A minor Prelude BK 96 is by Tomkins (MB 5/3), and the G major piece BK 97 (MB 20/46, 47), variously described as a 'touch' by Byrd or a voluntary by Gibbons, is certainly not by Byrd, for it abounds in untypical features: in the first part the passages in sixths and tenths (bars 3–7) and the sequence which rises a step only to fall back again (bars 8–10), in the second part the Gibbons-like harmonic progression at bars 7–8 and the unmotivated alto padding in bar 10. Tomkins knew two A minor fantasias by Byrd (see MB 5, p. 157); the second was presumably the first half of Fantasia C3, which occurs as a separate piece in a manuscript that Tomkins owned.

Of the four main keyboard genres cultivated by Byrd two are variation forms, respectively on grounds and treble melodies, and two freely composed – the pavans and galliards in stanza form, and the fantasias in what may be called prose form. Prose form is the factor common to the pieces considered in the present chapter.

Byrd's preludes are very brief pieces intended strictly for the function implied by their name; as a rule he preferred not to distract attention from the main composition by engaging in any preliminary development. At this period preludes normally occur as independent pieces in the sources, so that the player who needed one in a certain key could make his own choice. Byrd no doubt used his preludes in this way, but they differ widely in character and seem originally to have been devised for particular contexts rather than for general purposes. For instance, Tregian explicitly associated the A minor Prelude with Fantasia a1, and although both works occur separately elsewhere internal evidence suggests that he was right. The piece begins in the style of some of Byrd's earlier pavans, such as a1, and behaves like the first half of a 16-bar strain to the extent of basing bars 7–8 on a dominant pedal. The opening imitation of the fantasia echoes not only its general mood but the rhythm of the quaver groups in bars 7–8 and 10, and the descending triadic figure ECA with its variant EDB. Another apparent link between the two pieces is discussed below (p. 237).

Both the preludes in *Parthenia* are found in other sources and seem to have been slightly revised for publication. The **G minor Prelude** appears coupled with Pavan and Galliard g2, which had no prelude in Nevell. Whether or not it was composed specially for this pavan it cannot be much later in date because it occurs in Weelkes. In any case it fits very well, for it anticipates the salient harmonic moves in strain I, reaching its first pause on the dominant by way of VI^6, and then proceeding to VII (although for the same reasons it could preface Johnson's *Delight* almost as appropriately). The other prelude in *Parthenia*, the **C major Prelude**, accompanies Mary Brownlow's Galliard C4; as the latter is unique to the publication the two pieces were probably composed independently. They do not sound as though they belong together: the peculiar originality of the prelude lies in its slender, highly decorative textures kept largely to the upper range of the keyboard, and the piece contrasts oddly with the powerful galliard. Consideration of the remaining preludes will help to suggest its probable origin.

The preludes in F and G belong to the group of late works by Byrd to which Forster gives no ascription (see p. 23); the G major piece also occurs anonymously in Tregian. The relation of the **F major Prelude** to Pavan and Galliard F2, which has already been discussed (p. 210), proves its authenticity. The **G major Prelude**, unlike the others, is a tripartite structure capable of making a contribution in its own right to any work that it might introduce. It opens and closes with toccata-like runs, between which there is a section in fantasia style containing near-quotations from Fantasias C1 and G3.* It cannot, of course, have been intended for use with the first of these because it is in the wrong mode, nor surely with the second – a much earlier work which the composer had not seen fit to include in Nevell. These coincidences, which speak powerfully for the authenticity of the piece, may be felt to weaken any argument which involves accepting similarities with some other work as deliberate. Nevertheless the following points are striking: the prelude occurs only a few places further on in the manuscript from the anonymous text of the Echo Pavan and Galliard G5, with which it shares its spacious keyboard layout and forthright movement, and it introduces the first echo motive from the pavan in diminution and, in bars 15 and 18–19, at the same pitches (see Ex. 65).

It is just such similarities of general character and of detail that are lacking between the C major Prelude and the Mary Brownlow Galliard.

*Compare bars 11–13 with Fantasia C1, bars 28–31; and bars 18–21 with Fantasia G3, bars 84–86.

Ex. 65

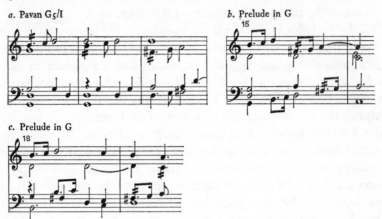

a. Pavan G5/I

b. Prelude in G

c. Prelude in G

However, the rich surface ornament and relaxed harmonic progress characteristic of this prelude are matched in another late work, the Pavan and Galliard C3. The opening of the prelude may be read as a parody of the pavan: it augments the slow rise from C to F in the treble and accompanies it with a very ornate version of the quaver group from the imitative point.* The dominant cadences at bars 10 and 19 balance the subdominant tendency of the pavan's first strain very well, and the low G and F at the beginning of the pavan make an excellent effect after the restricted range of the prelude. It looks as though Byrd transferred this relatively recent prelude to Galliard C4 when he was putting his contribution to *Parthenia* together, without much thought for its suitability.

Although the affinities traced here between the preludes in G and C and the relevant pavans and galliards cannot in themselves prove that the pieces belong together, the established connections between the G minor and F major preludes and their dance pairs would seem to tip the scale. The pavan and galliard pairs g2, F2, C3 and G5 are the most highly developed that Byrd composed. He provided the first two with preludes; it can hardly be an accident that he wrote two more preludes in the modes of the other two at roughly the same period, and fully in accordance with their respective characters and material.

*An inversion of this forms the basis of bars 16–17; bars 10–14 may be compared with bars 23–27 of the pavan. According to M. C. Bradshaw ('The Origin of the Toccata', *Musicological Studies and Documents* 28 (1972), 57f.) this prelude incorporates two consecutive statements of the eighth psalm tone. However, this reading requires a degree of rhythmic distortion to the chant incompatible with English traditions of cantus firmus setting, and the association of the chant with a galliard would have offended against contemporary notions of decorum – especially Byrd's.

Byrd's fantasias all belong to his early or middle years; none can post-date Nevell, and several show close ties with the organ music of an earlier generation. Fantasias C4 and C3, for instance, are very largely composed in two and three parts respectively. They belong to traditions of composition that originated in organ hymns and antiphons with decorated cantus firmus such as Byrd himself composed early in his career (see Chapter 6).

At first sight the little **Fantasia C4**, with its bright major tonality and complete equality between the parts, may seem remote from his 2-part plainsong settings, but the technical elements are essentially the same; they are able to develop more freely here simply because, it is safe to assume, no cantus firmus controls the lower part. Thus, while the secular ring of the opening finds a precedent at the close of the *Gloria tibi trinitas* (see Ex. 39), there is none for the freedom with which melodic segments are symmetrically transposed and varied in the interests of an equable balance between tonic and dominant regions. Again, the slower left-hand passages which accompany the more continuous quaver or semiquaver figuration in the right hand are typical of decorated plainsong style, but the resemblance is masked by the constant exchange of roles between the two hands, not to mention the use of quick runs in both at once. A lengthy semiquaver flourish of this kind ends the piece; it is the transition from the initial closed six-line stanza (bars 1–6) to the fluidity of the conclusion that constitutes the larger theme of the piece. To make the contrast more extreme Byrd ends each line of the stanza (except the third) with a falling third, thus forcing the implied harmonic pulse, which moves largely in crotchets, to a minim's halt.* He moves forward from the stability of this exposition by means of a developing series of phrases just as Redford might have done, given the greatly increased activity of Byrd's idiom and his gift for spontaneous gaiety.†

Redford's influence, direct or indirect, is still more marked in the 3-part **Fantasia C3**. Some account has already been given of a style of 3-part plainsong setting favoured by Redford and his contemporaries, in which elaboration of the cantus firmus leads to a freely imitative texture often involving all three parts (see p. 103). Pieces composed in this way were sometimes headed 'with a meane' in the sources, or simply entitled 'a meane'. Byrd was not the only composer who subsequently took the style up in free

---

*Cf. the stopped 4-bar phrases that hold the early stages of the Hornpipe in check, discussed on p. 121.

†The only 2-part piece in the repertory to resemble Byrd's in any way is Richard Farnaby's Duo (MB 24/55) which, however, is probably indebted to it. Bull's much larger fantasias (MB 14/10 and 11), though they show a better sense of line than many of his works, are untouched by Byrd's interest in popular melody.

composition; Tallis, Blitheman and Bull each left an example in which no plainsong has been identified.* Tallis and Blitheman still sometimes give the bass a non-imitative part in slower values; Bull's style in his presumably early piece is close to that of Blitheman's essay and the same composer's *Felix namque* (MB 1/32), though he coordinates the three parts more consistently by means of short imitative motives. Byrd's fantasia, however, is before all else imitative; in fact it is the most persistently imitative of all his keyboard works, comparable in general conception to such a piece as White's 5-part consort *Song* (see p. 63). As there, each point is cultivated intensively and then replaced by another derived from it, and as usual with Byrd, even in his early works, the paragraphs are very firmly marked out with cadences, especially in the earlier stages of the composition.

One technical feature in Byrd's adaptation of the 'mean' style stands out: at least half the points are never transposed, but always enter on the same degree, though in three different octaves. This procedure is rare in Tallis and Blitheman; there is no place for it, for instance, in the close, dissonant texture of Tallis's beautiful essay in free 'mean' style, which has all the sombre intensity of his keyboard hymns. Nor does it occur in Bull's piece. But it is common in earlier composers, above all in Redford who makes use of it, often extensively, in the great majority of his 'mean' compositions. Byrd's fantasia shares with these certain qualities that the technique entails by its nature: a steady, easy pace measured out by the insistent canonic echoes and a widely spaced texture. Bar by bar the music would sound very much like Redford were it not for Byrd's vastly stronger sense of harmonic direction. The influence of Redford's artistry can be felt in a number of details,† but the implications of Byrd's debt go deeper. The note-against-note imitative style of the intervening generation threatened to obliterate all memory of the freer melodic legacy of the previous century. It was the value that Redford set on melody that appealed to Byrd, his delight in the repetition in one part after another of an unchanged melodic statement, his skill in the contrary process of melodic variation and extension, and his concern for clear textures that would assure melodic supremacy. Byrd even revived (Ex. 66) decorative patterns of a crotchet and two quavers, or the reverse, used by all composers up to Preston, but not by Tallis or Blitheman because neither

---

*Two thoroughly unsatisfactory and widely divergent texts of Tallis's piece survive in Christ Church MSS 371 and 1034; the only printed edition (Tallis, *Complete Keyboard Works*, ed. D. Stevens (London, 1953), 8) apparently makes no use of the latter. Blitheman's undistinguished effort is in Add.31403 (fol. 9). For the Bull see MB 14/15.

†For example, at breves 24–26, where Byrd introduces a new point first on E and then on F before allowing it to settle at its standard pitch on G; or at breves 84–86, where he similarly lifts an imitative motive by a tone.

closely packed part-writing nor elaborate keyboard figuration could accommodate it.

Ex. 66

It goes without saying that Byrd did not leave the Redfordian technique where he found it. For instance he concluded the piece with a brilliant stretto (breve 86 to the end) in which closely related entries follow each other in the following sequence: 12 at the interval of a semibreve, 6 at the dotted minim, 2 at the semibreve, 2 at the minim. Such a passage carries the 'mean' idiom far beyond its original limits. In the main, of course, his long-range harmonic and structural thinking contribute most to its transformation, yet oddly enough it is in this field that the most striking evidence of the tradition's hold on him occurs: in his absorption with a style rooted in plainsong setting he was quite content to begin his piece in A minor* and end it in C major. In plainsong settings nobody worried about such things because the cantus firmus was held to justify what it dictated,† but in free composition to go 'out of the key' came to be considered, in the words of Byrd's stern pupil Morley, 'one of the grossest faults that may be committed'. The discrepancy is more blatant in Byrd's fantasia than in its cantus firmus forerunners because he establishes A minor so firmly at the beginning. While the modern listener is likely to accept this essay in progressive tonality as readily as Byrd himself accepted the prompting of his musical instinct when he wrote it, he may have felt abashed at the solecism in retrospect, and hit upon the idea of salvaging the conclusion by slicing the piece in half.

That this rough, ready and thoroughly unsatisfactory expedient had his approval is at least possible, because the second half is included in Nevell;‡ the first half also circulated independently. Unfortunately no suitable break occurs after the last A minor close because the transition away from this mode in the complete work has been most carefully calculated. There is a

---

*To judge by the cadences. The opening point could scarcely be more ambiguous: the first two entries begin on C and G, but sketch out the triads of A minor and E minor respectively.

†See, among countless examples, Byrd's own *Christe redemptor* settings for 4-part consort.

‡But Baldwin may have added it on his own authority; it is hard to believe that Byrd would have wanted it to occupy its present position at the very end of the manuscript, following two of the latest works contained in it (Pavan and Galliard g2 and Fantasia d1).

full close in A minor at breve 16, another at 33, a rather indefinite plagal cadence at 46, and a pair of interrupted closes at 52–53, after which the music turns to C major and stays there. The division was made at 46. This was no doubt the only possible place, but it leaves the first half with a final close weaker than the two intermediate ones, whilst the second half still begins in A minor. Moreover, whereas the first half starts with a sixteen-breve exposition of entries at the prime and fifth, the second half leads off with a fragmentary bass entry, and only three complete statements of the new subject follow, all at the prime, before further fragmentation occurs; the passage is obviously framed for the middle reaches of the composition. The piece should only be performed complete, in which form it makes an individual contribution to Byrd's output and takes a high place among his early works.

The two hexachord fantasias were intended as a pair, as Tregian makes clear by transcribing them in sequence and writing the direction *perge* after the first – the equivalent of *attacca*.* Tomkins too listed Byrd pieces with the same titles as a pair, adding the comment 'both for substance', in contrast to a piece of the same kind by Bull (presumably MB 14/18) which he labelled 'for the hand' (see MB 5, p. 158). The forms taken by the hexachord in the two pieces are shown on p. 221. In **Ut re mi** there are seventeen statements of the simple ascending and descending form woven into the fabric of the fantasia. An introduction of sixteen semibreves precedes the first, and there is a break of from one to six semibreves between each, except between Nos. 11 and 12. Byrd uses six of the twelve possible transpositions, avoiding those that contain A♭ or G♯. The first ten statements are based on G, D, C, C, C, F, G, A, B♭ and C. During statement 11 quaver movement sets in and continues up to the tripla section; in order not to inhibit the figuration with remoter harmonic twists Byrd starts all the later statements on the tonic, except for No. 14, which is on D.† Changes of texture or of imitative motive do not necessarily coincide with a new statement of the hexachord, and various sections of the work end on the third note of the rising scale, which provides a natural point of cadence. The tripla section, for example, does not begin until the third note of No. 13, although Byrd's general plan must have allowed for a round dozen statements

---

*Cf. the pair of consort pieces on the same pattern mentioned on p. 90.

†In the *Browning*, too, transposition becomes more restricted in the later stages (see p. 72), partly no doubt for similar reasons. However, the use of transposition in the two pieces cannot be compared in other respects because the hexachord does not play a fundamental structural role, and the Browning tune does.

in duple metre followed by four in tripla and a final one for the coda.*

Thus the work as a whole is planned in relation to the hexachord statements, but is not primarily controlled by them. There are four main sections, divided by tonic cadences. Roughly speaking, the first embodies statements 1–2, the second 3–6, the third 7–12 and the fourth (the tripla and coda) 13–17. The opening point begins with a rising hexachord, and since the rhythm changes at each entry, the first two statements of the cantus firmus, despite their long, even note-values, do not sound alien but take their place naturally in the 4-part imitative texture. The whole section down to the cadence in breve 23 is beautifully handled, the long undulating lines controlled by a balance between the inherent subdominant tendency of Mixolydian and dominant correction which is conspicuously lacking in the *Ut mi re* sequel.

Section 2 consists of three episodes, corresponding approximately to statements 3–4, 5, and 6 respectively; section 3 comprises four – roughly statements 7–8, 9, 10 and 11–12. It will be seen that in its earlier stages the third section is built to the measure of the second. The correspondence goes beyond questions of proportion: the structure moves in a spiral, so that the events in the third section mirror those in the second at a higher level of intensity. The related opening gestures in the two sections (Ex. 67a and b)

Ex. 67

serve an introductory purpose: they give birth to the main imitative motives

*Was the choice of the curious number seventeen influenced by the Second Ground (see p. 126)? The two pieces seem to belong to roughly the same period. (Bull's chromatic hexachord fantasia, MB 14/17, also contains seventeen statements, the last five all on the tonic G.)

in their respective episodes and then drop out. The first episode of section 2 proceeds relatively quietly to cadences on the Mixolydian seventh and sub-dominant; that of section 3 sets a livelier pulse and (with the help of the hexachord based on A) heads for dominant and supertonic regions.

The progress of the music in both sections is checked by the next episode. In section 2 this takes the form of a 2-part canon accompanying statement 5; it lowers the temperature considerably until the last episode takes over and closes the circle at Ex. 67b. The buoyant first episode in section 3 is abruptly terminated by a full close resolving in the tonic minor – tantamount in the context to an interrupted cadence. The ensuing slow episode in G minor and C minor (embodying statement 9 on B♭), corresponds exactly to the canonic episode in the previous section, but its effect is far more powerful because it follows on an episode of greater ardour and is much more chilling in itself. It is in every sense the central event of the work: the music hurries on unscathed, but the long lines of the melodious tripla section and the serene coda are enriched by the sense of a danger avoided.

It is disappointing to find that the companion to this fine work does not live up to it. There are fourteen statements of the cantus firmus in Ut mi re – only three less than in Ut re mi – but the work is little more than half the length because, despite the greater number of notes in the cantus firmus, Byrd uses shorter note-values to bring about the faster harmonic pulse and quicker divisions usual in a sequel. In statements 1, 2, 4 and 9 he keeps the rhythm of the cantus firmus flexible so that it can engage in imitation on equal terms with the other parts. Elsewhere he confines it very largely to minims (semibreves in No. 11); where such statements are placed end to end without a break (7–8, 10–13) the piece begins to resemble a set of variations on the kind of ground that moves from one part to another.

The feeling of variation form is reinforced by a harmonic trait. Byrd contrives to reach a chord of E major at, or soon after, the end of the first half of the cantus firmus in every statement except Nos. 1 and 3. The implied supertonic resolution at the beginning of the second half is often interrupted in some way, but the recurrent harmonic situation recalls the midway supertonic cadences in the Consort Ground and the *Browning* (see Chapter 4). By contrast this feature does not occur in Ut re mi until the more stable later stages, from statement 10 onwards.* Even in the more fluid earlier part of Ut mi re Byrd's tendency to think in terms of variations shows in strong cadences and breaks in the rhythm before every new statement

---

*In the transposed statements 10 and 14 of *Ut re mi* the harmony is correspondingly transposed, as in the two sets of consort variations, but in *Ut mi re* the transposed statement 10 and the canonic 7 and 8 do not disturb the pivotal E major–A minor progression.

except 4 and 6. The work was probably planned as a sequence of twelve statements (the most usual number for variations), with the usual acceleration through quavers to tripla. This scheme, however, would have reduplicated that of any preceding *Ut re mi* composition. Presumably as a means of incorporating faster divisions, Byrd added in the middle* a pair of statements accompanied by semiquavers, so that the work falls into three parts: statements 1–6, 7–8, 9–14. The semiquavers of the central pair enter halfway through 6, but it looks as though 9, which belongs technically with 1–5 rather than 10–13, may originally have been composed in sixth place, where it makes a perfect join.

Byrd begins the work 'out of the key' in C instead of G, evidently because he saw no reason why he should not. He makes no attempt to establish the tonic till the end of statement 2, but starts with a 3-part imitation† in which statement 1 provides the middle voice and the bass line departs from and returns to C. Throughout the piece he raises the Mixolydian seventh rather sparingly except at cadences. Thus he only once transposes the cantus firmus to D (statement 3), whereas he not only has a complementary transposition to C (statement 10) but imitates statements on G in canon at the fifth below in 1, 7 and 8. He also uses canon at the octave (2, 4 and the second half of 9) but avoids the fifth above except in 10 (second half) where the main statement is in C, so that the same combination of C and G results.

This modal influence, which is stronger than in any other keyboard work of his outside the hymns and antiphons, is one of a number of features that betray a very early date of composition. Another is the canonic writing in the two middle statements. In 7 the right hand has a canon at the fifth and at the minim against a free bass part in semiquavers, and in 8 the two elements change hands. The only parallel in the repertory for this texture is in Tallis, whose canonic keyboard piece‡ is laid out in precisely the same way as Byrd's statement 7, except that the running bass is in quavers instead of semiquavers. The tripla section in Byrd's piece has little of his customary melodic interest, each statement of the cantus firmus being accompanied by a slab of figuration altogether in the manner of Tallis or Blitheman. The

*Cf. the addition of the two central variations 11 and 12 in *Walsingham*.

†Cf. the reduced-voice variations at the beginning of *The Maiden's Song*, the *Browning* and *Walsingham*.

‡See MB 14/51. The later of the two sources, Add.31403, which is shaky in its ascriptions, gives the piece to Bull. Weelkes, who attributes it to Tallis, is far more reliable (he incidentally gives the earliest text of Tallis's *Felix namque* of 1564). No similar work is known by either composer, which tells more heavily against Bull, whose music survives in quantity, than Tallis, whose keyboard music is mostly lost. The dissonances between the bass and the canonic parts recall the treatment of figuration in parts of Tallis's two *Felix namque* settings, and would seem to settle the question.

figuration itself varies in quality: the semiquavers and some of the tripla passages are well handled and already typical of Byrd, but the stiff, old-fashioned syncopations of statement 11 are matched only in his early plainsong settings.

Above all the formal conception is uncharacteristic. Whatever the incidental merits of the later stages of the piece they do not serve a developing structure, but crop up in the course of an essentially static succession of textural patterns. Byrd very early rejected composition along these lines, though it lived on in the music of Bull and his imitators. Yet the imitative first half of the work shows real originality and establishes an individuality of tone that is never quite lost in the less satisfactory continuation, coming to the surface again in the little coda (statement 14). How does this piece come to form a sequel to the in every way maturer *Ut re mi*? The most likely explanation is that the latter work replaces another composed on the plain hexachord at the same time as *Ut mi re*. This would have started with the slower harmonic pulse of its eventual substitute, but would have shared the more variation-like structure and the less adventurous transpositions of its sequel. At some later date, probably in the 1570s,* Byrd decided to replace it, but still thought the *Ut mi re* worth keeping. By the time of Nevell, however, he had changed his mind, and so gave Baldwin the later *Ut re mi* by itself.

The fantasias so far considered are all special cases, subject to the conditions imposed by a limited number of parts or a recurrent hexachord cantus firmus. The remaining six are completely free. They divide into two groups. Three of them, G2, a1 and G3, progress from imitation to tripla, like the hexachord fantasias. The other three, C2, d1 and G1, abandon tripla and close with a decorated repeat of the last section. Byrd included all the fantasias of the second group in Nevell, but none of the first.

Fantasia G2, Byrd's longest, begins with proportionately lengthy treatment of the first point, lasting $28\frac{1}{2}$ breves. This, though unremarkable by continental standards, is considerably longer than the opening section of any other English piece of the period, for the English used imitation primarily to intensify the character of the music from moment to moment rather than as a means of structural prolongation (see p. 62f). Byrd gives his second point an even longer run, from breve 28 to 64, which suggests that his aim

*There are still a few small marks of inexperience in the new piece: the canonic statement 5 enters rather stiffly, the imitative motive in the alto at breves 68–69 is left incomplete because neither hand can reach the notes in comfort, and the accented tonic harmony at the beginning of breve 96 is anticipated on the previous semibreve.

here, as so often, was to outdo his forerunners in the field, especially as he betrays no direct knowledge of continental practice.

His basically 4-part writing shows none of the melodic grace and textural transparency of the 3-part Fantasia C3. The two points (Ex. 68a and b) are

Ex. 68

cut very square, with an eye to details like passing notes and suspensions rather than to complex contrapuntal combinations or melody for its own sake. They are worked out in the stiff note-against-note style of Tye, Tallis or White at their most pedestrian. If proof is needed that Byrd's 'old fancy', as Tomkins called it (see MB 5, p. 158), is an early work and not merely an essay in an early style, it is provided by the rhythmic monotony induced by numerous suspensions resolved with an anticipatory crotchet or pair of quavers. Similar troubles afflict some of the early consort hymns (see p. 58), but not the otherwise comparable opening section of the relatively mature *Ut re mi* fantasia.

Yet the suspensions point to something more positive: the musical thought is not primarily concerned with imitation, but with harmony, its power as a shaping agent and its ability to lend expressive colour to neutral melodic material. Thus the cadential implication at the end of the first point is frequently echoed in subsidiary voices, and there results a constant succession of resolutions of varying strength that serve to measure out and redirect the progress of the music with singular clarity, and incidentally to counteract the Mixolydian tendency towards the subdominant. This is not the only matter in which Byrd pays rather a high price but at least gets something in return. The point contains only four different notes and the thirteen entries occur only at the prime and the fifth; as the great majority of entries follow one another at intervals of from three to five semibreves, imitative tension is low. But the entries on the prime and fifth between them contain all the notes of the scale, and their liberal spacing helps them to assert their respective spheres, especially when, as happens rather often, they appear in the bass (three entries at the prime and two at the fifth). Consequently, before the second point enters the harmonic vocabulary has taken in both root chords and sixths on every degree of the scale.

The second point brings no great change of style, although entries occur on several degrees and are on average less widely spaced; there is also more play with melodic continuations. The point contains no F♯, and after a tonic cadence at the end of the first exposition (breve 37) Byrd finally lets the music make its way to the subdominant, though under supervision. After preliminary cadences in C (breves 44 and 48) a return to the tonic is forestalled by false relations, and the first C major cadence, together with the approach to the second, is repeated in only slightly altered form (breves 55–57). A fine closing passage in crotchets then supervenes, and leads by way of dominant and unestablished tonic to the first full close in C.

Here, at least, Byrd has found his form, and with a sense of relief, as the present-day listener may suspect, that the day's sterner duties are over, turns to a series of three shorter imitations on brisker subjects (Ex. 68c, d and e). The melodic shapes in the first two of these are quite common in Redford and Preston, but are here secularized almost beyond recognition by regular phrase lengths and frequent cadences.* There follows a transition in two brief sections (bars 100–104, 105–12), of which the first consists of an improvisatory melodic strand of widely varying speed with homophonic accompaniment; this style reappears briefly in the coda. The last main section is in tripla, beginning with the melody shown in Ex. 68f; it includes four bars (124–28) in the early, harmonically static tripla style found in Tallis's *Felix namque* of 1564 and Byrd's *The Hunt's up* (see p. 124).

The elements in all this that held Byrd's interest sufficiently for him to build on them were in the shorter run (Fantasia G3) the quick imitations of the middle stage, and in the longer (Fantasias C2 and d1) the free style of the transition at bars 100–104. But the work as a whole must have made a deep impression, for it turns up in unusual seventeenth-century sources, one of them continental, and was remembered by the expatriate Philips who used the first point as the sole basis for a hybrid English-Sweelinckian fantasia (Tregian No. 84). It is easy to forget how fresh and original the long section based on the first two points must have sounded to a contemporary. Where listeners with a background of Byrd's later music may find stiffness and some tedium, those accustomed, for instance, to White's consort

---

*They are also notated at twice the speed, and consequently look like the melody in Ex. 66. But the parentage of this is different, for most of its quaver groups return to the main note, the source being the written-out mordents notated in the same values in the earlier style.

fantasias* would have discovered unprecedented formal subtlety and a new tone of voice, natural, confident and eloquent.

In one respect this first half of the piece may be compared to the Consort Fantasia 6/F, which belongs to the same early stage in his development. Both betray a conviction that harmony is more likely to provide a secure structural framework for textless composition than imitation. As he was often to do again Byrd approached the two media rather differently, working more formally in the consort piece, more flexibly for the keyboard. Evidently neither experiment satisfied him, and Fantasia G2 was destined to remain his nearest approach to an extended ricercare-like structure. Whether or not he was already aware of his mistrust of the contrapuntal ideal when he wrote it, he quickly became so.

The only remaining fantasia which cannot be placed later than G2 with certainty is **Fantasia a1**. Its involvement with older traditions of keyboard writing places it early, but the two works differ too widely in style for either to have affected the other. They differ no less widely in quality, for a1 is the greatest large-scale instrumental work of Byrd's early years – perhaps only the *Quadran* Pavan among later keyboard pieces rivals it in scope and power to astonish. Byrd's mastery might raise a suspicion that it was a deliberate essay in early styles carried out at a later date, were it not that much of the detail exceeds the credible limit of conscious archaizing.†

The work starts with an imitative phase of 41 semibreves, and here at once a fundamental divergence in musical character from G2 (and the later fantasias) declares itself: the harmonic pulse is in crotchets instead of minims, and the difference affects not merely appearances but musical reality. That Byrd expects his notation to convey roughly the same meaning in both pieces comes out in Ex. 69a–c, which show a stock transitional flourish notated in the same way and, except perhaps in the second case, too closely integrated with other parts for free interpretation. But even so it is no less clear that he has a slightly slower absolute speed in mind for a1, because it contains frequent semiquaver passages and proportional divisions of eighteen notes to the semibreve, whereas he uses semiquavers sparingly in G2. The latter work begins, as has been seen, in a style not far removed from that of vocal or consort polyphony, but in a1 even the imitative

---

*No doubt such pieces played their part in the formation of Byrd's 4-part imitative style. The mid-century 4-part texture of Ambrose's keyboard piece in Christ Church 1034 or Alwood's voluntary (MB 1/17) is little more than an expansion of 3-part 'mean' style.

†E.g. the simultaneous parallel and broken thirds in octaves in bars 120 and 124, which are paralleled only in Redford (EECM 10/25, bar 93).

opening is indebted to keyboard style, though less obviously so than much
that follows.

Ex. 69

a. Fantasia G2

b. Fantasia a1

c. Fantasia a1

Its origins can best be traced by turning first to the final section of the
work. Here the usual episode in tripla in the proportion of six crotchets
(i.e. black minims) to the semibreve gives way to another in which the six
are increased to nine. This type of conclusion, though occasionally imitated
later, is found in only four other pieces of the sixties: Tallis's two *Felix
namque* settings of 1562 and 1564 and Byrd's *Clarifica me pater* 1 and 2.
Tallis's earlier piece appears to have influenced the two by Byrd (see p. 109);
his later one undoubtedly left its mark on Fantasia a1. Both composers use

Ex. 70

a. Tallis and Byrd (159)   *b.* Tallis   *c.* Byrd (162)

d. Tallis and Byrd (179)

the same type of figure where the 9 : 4 proportion begins: the bar shown in Ex. 70a is common to both pieces, and so is the right-hand melodic phrase in Ex. 70d.* The crotchet runs that come between these examples are also similar, as the samples in Ex. 70b and c show. Both works end in exactly the same way with a 10-bar coda in duple measure and toccata style, and based on alternating harmonies of D minor and A major (the final).† Among other signs of the deep impression made on Byrd by the style of Tallis's offertory is the bass pattern of Ex. 69c, which occurs in several passages in the Tallis piece but nowhere else in Byrd's music.

In the light of these connections more significance may be attached to certain other similarities than would otherwise seem justified. Thus Byrd's initial imitation, though more closely worked than the corresponding passages in Tallis's pieces, can be seen to have inherited their notation, harmonic pace and melodic character. Again some weight may perhaps be given to the correspondences shown in Ex. 71 between the intonation to the

Ex. 71

a. Tallis

b. Byrd   *c.* Byrd

1564 *Felix namque* and Byrd's A minor Prelude (see p. 222); common though such phrases are they tend to confirm that the prelude belongs to the fantasia. Ex. 72a may also be compared with Ex. 71.

---

*Tregian's slightly different version of Byrd's phrase, with ACB in the first bar, is also present in Tallis's piece, except that there the first note is G.

†Only Tregian and Forster transmit the coda to the Tallis piece. If the other three sources had all agreed in stopping where the duple coda begins, which makes perfectly good sense, it might have been thought a later addition. But only the untrustworthy Cosyn does this. Weelkes and Add.31403 stop a breve earlier, giving the last note of the plainsong the minimum duration possible within the terms of the piece (a breve, followed by a final chord). This altogether too abrupt end compares unfavourably with that of the 1562 setting and casts doubt on the authenticity of both the short versions.

Despite Byrd's debt to Tallis in superficial points of style, their pieces could scarcely differ more radically in conception. Tallis's is totally dependent on the plainsong, which remains unaware of the formal responsibilities thrust upon it; invention finds an outlet only in the sphere of figuration. Byrd's fantasia is, of course, freely composed, and it takes in a wider range of character than any other keyboard work of the time. Tregian divides it into four numbered sections, but these can have no authority because the fourth begins nonsensically in the middle of an indivisible phase of the composition, and the first is really divided into two by the cadence at bar 41. Like the sections in *The Bells* (see p. 122) they probably originate in the numbers assigned to separate leaves or fragments for the guidance of a copyist. For purposes of discussion, however, it will be convenient to accept the first two sections and regard the other two as making up a third.

The first phase of section 1 consists of imitations on the first two points. Although there are technical affinities here with the other early fantasias,* the differences are far more important – not merely the quicker pulse but the extreme clarity and concision of treatment. An exposition of six entries leads straight to a full close and a break in only eleven bars (i.e. semibreves). A short second exposition brings a plagal cadence (bar 17) and the introduction of the second point. This begins with the three repeated notes so popular with Tallis and his contemporaries (Ex. 72b), and forms the basis

Ex. 72

of a quiet and level episode in which, for once, something of Tallis's spirit is present – not the Tallis of the offertories, whose letter has been made to

*As in G2 the second point enters on a greater variety of degrees than the first, while the cadence scheme resembles that of C3 (and of the Consort Fantasia 4/a): a full close followed by a plagal cadence (both on A), and then a gradual move to the relative major.

spell something quite foreign to him in the taut opening sentences, but the essential, devotional Tallis. As this beautiful passage turns towards C major and the clear upper range of the keyboard, the mood lightens and prepares the way for the spirited second phase of the section, which Byrd also anticipates in the structural dimension by repeats (bars 17–20, 21–25; 27–33, 33–37).

For the next phase of the work is built on the principle, universally popular in both vocal and instrumental music during the first half of the century, of antiphonal exchanges between pairs of voices, often in imitation. The first pair to be treated in this way (Ex. 72c) draws on elements from the first two points (Ex. 72a and b). Two more exchanges are developed from it. The subject for the first is shown in Ex. 72d; the second employs four voices instead of two, so that the antiphonal answer becomes a straight repetition.* From here a lively toccata-like episode leads back to a very firm tonic cadence at the end of the section.

Up to this point the music has followed in its own far more succinct terms a course that can at least be compared with that of G2, with the antiphony and the semiquavers of the closing passage occupying an equivalent position to the quicker imitations and the tripla of the latter work. But no such parallel, however distant, exists for the second section, in which an extraordinarily heterogeneous train of ideas, none of them more than a few bars long, lead into one another as though by free association. The first four bars (78–81) perform a preludial function. To have started, even on a less remote degree than G, with a new subject as distinctive and as alien to what has gone before as the one that enters in bar 82 would have jeopardized continuity. The descending scales (see Ex. 69b) have no thematic value – they

---

*This repetition is omitted in Tregian and is not included in the BK text, though it is mentioned in the commentary (note to bar 60). It is clearly justified by the structure, and the nature of the bar that leads the music back is such that, if there is an error here, it is one of omission by Tregian rather than of reduplication by Tomkins, who transcribed the only other known copy. In performance it would seem preferable to play for safety and make the repeat, since it is certainly not wrong; but it is just possible that Byrd himself changed his mind and decided against it, for most of Tregian's more considerable divergencies from Tomkins look like revisions that only Byrd could have thought of. The most striking case is at bars 113–14. Ex. 69c shows Tomkins's version, which is clearly the original: the treble and bass echo the treble and tenor of the previous two bars precisely. It is hard to conceive anyone but Byrd breaking this sequence with the highly imaginative version given by Tregian (quoted in BK commentary). At first sight Tregian's version of Ex. 70d looks less attractive, but it strengthens the downward melodic movement in bar 180 to the now unanticipated G in bar 181. In a number of other passages Tregian gives superior versions; most are printed as ossias in BK. Tomkins omitted bars 84–86; here it is impossible to say whether he made a mistake, which would be easy at this point, or whether Byrd expanded the passage later.

merely serve to minimize the finality of the preceding tonic cadence by referring back to the semiquaver approach to it. But their very emptiness concentrates attention on the shift in the fourth bar from almost unbroken F major (the Aeolian sixth that Byrd uses so often to start a new strain in his A minor pavans and galliards) to G,* and builds up expectation.

The sequel is startling: out of nowhere, as it seems, but in fact out of an augmented reversal of the downward scale in the previous bar, there saunters a new tune as though from another planet, but with such natural self-confidence that the listener has no choice but to accept and follow it. And he needs to trust because, although all the keyboard fantasias take a progressive rather than a cyclic course, he nowhere else has the unnerving experience of suddenly finding himself travelling through a landscape which lacks familiar landmarks and changes too rapidly for new ones to establish themselves.

However, every step in the process of constant transition is completely assured. At bar 90 a sudden reduction in harmonic pace that would normally scarcely make sense is carried by rhythmic development: ♫♩♫ (bars 83–86) → ♬♩ (87–89) → ♩. ♪♩ ♩ (90, etc.) → ♪♩♬ (91, etc.). This passage introduces a 6-bar episode (90–95) in which each pair of bars pivots on a suspension, but the forward displacement of that in the second pair effectively removes any sense of repose that regularity might bring. The music then moves, in a space of twenty semibreves, through no less than five different syncopated patterns of a kind found in Redford, Preston and their contemporaries, but not in Tallis or Blitheman – yet another indication of Byrd's grounding in the earlier, more linear keyboard style.† His cogent harmonic sense, in conjunction with regular periods, characteristically transforms this legacy; by the end of the last span of six semibreves (bars 107–10) the quickening pulse and divisions have built up enormous propulsive energy which the masterly rallentando at bars 111–14 (see Ex. 69c) does not fully absorb, so that something remains to launch the closing episode of the section. The exhilarating idea that enters here, neatly compounded from the melody and bass of bar 114, might surprise the listener as much as the G major melody at bar 82 had he not become inured to shock. In the event it has a contrary, reassuring effect because its relatively expansive 12-bar development finally brings a measure

---

*The effect is strengthened in Tregian's text by a small alteration in bars 78 and 80 – a touch difficult to ascribe to anyone but Byrd.

†The older composers usually worked such patterns singly, but a crude precedent for Byrd's use of a string of them in succession survives in Robert Coxsun's *Veritas mea* (EECM 10/28).

of stability. The passage ends in the relative major, like the first half of the first section, and the tripla section enters at once.

The tripla divisions start in the normal proportion of six crotchets (black minims) to the semibreve, but without the customary element of caprice. After the vagaries of the second section Byrd needs to return to the broader handling of events of the first section in order to recapture a comparable sense of stability. He does not, therefore, at first make the relatively slow basic pulse of the piece the occasion of faster divisions than usual – that is held in reserve for the final phase – but adopts rather weighty, even keyboard textures. At the same time he returns to the technical procedures of the first section, first a simple form of antiphony (bars 128–38) and then (138–46) imitation. Here three parts follow one another at the octave and fifteenth in his 'mean' style; apart from the fitful presence of a free fourth part the passage resembles the three-beat portion of the final stretto in Fantasia C3 (see p. 227). From here seven bars of right-hand quavers, beneath which the left skilfully introduces harmonic subdivision of the semibreve into three, lead to the second tripla phase in the proportion of nine crotchets to the semibreve.

This begins with four well defined 4-bar phrases during which momentum gathers swiftly and culminates in an even more powerful accumulation of harmonic energy (bars 170–73) than does the comparable passage in the second section (107–10). Here once again technical affinity is used as a deliberate means of cross-reference. In both passages the harmonic pace is increased through syncopation, and both prepare the final phase of their section. But whereas the impetus is checked in the first case, in the second it carries straight through: at bar 174 the melody shoots forward in extremely rapid quaver divisions, and the harmonic movement slackens to allow them the greatest possible freedom. For the next twelve bars there is no stopping them; they hurtle on while the harmony takes just enough note of the 4-bar periods to prepare and execute the final full close with perfect punctuality. Duple measure, which returns with the tonic chord, breaks the harmonic rhythm and reduces the divisions from eighteen to sixteen notes to the semibreve. The relaxed plagal harmonic field takes a few more bars to bring the semiquavers to a standstill.

The fantasia had no direct successor, and many of its most striking technical features occur nowhere else in Byrd's music. He never again found a use for the syncopations that occupy the middle of the second section, no doubt because even his far from dated treatment of them could not disguise their connection with an obsolete liturgical style. Perhaps the G major melody and the high-spirited final phase of the same section embody no less personal reinterpretations of early secular styles now lost, for he was equally reluctant to return to them.* The work, although early, must have represented, like the *Browning*, the passamezzo pavans and galliards or the Consort Fantasia 6/g2, an end rather than a beginning and so needed no sequel. It is very unlikely, however, to have had precursors of comparable scope and variety, and through these qualities it eventually exerted influence, though in the rather different context of consort music (see p. 79). The later keyboard fantasias were not, of course, entirely unaffected by it, but in most essentials they followed Fantasia G2, accepting its minim pulse and more homogeneous stylistic range, at least as starting points. The compliment was two-edged, for Fantasia G3, which represents an intermediate stage between G2 and the fantasias in Nevell, embodies a good deal of criticism of its forerunner and probably owes its existence to a desire to salvage the best elements of the earlier work in one of more compact proportions. As its smaller scale sets the standard for the later works it probably also postdates Fantasia a1.

Fantasia G3 deviates most drastically from G2 at the beginning, where Byrd turns his back on the idea of a long initial imitative section in slow note-values. He starts with two short expositions on Ex. 73a separated by a

Ex. 73

tonic full close exactly as in Fantasia a1, but then rounds the passage off with another full close and a plagal extension so that the section makes the impression of a prelude or intonation. Then, after a 6-bar non-imitative

*The lively bass line of the latter, however, has a less distinguished counterpart in another early work, *The Hunt's up* (var. 9 in the revision), and remoter ones in considerably later pieces (Galliard G2, *Quadran* Galliard, Pavan F2).

phrase (Ex. 73b – the melody recalls Ex. 68a) and its antiphonal repeat an octave lower, he picks up the thread of G2 at the point where it reaches the quicker imitations on Ex. 68c–e, and follows it fairly closely to the end.

The cardinal change in the later work lies in the relation of each episode to the larger design. The main structural contribution made by the three central imitations in G2 is the increase in quaver movement, to which each successive point adds its quotient. In order not to disturb this process Byrd is obliged to pursue a rather level course, so that only the third imitation rises to a climax (which it does admirably). In G3 he paradoxically enables each episode to play a more effective structural part by allowing it more freedom in its own right. Thus the first of its three central imitative episodes (Ex. 73c) marches in smartly on the heels of the preceding triadic antiphony and takes possession of the work not simply through its more active character but by going ahead with its own succinct, self-contained contrapuntal development. Its deft and positive conclusion, far from breaking continuity, opens the way for a no less active second episode (Ex. 73d) to enter promptly with a rider in the form of a turn towards the dominant. This episode like-wise adds something to the whole by working out its own stretto and finally confirming the dominant.

For the third and closing episode of this part of the fantasia Byrd returns to the tonic and adopts a different technique, antiphonal as much as imitative. The melodic material here emphasizes the work's stylistic relationship to both G2 and a1. The first phrase (Ex. 73e) recalls a subject from G2 (Ex. 68d), and its related successor (Ex. 73f) one from a1 (Ex. 72d); imitative melodic lines in the Nevell fantasias are noticeably plainer than these. In contrast, another device used in this episode, that of decorated repetition, does not occur in the two longer fantasias but assumes importance in the Nevell works. Byrd employs it here to repeat an already repetitious passage. The three statements of Ex. 73f (bars 86–91), each skilfully introduced by a different interrupted resolution of a dominant preparation, would have sufficed to bring the central part of the work to a close; the decorated repeat, which results in no fewer than six consecutive 2-bar statements on the same degree, prepares for a completely different type of phrase structure in the last part of the work.

The first stage in this development follows straight away. The transition to the tripla section begins with six more repetitions, this time of a single-bar pattern; the first two bars are shown in Ex. 74a. The salient feature here is the harmonic rhythm. This receives the greatest possible emphasis because in every repetition but the fifth the harmony on the dotted minim is the same, and only in the sixth bar do the semiquavers run on through the

Ex. 74

fourth beat and allow the music to break free. The transition is completed in four bars of freer construction, but in the first half of the tripla section every bar is affected in some way by the pattern established in Ex. 74a. In the first nine bars the movement halts on the fifth crotchet (black minim) of the bar (see Ex. 74b); the resolution of a suspension on the sixth crotchet in several cases only strengthens the effect (Ex. 74c*). Later the harmonic rhythm comes even closer to the model (e.g. Ex. 74d). Finally, after bars 125–27 have neatly combined elements from Ex. 74b and d, the usual quaver phase steps in and breaks the pattern's hold.

It seems probable that Byrd devised this particular unifying pattern for the later part of the work on purpose to give the tripla quavers a positive role that would justify their presence, for having accepted them on the basis of tradition as the appropriate means of concluding the final phase in his earlier fantasias he found them troublesome. The stereotyped runs associated with them empty the music of content unless they throw some other element into relief. In certain contexts† they do this most effectively, but in a fantasia they can only draw attention to the harmonic framework that carries them, and this needs to be very strong indeed if it is to provide an adequate conclusion to a lengthy and varied composition. Byrd contrives this brilliantly in the special circumstances of Fantasia a1, where the harmonic preparation of the passage plays an important part, but in G2 and G3 his touch is less sure. In G2 he just makes port by keeping the passage short

---

*The reconstructed text is that of BK.

†For instance in variation forms when a clear restatement of the fundamental melody or harmonic scheme is needed at a later stage in the work, or in the *Ut re mi* Fantasia where the cantus firmus structure accommodates simultaneous contrapuntal strands of greater melodic value.

and prolonging the line into the duple coda, where it attains greater character. In G3 he risks a longer passage on a stronger and more appealing harmonic basis. It serves, but like the preceding episodes, which suffer from the stiffness of the unifying idea, it misses the excellence of the first half of the work.

The three fantasias in Nevell, as has already been mentioned, replace the tripla episode with a decorated repeat of the last section. They are linked in various other ways too, and together with the Consort Fantasia 4/g (see p. 93n) make up a group of which none is likely to have been composed before the later 1580s. One, **Fantasia C2**, still shows the influence of G3, but only in superficial matters. The initial imitation, based on Ex. 75a, runs to about

Ex. 75

the same length as that of G3 and comes to a well heralded tonic close with the same preludial effect. But there are no proper imitative expositions as there are in G3: some kind of cadence separates nearly every statement of the subject so that harmonically controlled phrase lengths rather than the requirements of contrapuntal structure govern the music. The antiphonal exchange that follows in G3 (Ex. 73b) is then quoted almost literally (Ex. 75b), though at twice the speed and as the basis of a rather longer episode. Then, once again as in G3, a new imitation begins (Ex. 75c).

Here, however, the two works part company decisively. Having given greater autonomy to the imitative episodes in G3, Byrd takes it away again in C2 and employs a quite different structural procedure, adumbrated in the regular phrases of the first episode, to suit a shift of emphasis in the conception of the whole. For in this work he erodes the features that in one form or another dominate Fantasias G2, a1 and G3 – the clear divisions and strong contrasts between sections, the over-all increase in speed – in the interest of greater unity. The range of character is comparable to that of G3, but the move from one episode to another is relatively lightly marked. The music progresses largely by short phrases which tend to group themselves in stanza-like sequences. The idea is borrowed from the later part of G3, but the metrical repetitions are no longer yoked to circumscribed harmonic patterns; on the contrary, they serve to draw attention to an unusually wide variety of cadential degree.

The effect of constant transition and renewal is less readily matched in the other keyboard fantasias than in the Canonic Fantasia C1 (= 5/C), another work based, though quite differently, on short phrases which sometimes fall into stanza forms. The structural analogy holds good in the sphere of motivic work, which Byrd always understood how to adjust to the particular formal needs of a piece. In the entirely imitative Fantasia C3 each point derives from its predecessor in the manner of White. This procedure would have had little effect in the extended paragraphs of G2, which establish themselves by their own weight, and the connections here are accordingly looser, as they are in G3 as well.* But in C1 and C2 a much more complex motivic network is needed to keep the less firmly articulated and less self-sufficient episodes within bounds.

*For G2 see Ex. 68: the emphasis on the supertonic and tonic in a recurs a fifth higher in b, approached from the tonic; the latter pattern is echoed in f and, by crab motion, in d; the central subjects c–e share only the closing stepwise descent to the tonic, which is not present in every statement. In G3 the subjects are related less by outline than by a constituent figure: a rising or falling five-note scale occurs in nearly all of them (see Exx. 73 a–d, 74c and d), and there is occasionally a more elaborate cross-reference (Exx. 73c and 74c).

The characteristic handling of phraseology, cadential choice and motivic derivation in C2 is illustrated in the passage represented by Ex. 75c. The two subjects derive respectively from the rising scale and alternating thirds of Ex. 75a. After four bars they settle into a series of five 3-bar phrases in which they exchange position but never transgress the cadences that close each phrase. Whereas the two earlier episodes keep close to the tonic and close there, the present series of cadences is much more varied and raises the music through the dominant to the supertonic. This prepares for the entry of a new 4-bar phrase (Ex. 75d) in the dominant; an antiphonal echo and a 5-bar extension of the same idea lead to the submediant at Ex. 75e. This example quotes the first two of five 2-bar phrases built on the model of the five 3-bar phrases that follow Ex. 75c, but with a new pair of subjects. The first of these is a version of Ex. 75a, and its companion, which enters in the treble in the second phrase, a sequel to Ex. 75b (bars 45–47). The five cadences lead by a devious route to the tonic, so that the episodes based on Ex. 75c–e are felt as a unit.

Here (bar 89) Byrd appears to prepare for continuous semiquavers, and listeners familiar with the earlier fantasias will expect a good deal of passage-work leading to a tonic cadence, possibly followed by a tripla section (the closing phase of the first section of Fantasia a1 starts very similarly, at bar 62). However, after only four bars another group of five consecutive 2-bar cadential periods begins (the first also functioning as the second half of a 4-bar phrase, bars 91–94), and soon breaks the semiquavers up into more varied patterns of rising scales and alternating thirds in quavers and semi-quavers. These patterns are not unique to the work – they occur together in the coda of G2 and in d1 – but by their nature they fit into its motivic field, with corresponding effect. They do not fall into step with the cadences so regularly as the phrases shown in Ex. 75c–e do, so that the stanza-like pattern remains a little below the surface and the musical progress becomes more fluid.

There is no real break at the final tonic cadence (bar 103), which introduces a new series of three 6-bar periods cadencing respectively on the supertonic, submediant and tonic (like the episodes based on Ex. 75c, d and e). The first two of these periods carry a brilliant development of the immediately preceding melodic patterns: in the first, phrases five crotchets long (see Ex. 75f), shifting up a degree at every repetition, play across a harmonic accompaniment that remains faithful to the bar line;* in the second, the phrases lengthen to six crotchets and bring the episode to an

*A simpler precedent occurs in the last episode of the second section of Fantasia a1 (bars 119–28).

end with a very firm submediant cadence. Once again Byrd avoids a decisive break by starting the new episode here and engulfing the tonic close six bars later in continuous semiquavers, which at this second attempt seem to establish their hold. The expectations aroused at bar 89 revive, but as before are not fulfilled: after a while Byrd slips in a reminder of the twin motivic sources of the piece in the shape of Ex. 75g which (like Ex. 75f) draws on both, and a little later arrests the passage-work temporarily on an interrupted tonic cadence (bar 129).

This proves to be the first step in a superlatively skilful transition to the closing episode. Bars 131–33 contain semiquaver runs in the context of a descending harmonic sequence; the outer notes of the root position chords at the beginning of each bar are shown by directs in Ex. 75h. Bar 134 breaks the semiquaver movement once and for all, but contrives to continue the same harmonic direction (and also to echo the progression at bars 129–30). The new subject enters as the harmonic sequence ends in bars 134–35; its first three notes derive from Ex. 75e, and since the whole phrase is twice repeated sequentially, rising a degree each time, the motive of interlocking thirds reappears as the dominant feature of bars 135–40 (the passage recalls the treatment of Ex. 75f). The episode closes with imitation on a version of Ex. 75d, and a lively decorated repeat of the whole episode follows, rounded off by a singularly apt 3-bar coda based on the figure quoted in the last four melodic notes of Ex. 75h.

An affinity between this inspired and subtle work and the no less beautiful **Fantasia d1** is more easily felt than demonstrated. It lies primarily in their concern for the integrity of their respective spheres of feeling. They also share a few details of vocabulary, but in the structural field their paths rarely cross. The dominating technical features in C2 are exactly contradicted in d1, which divides into clearly defined sections, favours asymmetrical phrasing and long paragraphs with few cadences, and makes only moderate use of motivic connections. The initial imitation is about the same length as those of G3 and C2, but takes the form of an unbroken contrapuntal development, and this is immediately followed by a second imitation. Byrd had not used this more conventional scheme in a keyboard fantasia since G2. It has been seen that the early part of G2 is indebted to the style of vocal or consort polyphony. This is precisely the aspect of the work that he did not follow up in G3 or C2, but he does so in d1 by turning, not to G2 itself, but to his more recent practice in 4-part consort fantasias.

In Fantasias 4/a and 4/g the imitations of the first section are followed by a passage of minim and crotchet syncopations, a sequence of events which the keyboard piece adopts. Moreover 4/g starts with two imitations of about the length of those in d1, and shares common material with it in the ensuing syncopations (see Ex. 76). Although the two works diverge beyond this

Ex. 76

a. Fantasia 4/g

b. Fantasia d1

point their over-all proportions remain similar, and Byrd must certainly have planned one in relation to the other. Since the obvious influence of consort writing in d1 is balanced by no trace of keyboard style in the consort piece, there can be little doubt that the latter served as the model. Reasons for placing its date of composition considerably earlier than its publication in 1611 have already been given (p. 93); the keyboard piece, as will be seen, belongs to the latest contributions to Nevell. Both were probably composed about 1590.

One of Byrd's aims in Fantasia d1 was thus to translate the special qualities of 4/g into keyboard terms, and work out the consequences. The piece starts in a similar sober vein, perhaps alleviated a little by more continuous crotchet movement. The workmanship shows all the economy of Byrd's mature manner: both forms of the second imitative subject (Ex. 77b) derive from the first (see the tenor in Ex. 77a). The first move away from consort style occurs during the second imitative episode where purely decorative runs of semiquavers are introduced in non-essential parts within the 4-part texture, rather like coloured passages in a continental keyboard intabulation. After a while these develop melodic interest by breaking up into more varied note-values (in the style already encountered in the coda to G2 and in C2), and then terminate abruptly by running up to the first high G in the piece and stopping dead. The underlying harmonic movement is thus left exposed; for five minim beats there is not even a crotchet passing note to deflect attention from a progression which turns out to be crucial (Ex. 77c).

Up to this point none of the natural major chords of the mode has been heard, but now all three suddenly appear. The Aeolian sixth which interrupts the II⁶ cadence leads to an excursion through the mediant and flat seventh before the final tonic cadence of the section. From here on major harmony in general, and the sixth in particular, have important roles to

Ex. 77

play in the work. Although Byrd carries this remarkable passage through in a style perfectly appropriate to a consort piece, in the more formal Consort Fantasia 4/g he admits no such disruption of the austere spirit of the opening, moving to the relative major only in the middle section, and then with the utmost circumspection.

The syncopations that follow the first section in the consort model have only a transitional function, but in d1 they become the foundation for the whole second section. Byrd uses the antiphonal homophony found at this

point in G3 and C2 (Exx. 73b and 75b) to give the greatest possible prominence to the alternation of duple with triple metre at the outset (Ex. 77d).
This leads to less emphatic use of the same rhythmic pattern in two statements of Ex. 76b, after each of which the metrical flexibility invades the
individual voices in such a way as to undermine the distinction between
strong and weak minim beats. As a result the tonic cadence at the end of the
section carries little weight, and the third section enters only one minim
beat later, on the Aeolian sixth (Ex. 77e).

The emphasis on this chord recalls Ex. 77d so strongly that the music is
able to slip almost unobserved from consort style into keyboard texture.
The conjunct melody of the new subject also helps to preserve continuity
with the previous sections (quite apart from its kinship with the important
countersubject in the alto at the end of Ex. 77b). Its treatment in quasi-
canonic dialogue over a strumming octave and fifth bass conforms to a
common convention in Byrd's keyboard music, but one that he had never
before admitted in a fantasia. This primarily harmonic texture provides a
context in which he can pursue the line of thought initiated in the major
harmonies at the end of the first section: with the aid of a circle of fifths he
builds three 4-bar phrases* using, virtually without repetition, the major
triads of every degree of the scale, and only them. The melody then develops
over the strumming bass in the varied manner already touched on before
the high G in the first section. Here rhythm and cadence sketch out a long
series of 2-bar phrases which group themselves into various stanza-like
formations.† Both technique and melodic style are reminiscent of C2, but
despite the harmonic variety (still predominantly major) Byrd keeps to a
more restricted cadential range, thus maintaining the level character peculiar
to the work.

The closing section, like the second and third, opens on the chord of the
Aeolian sixth (Ex. 78b). This has not been heard since the beginning of the
previous section, and makes an even stronger impact here because it interrupts a dominant preparation. At this point the full subtlety of Byrd's
structural plan becomes apparent. After holding the sixth chord in reserve
he gives it extraordinary emphasis on its first appearance (Ex. 77c), and
thereafter treats it as a counterbalance to the tonic. Each section after the
first progresses from sixth to tonic. But every tonic close at the end of a
section (apart from the expository one) risks implying finality, so that the

---

*That is, phrases of four semibreves. Although the BK text is barred in breves, it is
important to discuss this section in the same terms as Fantasia C2.

†Starting at bar 51: one of three lines, one of four, and, after two phrases that coalesce
in a single 4-bar phrase, another of four lines.

sixth has to step in with increased urgency on each occasion to set the process of gravitation towards the tonic in motion again. Hence the weakened cadence before Ex. 77e, and the interruption at 78b.

And that is not the end of the series. In order to press the claim of the sixth once again as the music draws to a close in diminishing spans, he foreshortens what should have been the first 8-bar period of the closing section. Towards the end of this 4-part canonic episode where two top As proclaim the climax of the work, he closes up the dotted crotchet and quaver rhythms of Ex. 78b into even quavers and forces the tonic final on to the second minim beat of the seventh bar, where it is even more weakly placed than the cadence at the end of the second section. The insistent sixth chord cuts in once more, initiating the decorated repeat of the episode. However, this extends to the full eight bars; the harmonic progression is laid bare and ends with the dominant preparation for the final full close of the work, so that this time the tonic receives a commanding position at the beginning of the 4-bar plagal period before the final chord.*

The first four bars of the closing section very closely resemble the 3-part canonic passage (Ex. 78a) in strain III of William Petre's Pavan (g2),

Ex. 78

a. Pavan g2

b. Fantasia d1 (earlier version)

composed during the compilation of Nevell (see p. 196) and entered immediately before Fantasia d1† near the end of the manuscript. Moreover both passages enter very abruptly on a cadential interruption in order to give special weight to the B♭ chord, which has an important structural

---

*Most editions print a C♯ in the ornament that precedes this chord, but this is surely a misreading. Weelkes's accidental is imprecisely placed, but seems to be intended for the B.

†Baldwin gives an early text of the fantasia; it had already been revised by the time Weelkes copied it.

point to make in both contexts, and both are associated with irregular phrase lengths. A guess may be hazarded that the fantasia is the later work. Having completed its third main section, in which the music enters the orbit of C2 without breaking faith with the balance and sobriety of Fantasia 4/g, Byrd felt the need to revert to polyphony briefly before the end. Imitation was out of the question at this late stage, but canon would suit the context and could be telescoped in accordance with the intricate metrical plan. The canonic episode in his recent pavan happened to begin on the right harmony, so he borrowed it, shifted the alto after the first two notes, added a tenor, and developed the line so as to echo the outline of his opening point (Ex. 77a, tenor); the textural rhythm could perhaps be heard as relating to the second section (see Ex. 76b). The graft took, even though the passage does not grow quite so naturally out of earlier material as its counterpart does in the pavan.

That Byrd should have had the very recent Fantasia 4/g and Pavan and Galliard g2 in mind while composing this work is hardly surprising, but it is interesting to note that he may also have been looking over his old In Nomines at the time. At all events, it is an odd coincidence that his systematic erosion of the strong minim beat in section 2, and his concentration on major harmony in section 3, should develop ideas first explored in much simpler terms perhaps a quarter of a century earlier, respectively in In Nomines 5/5 and 5/3.

Fantasia G1, the Voluntary for my Lady Nevell, is a less complex work than its nearest relatives C2 and d1. The structure proceeds on fairly familiar lines. The first section consists of two imitations, the subjects of which are prefigured in a short introduction of seven bars. Both close in the tonic, but the next subject (bar 39), which belongs to the same family as Ex. 75d and is worked out in the same partially antiphonal manner, leads to the subdominant. Two short homophonic phrases resembling those shown in Ex. 31b then lift the music back to the tonic. So far, so good – but here the composition begins to flag. Instead of signalling a new turn of events the homophony introduces another subject very like the one that preceded it; the treatment is also very similar, and it leads straight back to the subdominant. A rather uninteresting sequel rises again through the tonic to the dominant, where the closing section enters (bar 54), only to repeat once again the pattern of an antiphonal exchange and a third, slightly varied statement of the new subject. The piece ends with a decorated repeat of the whole section and a brief, ready-made coda (see *Monsieur's Alman* G1).

Byrd did Lady Nevell less honour here than in the vigorous ground and

Chi passa that he dedicated to her. It is true that the voluntary is the most intimate in expression of the three works, but formally it probably owes a good deal to Byrd's practice in improvisation. One detail points especially strongly in that direction: the introduction begins with a standard formula common in Italian organ music of an earlier generation. Ex. 79 shows it

Ex. 79

a. Jaches, Sanctus   *b.* Byrd, Fantasia G1

alongside one example, the *Sanctus* from Jaches Brumel's *Messa de la domenica.**

Nothing has been said so far in this chapter about foreign influences, because the fantasias differ radically in conception from anything composed on the continent. But the steady influx of continental music to England naturally did not leave them untouched. Imitation itself was, of course, a relatively recent importation, at least as a thoroughgoing principle, and Byrd's substitution of repetitions for tripla as a closing device in the later works very likely owes something to the Italian ricercare, where terminal (and internal) repetitions were common. Certain textures in these later pieces, which entail the stricter approach to part-writing necessary in consort music and favoured on the continent in keyboard style as well, are less remote from the standard international vocabulary of instrumental music than is the contrapuntal style of the early Fantasia G2.

But it is mostly in the earlier works that occasional borrowings of a far more interesting kind occur. Like Ex. 79, these seem to betray a knowledge of earlier traditions of Italian instrumental music. Thus little imitative figures like those at the end of Ex. 72c are common in the lute fantasias of

*From a Castell' Arquato manuscript; printed by K. Jeppesen in *Altitalienische Orgelmusik*, second edition (Copenhagen, 1960). There are several similar passages elsewhere in the work, and others at the beginning of Girolamo Cavazzoni's *Magnificat quarti toni* (*Orgelwerke*, ed. O. Mischiati (Mainz, 1959–61), ii, 48) and in a tiento by Cabezón (MME 2, ii/51). S. M. Kastner ('Parallels and Discrepancies between English and Spanish Keyboard Music of the 16th and 17th centuries', in *Anuario musical*, vii (1952), 77ff) mistakenly saw the parallel between the latter work and Byrd's as evidence for Cabezón's influence. His arguments based on a supposed likeness between two of Cabezón's tientos (MME 2, ii/26, MME 29/67) and Byrd's Fantasia d1 are equally fallacious.

Francesco da Milano, some of which are found in English lute sources of the 1570s and 1580s. The canonic treatment of statement 5 of the cantus firmus in *Ut re mi* may be compared with a passage in a ricercare by Giacomo Fogliano (Ex. 80), and strain II of Pavan G3 employs another type of canon

Ex. 80

a. Fogliano, Ricercare No.3

b. Byrd, Ut re mi

over a descending bass that can be matched in both Fogliano and Brumel (Ex. 81).

Ex. 81

a. Fogliano, Ricercare No.2

b. Jaches, Ricercare

c. Byrd, Pavan G3/II

The Italian pieces quoted in Exx. 79–81 are all contained in a manuscript at Castell' Arquato along with others by Marco Antonio Cavazzoni and Giulio Segni.* The group as a whole provides a valuable record of Italian keyboard music as it was before Willaert and his circle revolutionized instrumental composition in the years following the publication of the *Musica nova* of 1540.† Fogliano, the oldest of these composers by some twenty years, was born in 1468. Whether his four unassuming but charming ricercares reflect the tastes of his generation or simply the preferences of a composer who favoured the lighter vocal forms, they stand at the opposite extreme from the ensemble ricercares of the *Musica nova*. Their short phrases and paragraphs, their frequent and varied cadences entailing liberal application of *ficta*, their wide range of technical resource encompassing imitation, freer polyphony and homophony, their emphasis on the top line with occasional outbreaks of secular song-like melody – all were swept away in the 1540s in favour of consistently imitative texture, length of melodic line and seamless continuity.

Fogliano's younger contemporaries in the Castell' Arquato manuscript still share one or other of his salient characteristics. The elder Cavazzoni uses almost as many cadences, while cultivating in toccata style the continuity that was later to be sought in imitation. Brumel's style is as broken and as chromatic as Fogliano's but considerably less melodious. Segni, a pupil of Fogliano, shows his master's influence in an avowedly chromatic ricercare, in contrast to his severely diatonic contributions to *Musica nova*. None of these composers shows much interest in Fogliano's clear phraseology (though it can be paralleled in Francesco da Milano); the feeling of the time was against his directness of utterance, as the swift triumph of the new music confirms. Although some keyboard composers, such as Claudio Veggio, kept a place in their ricercares for toccata-like passages,‡ others, such as Girolamo Cavazzoni, renounced them. For instrumental music in general now took up the challenge of church polyphony, adopted its technical refinement and serious tone, and searched for its own means of attaining comparable scale. Perhaps it had also to meet a rather different challenge from which music suffered during the high renaissance, as in many other periods: the insatiable appetite of the consumer. The new style answered this demand too, for once mastered it enabled even the indifferent practitioner

*All those referred to here are printed by Jeppesen (see the previous footnote), and all except those of Brumel by G. Benvenuti in *I Classici musicali italiani*, Vol. 1 (Milan, 1941).

†Complete edition, ed. H. C. Slim, in *Monuments of Renaissance Music*, 1 (Chicago, 1964).

‡The elder Ferrabosco's only known keyboard fantasia (Weelkes fol. 49) belongs to this tradition.

to keep going almost indefinitely – Segni could even slip the same episode into two pieces in *Musica nova* (Nos. 4 and 6). Byrd's appreciation of this danger can be read in his short consort fantasias (see Chapter 5).

Although in general Byrd absorbed much less from continental traditions of composition than from English interpretations of them, one cardinal element in his style has no native root: his use of numerous and varied cadences to define melody and structure wherever the nature of a piece gives him liberty to do so. Nor does any obvious continental source present itself; early canzona style, for instance, is too square and limited, and in any case appears too late. In fact the surviving repertory of sixteenth-century instrumental music reveals only Fogliano, and sporadically the other composers in the older Italian style, thinking in comparable terms. Despite the far greater scope and subtlety of Byrd's practice, and his otherwise very different style, the parallel strikes the listener forcibly. The more direct reminiscences of this earlier Italian style, though few and scattered, suffice to prove the connection.

Throughout the century Italian musicians found a welcome at the English court. London – distant, damp and heretical – would scarcely have been their first choice as a place of employment, so that those who came were probably among the less enterprising or less talented who had failed to get better jobs nearer home. Their musical tastes would have been unadventurous and the repertory they brought with them old-fashioned. Thus the imported music that Byrd heard at an impressionable age in the 1550s or early 1560s could easily have been a quarter of a century or more behind the Italian times. And just as Redfordian conceptions of melodic pre-eminence entered his musical sensibility for good, their influence extending far beyond his early essays in Redford's style, so the Italian feeling for cadential spacing and chromatic inflection became a permanent element in his thought. The unexpected combination of these two influences lies at the root of all his textless music, but especially of the fantasias, where the interplay of melodic development with harmonic measurement becomes the primary vehicle for his extraordinarily diverse formal inventions – and also mirrors at a purely local level his wider structural thinking.

For the individuality of the fantasias, whether for consort or keyboard, arises above all from the relative importance accorded in each particular case to the conflicting but never wholly incompatible principles of the continuous and the sectional. By comparison the relation of imitative to homophonic texture is a subsidiary matter, as a comparison of the two early fantasias 6/F and C3 demonstrates. Both are wholly imitative, but the brief and all too tidy sections of the consort work stand at the opposite extreme to the almost unbroken continuity of C3. The idea of larger sections of broadly contrasting character begins to establish itself in the other early keyboard fantasias. The long forward development of G2 is saved from shapelessness by the firm divisions between the successive stages, and sectional planning takes an even firmer hold in the more compact sequel G3. From here a straight road leads to the various versions of tripartite structure in the late Fantasias 4/g, d1 and 6/g2.

But Byrd's growing realization of the advantages of sectional structure was accompanied by new ideas about the uses of continuous development (which in any case retained its place within sections), and the forms it might take. As early as a1 he chose the security of the enclosed central section as the arena for a sequence of contrasts so daring that he only once followed it up, and then characteristically in order to work the idea out in terms of consort style, in Fantasia 6/g1. Here he sectionalized the sequence of contrasts, but still found it necessary to add the greater contrast of a dance section, and then a coda, to stabilize the whole. In two other late fantasias, however, one each for consort and keyboard, he achieved within a narrower range of character a unified continuous development by intensifying motivic work. In 5/C (= C1) the process carries right through a tripartite structure so that the two formal principles subtly combine; in C2 potential sections dissolve into more gradual shifts of character which nevertheless remain strong enough to hold the work in shape.

12

Conclusion

The problems encountered in establishing some kind of chronology for Byrd's instrumental music genre by genre bedevil even worse any attempt to fit the various sequences together to form a more general picture of his development. As has been seen, very few compositions can be dated by external evidence. In certain genres, such as the grounds and the pavans and galliards, the presence of a common principle of construction allows the progress of the composer's thought to be traced, even though the different stages along the way cannot be accurately dated. But in, for instance, the variations, where each melody requires its own structural approach, the lack of such a guiding thread creates almost as many difficulties for relative as for absolute dating, while unique pieces such as *The Barley Break* or *The Bells* are extremely hard to pin down at all. In the same way the many genres cultivated by Byrd resist amalgamation in any but the most general over-all chronology because they present so few points of comparison. Nevertheless, a fairly convincing outline can be constructed on the basis of arguments advanced in the foregoing chapters.

Byrd's earliest pieces, at least in the instrumental field, are all based on cantus firmi. Some of them, both for consort and keyboard, are clearly the work of a beginner, though one who had access to the music not only of established composers, but of young men only a few years his senior, such as White and Parsons. Byrd's extraordinary originality, which shows itself almost from the beginning and at first tends to outstrip his technical experience, makes his early appointment as organist at Lincoln readily understandable. Probably only the more mature 5-part In Nomines and the last consort hymns among the plainsong settings postdate his arrival there in 1563, and all were written by the mid-sixties. Various other works still partially dependent on obsolescent mid-century styles must also belong to the sixties: *Ut mi re*, the Short Grounds, the Hornpipe, the Galliard Jig, Fantasias C4, C3, 6/F, G2 and a1, *The Hunt's up*, *Gipsies' Round* and *The Maiden's Song*.

A large body of work of Byrd's earlier maturity spans the gap between the early pieces and those of the 1580s. The period is a long and rather ill-defined one. Some pieces, while not employing any obviously early technique, probably go back to the sixties; a few may reach forward into the eighties. The earlier development of the pavans and galliards up to such pairs as c2 and C2 belongs to this time, and so do most of the almans (nearly all the early consort pavans and galliards have been lost – perhaps the fragmentary Fantasias 4/G and 4/a were contemporary with them). Works in other forms include *All in a garden green*, *Fortune my foe*, *Sellinger's Round*, Fantasia G3, the *Ut re mi* Fantasia, the Prelude and Ground for consort, the *Second Ground*, *Hugh Aston's Ground*; they culminate in the *Browning*, *Walsingham* and the *Passing Measures* Pavan and Galliard.

The masterpieces of the sixties and seventies, however original, build for the most part on established formal traditions. In the majority of later works the basis is either completely new, as in the magnificent series of fantasias which dominate the music of the eighties and earlier nineties (5/C, 6/g1, C2, 4/g, d1, 6/g2) or is made to serve an entirely individual technical invention, as in the important group of pavans and galliards of about 1590 (g2, F1, d1, the *Quadran*). The keyboard writing here achieves a new density of content. A unique work in a different vein, *The Woods so wild*, is actually dated 1590. A few pieces which anticipate one or other of these later developments must be placed in the eighties (Pavan and Galliard G2, Pavan G6, *The Carman's Whistle*); five more written mostly for Nevell at the end of the decade, though brilliant and substantial, are less exploratory in intention (*My Lady Nevell's Ground*, the *Chi passa*, Fantasia G1, Galliard G10, *Lord Willoughby's Welcome home*).

After the mid-nineties Byrd wrote, so far as is known, no more fantasias or grounds and very little consort music of any kind. The only consort pieces from the late period are the Pavan and Galliard 6/C (and possibly the little 3-part fantasias). The few late keyboard pieces are as eventful in texture as the major works around 1590, but even more refined in detail: *Go from my window*, *John come kiss me now*, *O mistress mine I must*, Pavans and Galliards F2, C3, G5, a2 and C4, the preludes in F, C and G, Alman C2 and the arrangements of Dowland's *Lachrymae* and Harding's Galliard.

The scarcity of late pieces raises the question of losses. No doubt many early pieces have disappeared; but in the seventies and eighties, when Byrd was at the height of his fame, his music circulated very widely and the bulk of his keyboard music from these years has certainly survived, even though the smaller consort works have suffered. Later, as his tendency to make every piece entirely individual increased, he inevitably produced less; it is significant that the two fantasias which he published in 1611 were about twenty years old. Nevertheless, some of the music of the last phase has probably been lost. Although he remained a respected figure, interest in his work waned. Those seventeenth-century copyists of consort or key-board music who turned their attention to younger composers virtually excluded it.

The extent to which Byrd drew simultaneously on English and continental traditions in the creation of this extraordinarily independent body of work has been emphasized many times in the course of this study. From Henrician times onward English music, like English poetry, benefited increasingly from continental, and especially Italian example; without it the achievements of Elizabethan and Jacobean composers would not have been possible. But it would be altogether too simple a formulation to see Byrd's music merely as the product of the belated action of renaissance developments on an ossified mediaeval tradition, resulting in a moderately interesting variant of what had been done on the continent a couple of generations earlier. The literary parallel is useful here. Byrd's music can no more be branded old-fashioned for its debt to an indigenous melodic tradition with roots in the previous century, than the plays of Marlowe and Shakespeare can for their descent from mediaeval drama. To measure Byrd's work against con-temporary Italian practice would be as pointless as treating the dramatic tradition of *Aminta* and *Il Pastor fido* as central, and finding *Hamlet* and *Lear* provincial by comparison. A brief consideration of continental in-strumental music in Byrd's time will bring the situation into sharper focus.

The types of composition cultivated in Italy had grown up in response to developments which had largely passed England by. The music of Josquin's generation had opened up such a wide range of possibilities in all spheres of composition that a need arose for limiting factors. Towards the middle of the century Willaert and his circle averted confusion by canalizing the new forces in a number of genres, each rather strictly governed by its own conventions. The pattern thus established held good till the end of the century: later composers tended to become specialists – church musicians, madrigalists, organists and so on – and the developments in one genre, however striking or revolutionary, were slow to find acceptance in others. A very important feature in this rather self-conscious programme of codifica-tion was the treatment of chromaticism, which was locked away and allowed the occasional airing only under special conditions; it was to remain a thing apart for many years to come.

In instrumental music the ricercare became the most important genre – and a very severe one, purged not only of the chromatic inflections necessary to cadential variety, but of any vestige of stanza-like melody or dance rhythms. Little distinction was drawn between pieces for ensemble and for keyboard; many were intended for either. In keyboard writing the parts were often decorated, as they were in intabulations of vocal pieces, and in time accommodated a considerable degree of toccata-like display, but the texture remained limited to a set number of parts, usually four. Accompanied melody and extra parts for the sake of sonority were banished to dance music, which was not encouraged to rise above its utilitarian station.

Music in England could scarcely have presented a greater contrast. Although it had by no means stood still in the first half of the century its horizons had not broadened in any spectacular way. No embarrassment of continental riches perplexed the English composer, and Byrd's early experience made him heir to long-standing habits of mind still not greatly affected by outside events. But the education which instils a narrow outlook in one young composer may provide his more gifted fellow with the advantage of a positive standpoint. Moreover Byrd was endowed with an extraordinarily keen analytical intelligence which discovered opportunity in everything that came its way. Just when Italy, with the rest of Europe in her wake, was bent on definition and control, new lines of thought opened out for Byrd on every side, much as they had for Josquin a hundred years earlier. He dissected and rejected, reconstituted and transformed, leaving nothing as he found it.

In the instrumental field he was already combining the most heterogeneous techniques at a very early date, using tonal excursions and symmetrical phraseology to articulate the form in the unlikely context of cantus firmus composition. He was soon displaying unprecedented flexibility in the interdependent spheres of phrase structure, texture and harmonic control. Having raised idealized dance forms to equal status with variation forms and the fantasia, he could range within a single work from the prose rhythms of polyphony to the stanza patterns of dances and popular song (he even quoted popular tunes in *The Hunt's up*, the *Passing Measures* Galliard and Fantasias 5/C and 6/g1), and from fully imitative counterpoint, through every kind of intermediate texture such as antiphony and accompanied dialogue, right down to melody with purely harmonic support. His sensitivity to the power of the top line as a shaping agent brought unity to the constantly changing textures, his acute feeling for cadential degree, weight and timing made the remotest transition appear inevitable, and at all times the interplay of a varying harmonic pulse with fluctuating rates of divisions enabled him to control the progress of the music by means of the finest nuances of pace and density.

All these qualities are equally apparent in his consort and keyboard styles, but in quite different guises. For Byrd, far from treating the two types of instrumentation interchangeably, cultivated entirely separate modes of composition in each. When he wished to work out the principles underlying a particular consort work in keyboard terms he would write a completely new piece (as with the Consort Ground and *Second Ground*, the *Browning* and *Walsingham*, Fantasias 4/g and d1, Pavans and Galliards 6/C and G5).

This catalogue of technical opposites in the music of Byrd and his continental contemporaries reflects a deep division on the aesthetic level. The parting of the ways may be traced back to the time of Josquin, when continental composers began to explore the power of music to enhance the meaning of a sung text. Their best energies went into this new kind of expression. As a result they tended to think of musical structure as a sequence of episodes governed by the requirements of words, whereas right down to Byrd's early years England remained content with more generalized expression coupled with a rather abstract structural approach.

The continental preoccupation with word-setting affected instrumental music in many ways. Although cantus firmus schemes lingered on, the commonest types of ricercare, tiento and toccata all adopted the chain-like construction of the motet. Their manifold departures from the motet in other respects could not remove the problems posed by the absence of a guiding text, and it is not surprising that the successive subjects of a piece were sometimes drawn from some well known vocal composition in order to provide extra-musical coherence. The ricercare shared the serious cast of the motet – in certain circumstances it could find a place in the liturgy – but the same dependence on vocal models is found in the purely secular sphere, where decorated intabulations of chansons and madrigals enjoyed enormous popularity. Even when, late in the century, instrumental music finally began to assert greater independence, it took courage from the pronounced verbal rhythms of the canzona. The average continental musician can be imagined anticipating Fontenelle's famous sally against music without words with the question 'Ricercare, che vuoi da me?'

In England vocal music was often played on instruments, but hardly ever taken as a basis for music written specially for them. A growing interest in absolute music favoured abstract schemes, notably variation forms. Some of these, of course, came from abroad; but Byrd showed how the passamezzo basses, for instance, could contribute to compositions of an altogether different order from any built on them elsewhere. Although the variation principle, which is present in some form in a great deal of Byrd's instrumental music, often entails a somewhat static approach to structure, no attribute of Byrd's structural thinking is more striking than its dynamic quality. In work after work he achieved a progression of feeling within abstract ex-

pression far outstripping anything of the kind that music had hitherto
known. Such progressions are both the reason for and the means of attaining
self-sufficient forms.

Byrd's techniques of construction have already been summarized; the
point to recall here is their extraordinary fluidity – they are processes rather
than schemes, and are capable of simultaneously profiting from and over-
riding the limitations of a precompositional framework, as well as building
entirely original formal conceptions. Consequently the possibility lay open
for every work to take its own individual course. Byrd was in fact a composer
quite exceptionally impatient of repeating himself. Except in a handful of
immature works and some unpretentious dances and arrangements he
rarely undertook a composition without some special technical idea and
aesthetic intention in mind, and wrote two closely similar pieces only
where he felt that he had not done justice to his conception at the first
attempt (compare *Gipsies' Round* and *Sellinger's Round*, *Monsieur's Alman*
G1 and 2, Fantasias 6/g1 and 2, and various partial examples such as *The
Hunt's up* and *Hugh Aston's Ground*).

Byrd's development of a more dynamic mode of thought and feeling
required a vastly extended range of character and contrast, and to encompass it he so far expanded the scope of his style as to absorb characteristics from dance measures, popular tunes and the like as a part of his
normal vocabulary. As a result his instrumental music, apart from the early
plainsong settings, is manifestly secular. He is not concerned here, as he is
in the greater part of his vocal music, with divine immutability, but with a
changeability that belongs to the human sphere. There is no lack of serious-
ness: if the 'pietie' for which he was noted finds no direct expression, his
'gravitie' frequently does. But the transitions of mood move through a
different spectrum, taking in the exuberance and gaiety that appear very
occasionally in the secular songs, and a special vein of poetry which often
carries pastoral overtones. This in no way suggests the classicizing pastoral
idyll or any of the vocal genres through which popular strains gained
admittance to sophisticated music on the continent. Byrd's native wood-
notes so wild would have jarred a continental ear, just as the unprejudiced
combination of widely disparate styles and techniques in his instrumental
music as a whole – and no doubt some aspects of his vocal music too – would
have offended against a foreigner's sense of propriety. It is worth remember-
ing that two centuries elapsed before Shakespeare became acceptable to
Latin taste.

At home, of course, there was no obstacle to the early recognition of
Byrd's stature. His music held the centre of the stage unchallenged until the

1590s, and retained an honoured place there to the end of his productive life. To the many gifted composers who grew up in its shadow it was an inescapable presence; its scale, assurance and breadth of humanity gave confidence. But that does not mean that they understood his achievement fully, still less that they necessarily wished to emulate it. Like the early romantics faced with the example of classical Vienna, they turned to the cultivation of individual sensibility. Byrd himself had not neglected to do that, but the tougher fibre in his deeply poetic qualities eluded even men of real genius such as Dowland, Wilbye and Gibbons. They lacked his inventive power on the intellectual level, and so missed not only his range of successive contrast but the richness of meaning arising from his more complex musical language.

Byrd's distinctive modes of thought in abstract composition were never followed up. Keyboard composers continued to show his influence in superficial respects during the brief period before the collapse of the English school, but their view of each of the main genres differed from his. The variation forms increasingly fell a prey to repetitive figuration. Sweelinck, whose variations on popular tunes owe a good deal to English practice and so, at least in a general sense, to Byrd, did not attempt to develop a totally individual conception from the characteristics of the chosen melody as Byrd invariably did, but looked upon it as the framework for a much more formal type of composition. The pavan changed radically: its stanza form slackened where it survived at all, and lost its hold almost entirely in Bull and Gibbons, so that the special subtleties of phraseology and harmonic structure that Byrd had brought to it became irrelevant. Gibbons's justly celebrated Lord Salisbury Pavan scarcely belongs to the genre as Byrd understood it; it could be described as a short three-section fantasia in pavan style. It was in the fantasia that Gibbons excelled. No doubt he was inclined to fall too easily into sequential writing, but at his rare best, as in the big G minor and A minor fantasias (MB 20/9 and 12), he surpasses all Byrd's English successors in keyboard music (except perhaps Bull). Although these pieces could scarcely have been written without Byrd's example, Gibbons avoids meeting him on his own structural ground. For the most part he adopts the chain-like imitative structure of the ricercare that Byrd had always treated with such suspicion, and attunes it perfectly to the needs of his less robust but wonderfully personal inspiration.

In some of his consort fantasias Gibbons did echo Byrd, distantly but distinctly, using regular song-like phrases and short repeats to offset his fine-spun polyphony. But no other younger composer of consort music showed Byrd's influence in any significant way. Whereas in keyboard music the presence of a continuous tradition gave Byrd the status of an older contemporary until late in his life, he had virtually stopped composing consort music some years before its resurgence early in James's reign, and the break made him appear the representative of a past generation. The new fantasias were madrigalian, standing in much the same relation to the vocal form as the ricercare had to the motet. Skilfully handled the scheme worked well enough, but unfortunately it gave a new lease of life to the dangers inherent in vocal forms robbed of their words, and composers soon began to indulge the English propensity – amply exemplified in the Eton Choir Book and virtuoso keyboard writing – to cultivate texture at the expense of form.

Byrd's instrumental music is thus of very small historical importance in the evolutionary sense usually implied by that phrase. Yet in some respects it looks a long way into the future. As time went on many of the features which set it apart from the music of his contemporaries entered general usage, though naturally in rather different guises. Comparable variety of character, having first emerged in a somewhat improvisatory form in the toccata (and in the contrast between the separate movements of the early suite and sonata), gradually became a factor in larger continuous structures, whilst symmetrical periods and tonal excursions established themselves as attributes of major and minor tonality. These were baroque developments; any parallel for Byrd's flexibility of texture, and the particular kind of emphasis that it imparted to his musical ideas, must be sought even later.

Analogies of this sort do not, of course, place his music ahead of its time; the norms by which such things are measured are illusory. Byrd's seemingly advanced technical procedures were not so much harbingers as closely interdependent elements in a unique musical language. He never reduced them to readily imitable patterns through which his work might have become more influential, because his intensely creative cast of mind precluded routine of any sort. But from this last characteristic his music drew an abundance of life which has ensured its survival in a much more important sense. After three centuries of oblivion it has reawoken as fresh as when it was written, capable of endearing itself to the player or listener to the point where it becomes indispensable to him as only the work of the greatest composers can.

Index of Byrd's Instrumental Works

(including doubtful and spurious pieces)

The reference to the main discussion of each piece is given in bold type.

Index of Names